1988

CW00420464

B1

A Life on the Line

A Life on the Line
Ashton Wade

British Library Cataloguing in Publication Data
Wade, Ashton, *1898* –
    A Life on the Line
    1 Great Britain, Army, Wade, Ashton, 1898 –
    I Title
    355.3'31'0924

ISBN 0–7104–3039–6

First published in Great Britain 1988

All Rights Reserved. Enquires to:
D J Costello (Publishers) Ltd
43 High street
Tunbridge Wells TN1 1XL

Typeset in 10 on 12 pt Times Roman.
Typesetting processed by Composing Operations Ltd, Tunbridge Wells
Printed by Adlard & Son Ltd, Dorking
Jacket design by Greenway Graphics, Tunbridge Wells

Contents

Acknowledgements

To all those who have helped and advised me in the preparation of this book I express my most sincere thanks. In particular I would like to thank Lyn Putnam formerly of the Womens Army Corps (India), John Whitney Director-General of the Independent Broadcasting Authority, Christopher Dowling of the Imperial War Museum, Anne Cree of D J Costello (Publishers) Ltd, the editor of the Army Quarterly and Defence Journal for reproduction of chapters 3 and 5, and above all Cynthia, my wife, without whose encouragement and endless typing this volume would not exist.

Foreword

I started writing this book in 1979. I was then 81 and had recently retired from what is commonly called active employment. I can honestly say that most of my 63 years of employment were active in the sense that they entailed a life of constant variety and movement, both at home and abroad; so much so that I was never able to make my home in any one place for more than a few years.

When eventually I retired and found time to write what is in effect an autobiography, I did so with a view to leaving some record of my life and the times in which I had lived for the benefit of my descendants. I suppose that from a comparatively early age I had had some such intention at the back of my mind, because since 1931 I have kept a daily – albeit a pocket – diary.

Eventually my wife persuaded me that I should seek a wider readership by getting it published. So here it is – a record of the main events in my life and some account of the times in which I have lived, covering incidentally the reigns of five monarchs.

People of my generation often recall with dismay the principal events of the present century: the two World Wars, the decline of the British Empire, the rise of the permissive society, the failing influences of the churches, to give but a few examples. They forget that they have lived through what is undoubtedly the most exciting and interesting period of British history; that the advances of sciences and technology have brought happiness to the lives of millions who formerly existed in misery and poverty. They forget that they have been privileged to witness the birth and growth of the motor vehicle, wireless, aviation, television and computers, all of which have revolutionised transport and leisure. They overlook the tremendous advances in the science of medicine – surgery and nutrition – which have resulted in the virtual elimination of such diseases as tuberculosis in this country, and increased the expectancy of life by something like a decade.

All these developments and the social changes which have accompanied them have had a vast, and, in practically all cases, beneficial effect on mankind. The one possible exception lies in the field of atomic science with its almost unlimited destructive potential. Here I incline strongly to the view that within it lies the key to energy requirements in the long term future, and that without its overwhelming deterrence World War III would be inevitable.

These are some of the factors which have prompted me to put pen to paper. An additional incentive has been the changed attitudes of the young generation of today. Ten years or so ago it appeared that the young regarded their parent's and grandparent's generations as portents of failure. They regarded them as responsible for the disarray in which the world stood. Their generations, so they argued, spawned the greed, hatred and jealousy which resulted in strikes, riots, terrorism and, in places, open warfare, eg, in Korea, the Middle-East and Vietnam.

Today the attitude of the young seems to have changed. They express interest in the causes and effects of the vast economic and social revolution through which the western world has passed since 1914. They are interested in the First World War and the failure of statesmen to prevent a repeat performance in the second. They seek to learn how to avoid the errors of the past, and how to apply modern scientific knowledge to the benefits of all mankind, and not just of a selfish minority. The popularity of books, films and TV covering the first half of the 20th century are evidence of this interest.

I hope, therefore, that my own experiences and thoughts may be of some interest to other than mine own fast disappearing generation.

Although just over half my working life was spent in the Army, I have made no attempt to contribute to military history in the conventional sense. I have, however, attempted to give some account of events which might be described as peripheral military activities, in as much as they were not directly connected with operations in the field and consequently have received little publicity. The trial of war criminals and the partition of the former Indian defence forces fell into this category.

As for the remainder of my working life I look back with gratitude and pride that I was able to play my part – albeit behind the screens – in the formation of what has now become a national institution, namely Independent Television, and also in the application of the small screen to the art of teaching.

D A L W
Norwich 1987

8

1

Childhood—4th August 1914 War declared

My childhood was spent in the market town of Saffron Walden, which lies in the north-west corner of Essex bordering on Cambridgeshire and Hertfordshire. It had the reputation of being a sleepy backwater, so much so that it was jokingly stated that when a passenger at Liverpool Street station asked for a ticket to Saffron Walden the booking clerk replied, "Suffering Walden! God help you."

In 1850 my grandfather, Charles Martin Wade had started practising as a solicitor in the town. He must have prospered as in 1890 he sold his house there and moved to Spaynes Hall, Great Yeldham, a village in the Colne Valley about midway between Cambridge and Colchester.

He had married Elizabeth Nockolds, a member of a well-known Walden family, who bore him two sons and a daughter. Both Stewart, my father, and Campbell, the younger son became solicitors and joined their father's firm. By the time I arrived on the scene in March 1898 the brothers had split up, Campbell having joined a firm in London, leaving my father to carry on the country business.

After the death of my grandfather in 1899 my grandmother continued to live at Spaynes Hall. It was there that my brother and I spent some of the happiest times of our boyhood. My grandmother was a gentle soul never known to utter a cross word and invariably considerate of those less well-off than herself. Following the custom of the Victorian era she, as a widow, invariably dressed in black with a white lace cap, and occasionally went out in her brougham – later replaced by a chauffeur driven Benz motor-car.

As the eldest son my father should normally have inherited Spaynes Hall; but unfortunately he had squeezed so much of his inheritance out of his parents during their lifetime that the estate eventually passed to his young brother Campbell.

My mother was one of the thirteen children of the Revd Hubert Ashton Holden, a well-known classical scholar and a schoolmaster. He died before I was born. My grandmother had been a Miss Lofft, a family which at one time owned estates in Suffolk. In the course of time she inherited a share of the Troston Estate, 6 miles from Bury St Edmunds, including the Hall, an outstanding example of Elizabethan architecture, which in my time was occupied by Sir Max Pemberton the well-known novelist. This statement is not entirely accurate, since Sir Max seldom visited the place, but his wife and three of his family lived there permanently. The latter included two teenage daughters, for the elder of whom, Barbara, I developed a secret passion. Alas I was too shy and inexperienced to show my feelings. A few years later as a young officer I tried to rekindle the flame, but unfortunately I could not contact her at the address given me.

During her lifetime my grandmother retained a somewhat gloomy house at Troston which she visited for a few weeks each summer. For the rest of the year she lived with her three unmarried daughters at Hove, where she owned a house in Brunswick Square, one of those beautiful Regency Squares which are such a feature of Brighton and Hove. It must have been on my first visit to Hove that I was lifted up in somebody's arms to catch a glimpse of King Edward VII arriving for lunch with a member of the Sassoon family who lived in the square. It always strikes me as a curious feature of the human brain that after eighty odd years one can vividly recall certain incidents which occurred in infancy, whilst to recall events which happened in recent weeks requires a considerable mental effort.

As a country solicitor my father found it compatible with his professional interests to hunt and shoot. By so doing he made friends with the "County", ie, the wealthy landowners. Although our house, "The Grove" standing in its own grounds and facing Saffron Walden common, had ample stabling and coachouse facilities the only occupant of them was my father's hunter, so when my mother wanted to pay visits outside the town she had to hire a carriage.

My mother's main interests apart from the house were the garden and the Primrose League, a Conservative party organisation which flourished and had considerable influence in the years prior to World War I.

My brother and I saw little of our parents. As was the custom in those days we were placed in the care of a nurse; later to be replaced by a

10

governess. My first infant memories are like early photographic plates, blurred in outline but historically in focus. I am being wheeled in my pram past the top end of Castle Street, then the poorest street in Walden, but now a 'desirable residential area' in house agent's jargon. Again in my pram I am parked outside the butchers. The butcher comes out with my nurse and presents me with a miniature stretcher made out of two meat skewers and a piece of cloth. The Boer War was still being fought and I can only conclude that one of the butcher's relations must have been wounded; otherwise why this macabre gift for an infant? Later in the post-nanny era my happiest memories are of tea in the garden on summer days with home-grown lettuce (Cos, of course; we did not grow the new-fangled cabbage variety) and cherry jam; of croquet parties over which my mother presided, and which we children were allowed to watch from the touchline, or to be accurate the herbacious bed which bordered the lawn; of my mother's sudden addiction to photography and as a special treat being allowed to share the mysteries of the dark room to watch the image gradually materialise as she gently swayed the developing tray containing the plate.

Occasionally in the winter we were invited to children's parties in the houses of some of my father's wealthy clients. Being extremely shy and having no sister to accustom me to the opposite sex, I came to dread these events, especially when they involved dancing – an art in which I received no instruction or encouragement. Our governess usually accompanied us, and we travelled in a closed carriage smelling faintly of ammonia and damp straw.

In the summer we sometimes accompanied our mother to a village fete. These were fun and always included some side-shows and a large marquee full of flowers, fruit and vegetables laid out in competition. For some reason the prizes in the fruit classes always seemed to go to yellow tomatoes, yellow raspberries and so-called white currants – varieties which are now quite out of fashion.

It was about this period that I became aware that my parents were drifting apart. As so often happens when the marriage is disapproved by the parents of one partner – in this case my mother's – it starts under a handicap which eventually proves fatal. My mother was comparatively old for a bride of those days being over thirty and a few years older than my father. She had travelled; was well-educated in so far as girls were allowed to be in Victorian times; and was well-read. She was artistic and painted quite well. My father on the other hand had lead an insular life. His horizon was limited to the local Essex countryside. He had been educated at home (his only experience of boarding school had been brief, having run away from Repton in his first term and never returned) until he graduated at Cambridge before joining my grandfather's firm of solicitors in Saffron Walden. Being a good shot he was invited to most of the leading shoots in the vicinity. In season we were never short of game. He also liked dancing, a pastime in which my mother took no interest.

The first occasion on which I fully realised the rift between my parents was at lunch one Sunday, the one occasion when we boys were allowed to feed in the dining room. A furious quarrel broke out between them over my father's insistence on some unmarried woman being invited to stay in order to accompany him to a society ball. My father in a raging temper threw down a carving knife he was using and strode out of the room. I was under ten years old at the time. The incident created mingled feelings of horror and misery which hung over me like a cloud for many years. I think it was from that moment that I was seldom, even when grown up, at ease in my father's company. By stating this I in no way wish to give the impression that my whole character was adversely affected by the unfortunate relationship between my parents at that period, or later in life when they were virtually separated. On the contrary, being denied the blessing of a happy family life, I believe, forced me at an early age to be self-reliant and to paddle my own canoe rather than being a member of a happy and homely crew. This was not altogether a bad thing for a youngster like myself who suffered from constant ill-health, was physically weak and, as so often happens in small families, had to play second fiddle to my elder brother.

In due course it was decided that my brother should go to a preparatory school as a boarder. To lessen the shock it was also decided that I should accompany him. I was eight at the time. The school chosen was St Faith's at Cambridge. It had, needless to say, a high academic record, since the majority of the boys were dayboys and mostly the sons of University dons. The number of boarders was small – about 20 or so. The school was owned by a man called Goodchild, who lived in the school building with his wife and two unmarried daughters. Despite his formidable appearance – he was tall and invariably wore a black suit – his severe countenance concealed a kind heart, and we boys regarded him with a kind of awed affection. Living conditions at St Faith's, as I suppose was common at other "prep" schools at that period, were hard. My brother and I were placed in a dormitory of about ten beds down the centre of which ran a series of basins with cold water taps. Even in the coldest weather the windows were always kept open. Once a week we were allowed a hot bath in the one bathroom provided. The boy's lavatories – we aptly called them bogs – were a battery of earth closets built on to the back of the building. The stench from them was over-powering. In the afternoons we played games – soccer in winter and cricket in summer – but apart from matches at the weekends we did not change our clothes. One got used to sitting in class soaked in sweat from some outdoor activity.

Mrs Goodchild was a large and formidable person whose one passion in life was stamp collecting. She took little part in the school life, delegating one of her daughters to act as school matron whilst she contented herself with her daily appearance at lunch. Here she presided over a ritual which Charles Dickens would have delighted to describe. The school dining room comprised two long tables for the boys, and a top table at which the Goodchild family and a few of the staff sat. On the sound of a bell the boys filed in with military precision and proceeded to the top table where Mrs Goodchild sat in regal state. Each boy in turn was required to hold out his hands for her inspection to ensure that they were clean enough to partake of the indescribable food to follow. Those who did not pass the test were sent away to have another scrub.

It was this ritual that led to the downfall of one of our fellow boarders, a boy of about my age who like me had an elder brother at the school. One day after lunch, instead of going out to play games, the school was summoned into the largest classroom. Having assembled under one of the masters, the Head made a dramatic entrance be-gowned and wielding a large cane. He then announced that to the utter disgrace of the school one of our number had stolen money from a fellow pupil. To catch the criminal a trap had been set. The money was the weekly pocket money allowed to boarders and the thief had extracted it in the changing room, where the victim was in the habit of hanging his jacket during break. On hearing of the theft the headmaster had arranged for permanganate of potash to be inserted in the jacket pocket together with the pocket money, so that the thief's hand would be stained violet. This duly happened and Mrs Goodchild had caught the culprit during her daily hand inspection ritual. The miserable little creature had then confessed. For this disgraceful act the Headmaster announced that X Junior was to be expelled from the school; but not before receiving six of the best in front of the assembled boys; being reduced to a picture of abject misery in floods of tears; and then told to report to matron, who would see that his trunk was packed and subsequently escort him to the railway station. Needless to say none of us ever saw this unfortunate boy again. His elder brother left at the end of term.

On looking back one feels horrified at the class barriers which existed at the turn of the century. Society was roughly divided into four main classes, the aristocracy, the upper middle class, the lower middle class and the working class. Of the aristocracy I knew little and even today would be at pains to define them. Within the boundaries of my limited horizons in north Essex the old aristocratic families were giving away, or selling out to be more specific, to a new class. These were the business empire builders, which the jealous called "nouveau riche", whilst the ambitious sought their patronage. Within a few miles of Saffron Walden Sir James Bailey, the founder of Bailey's Hotel, Sir James Mackay, soon to become Lord Inchcape of the P&O fame, and Lord Strathcona, the principal architect of modern Canada, all owned large mansions and estates; whilst not far from my grandmother's house at Great Yeldham, Samuel Courtauld was building up his textile empire. If the aristocracy, willingly or unwillingly, admitted these new and hardworking industrialists to their society and their exclusive west end clubs, I doubt whether the upper middle class were so indulgent to the lower middle class. Perhaps one can best define the upper middle class as those who sent their sons and daughters to private schools, ie, the "prep" and public school routine, followed preferably by a spell at one of the older universities, usually Oxford or Cambridge, though Scots might go to Edinburgh and medical students to Trinity College, Dublin without loss of face. Professional people such as bank managers, clergy, doctors, lawyers and Service officers were automatically accepted into the upper class social circle, but those connected with commerce and industry had to fight to squeeze their way in. It was the age of snobbery and, of course, we youngsters were the biggest snobs of all. I well remember at St Faith's how we despised two boys called Pascall because their father was head of a sweet manufacturing firm. A day boy called Bird, whose father was erroneously reputed to make custard, was only accepted by us boarders because his parents had a large house and offered us hospitality at weekends.

The lower middle class embraced anyone between the upper middle class and the working class. It included such people as shop-keepers, clerks, owners of small businesses, the postmaster and the station master. They lived in neat well-kept houses; their wives managed with little or no domestic help; their transport was the bicycle and they spent their holidays at Southend-on-Sea or Great Yarmouth.

Finally there was the working class. They were the labouring class in the sense they earned a meagre living by the use of their hands, be it in agriculture, industry or domestic employment. Their wages sound pitiful by any standard. Ten shillings a week for an agricultural worker, (or farm labourer as they were known), plus a few perks, eg, milk and potatoes; twenty pounds a year for a resident parlourmaid; fifteen shillings to one pound a week for a non-resident groom or gardener. These were typical rewards for a 50-60 hour week.

And yet in the rural, as opposed to the urban, areas the really poor were not very numerous. There was very little unemployment, and for the working man and his wife only Sundays provided a few hours for leisure, apart from a pint or two at the pub on Saturday nights for the husband and an occasional outing for his family. So long as the husband was in work life was tolerable, but if he was sick or invalided there was real trouble. There was a form of health insurance. For a penny or so a week people could "join the club", ie, a Friendly society, and get free medical and hospital benefit. But if the rent became overdue the workhouse became the last refuge of the destitute and in the case of the elderly and disabled the dreaded prelude to a pauper's grave.

Today these distinctions and barriers between various strata of society seem rigid to the point of absurdity, but they certainly existed. They continued up to 1914, but under the stresses and strains of battle conditions the barriers broke, or at least were lowered. This is one of the few good features which emerged from World War One. I suppose that in an imperfect world, class distinctions in one form or another are inevitable. Nowhere today are they more significant than in the Communist countries. The distinction there is not, of course, between aristocracy and the lower orders, but between the rulers and the ruled. But in this country it appears to me that such distinctions as do still exist are minimal. For example at the end of the social scale life peerages have partly democractised the House of Lords, whilst at the other end Lord's cricket ground no longer sees the "gentlemen" competing against the "players".

In 1910 my brother, having won the top scholarship to St Lawrence College, Ramsgate, left St Faith's. So I left also. Being too young for the College I was destined to spend a year at the junior school, which stood in the same grounds. For reasons best known to the authorities the senior and junior schools were not allowed to mix. The one exception to this policy of segregation was on Sunday afternoons when brothers from the two schools were allowed to meet for a walk. These occasions were

15

somewhat marred for me, because as a junior I was forced to wear a hideously conspicuous black and white straw boater whilst my brother sported a neat school cap. I felt a sense of inferiority which increased when I joined the college and found that my brother was making his way up the school ladder, both academically and on the playing fields, whilst I with my poor physique was hopelessly inadequate at games and began to loathe everything connected with them. As some compensation I was able to hold my own academically and eventually found myself in the classical sixth form enjoying Latin and struggling with Greek verse. By the time war broke out in 1914 my brother was school captain, had won his colours for cricket, hockey and soccer, and was company sergeant major in the Officers Training Corps. I was an undistinguished member of the classical sixth, a nobody at games and a recently promoted lance-corporal in the OTC.

The first week of August 1914 found us both in camp at Tidworth Pennings with other public school contingents of the OTC. On 4th August War was declared. That night for the first and last time in my life I was on guard duty. The next day all the cadets were sent home wearing uniform and the camp ended prematurely. I always remember the thrill and pride with which on Liverpool St Station, when asked by complete strangers if we had been called up, we were able to give sufficiently evasive answers to imply that that was the case.

In these OTC camps the various contingents from schools were grouped together to form battalions under the command and adminis-tration of officers of the regular army. The Tidworth Pennings camp that year was, I assume, under the charge of the Depot of the King's Royal Rifle Corps, Winchester, because our battalion commander was a Major Hereward Wake* of that regiment. I bought a picture postcard of him mounted and in dress uniform. Years later he was to have a very close connection with St Lawrence. During the Second World War the college moved from the vulnerable area of Ramsgate to the comparative safety of Major General Sir Hereward Wake's country estate in the heart of Northamptonshire. He took a keen interest in the school and remained its active supporter until his death. That was not the first time that the school had been forced to leave Margate. In 1916 under the threat of raids by air or sea it was decided to evacuate it to Chester. This

---

*Major-General Sir Hereward Wake CB, CMG, DSO, died on 4th August 1963

16

decision no doubt was influenced by an event which took place one night about the end of April 1915. In the early hours some of us were woken by the noise of gun fire. I happened to sleep in a dormitory facing Ramsgate. We rushed to the windows and some of us had a fleeting sight of a zeppelin caught by searchlights over the centre of Ramsgate. Next morning many of us, with or without permission, rushed into the town, where we joined the crowds staring at the burnt out shell of a public house in the narrow high street. The publican and his wife had, we were told, lost their lives.

In the summer of 1915 my father broke the news to me that my school days were numbered. He could no longer afford to keep me at St Lawrence, although my fees were partially offset by an exhibition I had won from the junior school. He gave his reasons as a heavy reduction in his income. This was due to loss of clients in war-time. Coupled with this was the cost of maintaining a separate house for my mother.

My mother by this time had suffered what today would be called a nervous breakdown resulting from the strain imposed on her over the past six or seven years by the breakdown of her marriage. Contributory causes had been her ceaseless activities as an official of the Primrose League before and during the election of 1910; and, after the war started, the effect of the Zeppelin raids over East Anglia, where she was now living in one of the houses owned by my grandmother at Troston outside Bury St Edmunds.

Those were the days when divorce or legal separation were frowned upon in polite society. And so, like countless other couples, my parents outwardly appeared to lead a normal married life. For appearances sake my father frequently spent the weekend at Troston. Inwardly and in private their feelings and behaviour towards one another could only be described as hostile. Undoubtedly under similar conditions today they would have been divorced after two years separation. Subsequently my father would probably have re-married, leaving my mother free to pursue her intellectual activities in peace. More important she would have avoided the distress and humiliation of being incarcerated in a mental home and classified as a lunatic until such time as the Master in Lunacy saw fit to release her. This happened on more than one occasion. Up to the time of her death in 1938 she remained one of those unfortunate individuals, in my experience usually female, whose mental stability was poised on a knife edge. Consequently I, for one, shall always feel grateful to the late Sir Allen P Herbert MP and others to whom this country owes a sensible and humane relaxation from the archaic divorce laws of my youth.

2

Cadet at The "Shop" – The Western Front – Red X Hospital in London

In August 1915 my father, through a mutual friend, arranged for me to be interviewed by a senior official of the Great Eastern Railway Co. As a result I was offered the job of a trainee booking clerk at Liverpool Street Station. I was seventeen and had ambitions of becoming a surgeon. My immediate reaction was an inclination to falsify my age and enlist. Thanks to my mother wiser counsel prevailed. She persuaded me to seek the advice of my uncle Capel. I had never met him, but had heard much about him from my mother who was naturally proud of his achievements. Brigadier-General Sir Capel Holden was commissioned into the Royal Artillery in 1875. He had spent most of his Service as a senior officer at Woolwich Arsenal, where his scientific inventions and improvements in the art of gunnery earned him an international reputation and a Fellowship of the Royal Society. He was also a pioneer motorist and as chairman of the Royal Automobile Club was responsible for the construction of Brooklands motor racing track, portions of which can still be seen forming the perimeter of the Weybridge aircraft works. One permanent memorial to his genius remains in the Science Museum, South Kensington. This is the motorcycle which he designed and which subsequently went into limited production. It is a debatable point whether the Holden machine was the second motorised cycle (as opposed to tricycle) in the world. It was certainly the first to employ four cylinders.

My uncle arranged to see me at the War Office, where he had been recalled from retirement on the outbreak of war to head the Department of Mechanical Transport. His inquiries confirmed that entry to the Royal Military Academy, Woolwich, where potential officers for the Royal Artillery and Royal Engineers were trained, was open to boys of my age, and that the next intake was due in November. All I had to do was to pass a medical test and the written examination. In this I duly succeeded. And so on a cold day in November 1915 some 200 of us "snookers", as the junior cadets were called, presented ourselves at the RMA, Woolwich, all wearing, as instructed, dark suits and bowler hats. As each cab load of us arrived from the station we were assailed by shouts of "turn them down" by senior cadets assembled at the entrance to welcome us. Trousers with turn-ups were *de rigueur* for the young at that time. We obediently turned down our turn-ups. What the origin or purpose of this introduction to military life was I have never discovered. It did, however, give some warning of the rigorous and disciplined life which lay ahead of us for the next six months.

At school one had come to regard a certain amount of bullying as a necessary part of the educational system. At the "Shop", as the RMA was called, my initial attitude was much the same. Needless to say all the cadets had come from public schools. Bullying at school was to my mind a personal matter; the strong taking advantage of the weak, until, as quite often happened, the strong met their match and were shown up in their true colours. But I soon realised that at the "Shop" bullying, if that is the right word, was directed solely against those who failed to maintain the standards expected of a potential officer. I was to experience at first hand a notable example.

In the room, which I shared with three other Gentleman Cadets – GC's – as we were officially known, was one Rawlinson. For some reason he appeared incapable of maintaining the very high standards of dress and punctuality expected of potential officers. He was invariably somewhat scruffy in appearance and often late on parade. For those offences he suffered the official penalties of extra drills under the keen eye and sharp tongue of one of the Guards drill-sergeants attached to the staff. But for the senior cadets in our company that was not enough. In their eyes GC Rawlinson was letting the side down; and so, on more than one occasion, they dragged him out of bed and chased him with swagger sticks across the parade ground or into the swimming baths. Had he been at Sandhurst instead of the "Shop", his fate would no doubt have been an ink bath. I must add that at that time a near relative of Rawlinson, an uncle I believe, was a general commanding an army in France.

The shortened war-time course was dominated by foot drill, gun drill, physical training, lectures and equitation. The timetable was tight and allowed little time for relaxation except at the weekends. For example

15 minutes was the appointed time between the end of a lecture and the start of a session in the gym. In that time we had to rush back to our rooms, change from uniform into gym kit and parade in the gymnasium. Anyone late on parade was certain to be given extra drills by one of the officers of the staff. The latter were mainly men who had seen active service, and in some cases been severely wounded. The more senior ones delivered lectures on purely military subjects, which naturally formed the bulk of the curriculum; whilst a few civilians from the Royal Arsenal dealt with some technical subjects, eg, explosives. The proportion of teachers to taught was much lower than was the norm in schools and universities, and there was none of that intimacy out of working hours to which one had been accustomed. Under the stress of war this was no doubt excusable, but not inevitable. Out of working hours it should, to my mind, have been possible for the staff to have made efforts to get to know the GC's on a personal basis. They did not do so. Today such behaviour would be out of the question.

In 1915 mechanisation was in its infancy and all officers were required to be able to ride a horse, and have some knowledge of animal management. Riding school, therefore, played a conspicuous part in the curriculum. The "Shop" had no riding school of its own, so once, or maybe twice, a week we marched, or to be more accurate bicycled in formation, to the riding school at the RA Barracks in Woolwich. There we were put through our equitation paces by NCO riding instructors. The instructor who took our ride was a bully. He epitomised the type of sergeant-major cartoonists like to portray.

Being mounted on strange horses of varying temperaments and agility provided a severe test for those without previous riding experience, especially when the order was, "Drop your reins and cross your stirrups." Without the aid of stirrups a trotting horse provides the rider with the very minimum of rapport with his mount, resulting in strains and pains in the anatomy which have to be experienced to be believed. One of our fellow cadets, Penfold, was, to say the least of it, not athletically built. In particular his legs appeared not to lend themselves to the chassis of a horse. He excelled us all in the number of times he fell off. One day during a particularly uncomfortable session, in which our instructor in a fit of more than usual bloody-mindedness flogged our mounts into a state of pandemonium, many of us bit the dust of the arena – in some cases more than once. Needless to say GC Penfold was amongst the latter. Finally our sadistic instructor ordered him not to attempt to remount, but to run behind the string of horses as they careered around the riding school. Nearly sixty years later I encountered Penfold again. The occasion was the state funeral of Field-Marshal Lord Alexander at St George's Chapel, Windsor. The cortege accompanying the coffin was provided by the Military Knights of Windsor in their historic tail-coated scarlet full dress uniforms. Amongst these distinguished figures was Colonel Penfold RA (retired).

On the outbreak of war it was decided for obvious reasons to increase the supply of officers by, amongst other measures, reducing the length of the courses at both the "Shop" and the Royal Military College, Sandhurst. It is not so obvious why in the autumn of 1915, the former was reduced to six months, whilst Sandhurst stood at nine months, since Sandhurst trained infantry officers amongst whom casualties were tragically high. I believe the reason given by the War Office was that gunner casualties were proportionately even higher. This was due to the practice of placing artillery close behind the infantry they were supporting. In mobile warfare, when gun positions were constantly changing, this was reasonable; but once the front stabilised into trench warfare, batteries remained in the same positions for long periods. Consequently they could more readily be spotted by the enemy and subjected to destructive counter-battery fire. With the increasing use by both sides of observation from aircraft and balloons, the siting of artillery in concealed positions became of paramount importance. As an aid to concealment, camouflage netting eventually came into general use. Other compelling reasons for turning out more artillery officers were the increasing need for more and heavier guns in trench warfare as the only means for destroying troops well dug in to the ground, and the advent of anti-aircraft artillery.

The introduction of the six months course at the "Shop" meant that our term was due to pass out within a few days of the end of the existing one year course. The latter's passing out was memorable on two counts. Firstly, the traditional passing out parade was taken by Field-Marshal Lord Kitchener, Secretary of State for War. This controversial figure, whose face is familiar, to this day, by the reproduction of posters in which his outstretched finger called for recruits to the new armies bearing his name, was shortly to lose his life, when HMS *Hampshire* carrying him to Russia was sunk by enemy action on 5th June 1916. Secondly, the passing out night was marked by a post-prandial rag in which chamber pots played a prominent part. Next morning the people of Woolwich were entertained by the sight of every pinnacle of the RMA crowned with jerries. It was some time before the less accessible of these articles could be retrieved from the chapel and the statue of Prince Napoleon – a former GC, who was killed in the South African

War – which overlooked the main road from Woolwich to Eltham.

The Commandant, Major General Jelf was not amused and as a deterrent persuaded the War Office to antedate the commissioning of a few of the senior cadets concerned.

This had its effect, and when on 26th May 1916 our term passed out it was on a sober and sombre note. It is, perhaps typical of that period that in his final address to us, Jelf, amongst other advice as to what was expected of an officer and a gentleman, included this exhortation as to headwear, "Gentlemen, when in mufti you must never wear a cap, only a bowler or a homburg." Next day with one pip on our shoulders and a Sam Browne belt we departed.

Apart from something of the theoretical side of gunnery, the ability to drill like a guardsman and an antipathy to all forms of riding instruction, I cannot recall learning much of value at the "Shop". My time there did, however bring me one great benefit in that it enabled me at the weekends to spend much time with my Uncle Capel and his wife Bessie. They lived in a comfortable house at Blackheath and many Sundays after church parade I bicycled over to spend the day with them. My uncle had a well-equipped workshop in which he had carried out many of his inventions in the electrical and mechanical field. It was he who opened my eyes to the enormous future which lay open to electrical communications. Amongst items in his collection of instruments were many forms of telegraph and an early telephone with which he was credited as having established the first telephone circuit in India, when stationed at Darjeeling in 1880.

My place in the entrance examination to the "Shop" was not high enough for me to aim for a commission in the "Sappers" who at that time were responsible for army communications, so I became a "gunner". I could have joined the Royal Field Artillery (RFA) which was horse drawn, but chose the Royal Garrison Artillery (RGA) because they were in the process of being mechanised. The term 'garrison' was somewhat misleading, and was abolished after the war. It had originally been introduced to mark those gunners who manned the static defences of ports and harbours. In war-time some of the guns embracing these defences were made mobile by mounting them on carriages to accompany a field force on special operations such as the siege of a fortress. During the South African war much mention was made of the "Long Tom", a 4.7 inch gun which accompanied the various columns. In 1914 those which had survived were taken out of store and sent to the

23

Western Front until such time as something more up to date could replace them. By the spring of 1916 the flow of modern medium and heavy artillery was underway. The main weapons in the medium class were the 6 inch howitzer and the 60 pounder gun; whilst in the heavy class the 9.2 inch and the 12 inch howitzers were seen in increasing numbers. For reasons best known to Whitehall the new batteries, which were being formed almost weekly, were entitled, "Seige" batteries, although the formations to which they were allotted were called, "Heavy Artillery Brigades".

After a short spell at the School of Artillery at Lydd, Kent I was posted to No 168 Siege Battery forming at Plymouth. Whilst at Lydd I flew for the first time as an observer in a "string and canvas" biplane, the famous FE2b. I was thrilled by the experience. Although I have flown many thousands of miles since that day, I can still recall the slightly sweet smell of the machine – a combination of engine oil and the dope used to cover the linen wings – the roar of the propeller as we bumped over the grass, that indescribable feeling of freedom as the machine became airborne, and familiar landmarks spread out like a map below.

In August we received our equipment as a battery of 6 inch 26 cwt howitzers. After two weeks practice on the firing ranges at Lydd, we were deemed to be trained and ready to go into action.

On 20th September 1916 I left England with the advance party and eventually ended up at Ypres. The battery joined us a few days later and immediately went into action on the western outskirts of the shell-torn town, which was invariably known to the British Army as "Wipers". My first few days at the front were spent with a battery whose position we were due to take over, so that my task was not too onerous. I had time one day to spend an hour or so wandering through the ruins of the town, which was fairly free from shelling during the hours of daylight. I cannot recall seeing a single building that was intact. The magnificent cloth hall was completely in ruins. Only a few buildings on the outskirts were occupied – by soldiers – all the civilians had long since departed. In one such building we settled ourselves. The walls of the room in which the officers messed were decorated with humorous sketches executed in crayon. An endearing figure of a be-whiskered private soldier featured in most of them. That figure of "Old Bill" was shortly to become famous. It would appear that the cartoonist Bruce Bairnsfather had occupied the room earlier and practised his art on the walls.

Our battery commander, a middle-aged militia man, invariably wore his tin hat in the mess, even at meals. Behind his back we junior officers categorised him as "a windy dug-out", and rather despised him for the example he was setting. A few weeks later a report was received in which the infantry accused our battery of causing casualties amongst our own men in the front line trenches by firing short. Our CO went out at night into no-mans-land groped about in the offending shell holes and returned with conclusive evidence in the form of fragments of shells that it was a German 5.9 inch howitzer which had caused the casualities. Later he was awarded the DSO for another act of bravery; which only shows how deceptive first impressions can be.

At night long convoys carrying supplies to the front were forced to pass through "Wipers". The Germans harrassed these movements by long range artillery fire, causing a nightly toll of death and destruction. Apart from that, the most lasting impression this introduction to war created in me was that of smell. The sweet, sickly odour of chloride of lime combined with human sweat, urine and rotting vegetation struck the nostrils with increasing intensity the nearer one approached the front. Existence in water-logged trenches in the flat fields of Flanders, where to show your head for an instant above the parapet invited a sniper's bullet, called for courage and morale of a high order. It was only by pulling the infantry out of the front line periodically and resting them in the back areas that life became sustainable. There at any rate, with luck, they could be sure of a shower, a change of clothing and a decent night's sleep. We gunners admired them, and although we did not get pulled out of our positions for periods, we were in most cases able to sleep under some sort of cover, change our clothes, and keep ourselves reasonably clean.

My time in 168 battery was brief. The signal officer of the brigade, of which the battery formed part, became a casualty. To my delight I was appointed to replace him. It meant that I had my own independent command of about 25 men and came directly under the Brigade Commander, Lieutenant-Colonel Buzzard. Buzzard was a regular gunner who had already seen considerable active service. He was one of those mild mannered, kindly characters whose outward appearance concealed a strength that inspired confidence when things were critical, and who never failed to address words of encouragement or thanks to those under him. I consider myself lucky to have served under him at such an early stage in my career.

As brigade signal officer my main task was to maintain communications between brigade headquarters and the batteries and to certain observation posts (OP's). The brigade formed part of VIII Army Corps, which was commanded by Lieutenant-General Sir Hunter Weston, a Royal Engineer officer, who became quite a well-known personality. After the war he served as an MP for some years. At the time the Germans were unusually quiet in the Ypres salient, which normally was one of the hot spots of the Western Front. No doubt in order to ascertain whether or not the enemy were preparing for an offensive VIII Corps carried out frequent raids with the object of capturing prisoners. After one such raid "Hunter Bunter", as the Corps Commander was affectionately known, ordered a parade at which he was to present medals to certain individuals who had distinguished themselves. The parade was held in the grounds of the chateau occupied by Corps Headquarters. For some reason I was present in the parade. "Hunter Bunter" was nothing if not a showman. The parade was drawn up facing the exit from a ride in a stretch of woodland. Out of sight from the parade was the chateau. At the appointed hou with a fanfare of trumpets and accompanied by a mounted escort with pennons flying "Hunter Bunter" suddenly appeared in the distance from a side-turning, galloped down the ride towards the parade and as suddenly drew up facing it. He addressed the parade, presented the medals, turned smartly about and galloped off by the same route from which he had arrived. It was an impressive display by an unusual general. I use the expression unusual, because many historians of World War I have depicted the British High Command, particularly on the Western Front, as autocrats with no imagination and little regard for those under their command, who spent most of their time living in comfort and safety, in chateaux well behind the lines. If this is a true judgement of the majority of those in high command, I can only say that the only two generals I encountered in the 1914-18 war must have been exceptions. Hunter Weston was one and General Plumer the other.

The stories told about "Hunter Bunter" were many. The best known relates to an occasion when he was visiting troops holding the front line. As he was about to reach one company position it was discovered that Private Snooks had somehow obtained more than his fair share of the rum ration which was daily issued to troops in the line. The offender was quickly bundled on to a stretcher, covered with a blanket, and told to keep his mouth shut. Unfortunately the Corps Commander caught sight of the stretcher and inquired as to the nature of the casualty. To which the Company Commander replied, "That's Private Snooks, sir. I'm sorry to say a sniper got him just before you arrived." Drawing himself up Hunter Bunter raised his right arm and said, "I salute the gallant dead." Whereupon from the stretcher arose a resounding belch which nearly lifted the blanket, followed by, "Watch-er old baaastard shaying?"

General (later Field-Marshal) Plumer was a very different character. I met him twice. On both occasions he was visiting units in action. He was accompanied only by an ADC. He talked freely to all ranks and showed an obvious interest in all whom he met. His headquarters may, for all I know, have been in a chateau, but it was generally recognised that he spent as much time as possible visiting the troops under his command. He was as much a "soldier's general" as, say, Alexander, Auchinleck and Montgomery of the Second World War. Unlike them, however, he never had the opportunity to exercise his professional skill in mobile warfare.

On 14th December, 1916 I, in company with one of our battery commanders, Major Colson, was reconnoitering in the trenches for an Observation Post from which to carry out a counter-battery shoot against a German field battery which was causing considerable casualties to our infantry. Unfortunately our potential "target" opened fire and treated us to a brief dose of the medicine we were planning to give them, during which one shell exploded on the parapet of the trench down which were were proceeding. We were thrown flat down on to the duckboards lining the trench. After what seemed an eternity, but in fact was probably only about one minute the shelling ceased. I raised myself on my knees and called to Colson, "Are you alright, sir?" There was no reply. My sergeant who had been following us and had escaped injury then came and tried to help Colson to his feet. He had been killed instantly. I struggled to my feet, but found I couldn't stand. I could not make this out as the only sign of injury appeared to be a scratch on my cheek from which blood was oozing. A stretcher party quickly arrived to remove Colson, and one of them, a tall guardsman, picked me up and carried me pick-a-back to the nearest regimental aid post. I recall receiving an injection and then presumably passed out. That evening I remember being wheeled into a Casualty Clearing Station at Poperinghe (of Toc H fame) where my immediate destination was a large Nissen hut full of operating tables and figures in white. Next morning I came to in another Nissen hut – this one a ward – with a contraption of rubber tubes attached to my left thigh. A shell splinter had entered the back of that limb and ended up partially embedded in the bone, where it remains to this day. In doing so it had damaged the main artery and created a blood clot which luckily the surgeon was able to remove.

In due course I was evacuated to England, where I was fortunate enough to find myself in a most luxurious emergency hospital run by the Red Cross. It was in a corner house of London's exclusive Belgrave Square. The owner was, if I remember rightly, Lord Dudley, whose wife, an American heiress, together with another lady similarly placed, met most of the expenses. Many of the pre-war staff had remained, including the butler and cook. The former waited upon us in our wards, which in my case was the ball-room, the latter produced the most delectable meals. The small nursing staff was headed by a charming Scotch sister. Those of us who were able to get about on crutches vied with one another to take her to the theatre. This cost us little since theatre managements were generous with the distribution of complimentary tickets to the wounded. "Chu Chin Chow" had just started its highly successful run at His Majesty's with Oscar Ashe and Violet Essex in the leading roles supported by a large cast, including camels, donkeys, goats and other animals. I saw it three times and lost my heart to Violet Essex. Another very popular and highly successful musical at that period was "The Maid of the Mountains", some songs of which have survived the passage of time.

The surgeon who attended us daily was a Harley Street man. He was involved in an accident in a taxi as a result of which he lost the sight of one eye. To our admiration he was back on duty again within a week or two. He attributed the accident to the black-out which was still in force, since the danger of Zeppelin raids had not entirely faded despite their heavy losses. One afternoon soon after my arrival those of us who were taking a nap were woken by a series of distant explosions. From the evening papers we learnt that London had been bombed for the first time by bombers – as opposed to airships – and in daylight.

Compared with conditions during the blitz of 1940-1 London, during the winter of 1916-17 was comparatively normal. The black-out was minimal, except when raiders were reported having crossed the coast and heading towards the Capital. In that event street lamps and public lighting generally were cut off or reduced to a minimum. Vehicle lighting was reduced to the equivalent of present day parking lights. Petrol rationing had reduced the number of private cars in circulation, but taxis were plentiful.

There was little shortage of food. Theatres and cinemas were flourishing. The one depressing feature was the appalling toll of casualties, which mounted week after week, and turned the humble telegraph boy into a figure of doom for those whose husbands and sons were "at the front".

By the autumn, after convalescence and a short spell of light duty, I was passed fit again for active service. I was by now nineteen. I mention this because a year previously, after a debate in the House, it was decided to limit active service to those over that age. Those under it were being sent home when I was wounded, and my turn would have followed despite Colonel Buzzard's effort to retain me. Whilst I was in hospital at Poperinghe, Buzzard had visited me and cheered me up with two pieces of good news. First, our brigade had virtually destroyed the enemy battery which had killed Colson. Second, he asked me to keep in touch with him as he wanted me to rejoin him, if possible. This I had, of course, done and he had successfully applied for me. His brigade had recently been transferred from the Western Front to Italy.

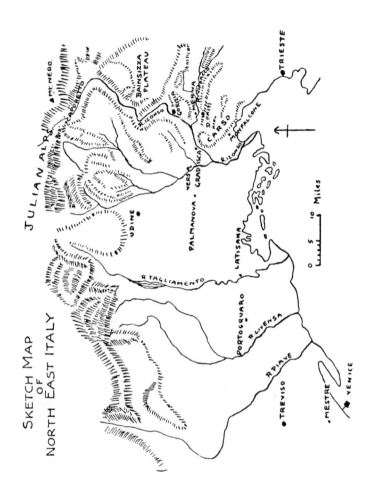

SKETCH MAP
OF
NORTH EAST ITALY

JULIAN ALPS

MT. NERO.
CAPORETTO
BAINSIZZA PLATEAU
R. ISONZO
GORIZIA
VERBIA
R. ADDA
CARSO
MONFALCOME
R. ISONZO
VERSA
GRADISCA

TRIESTE

UDINE

PALMANOVA

LATISANA

R. TAGLIAMENTO

PORTOGRUARO

R. LIVENSA

R. PIAVE

TREVISO

MESTRE
VENICE

0   5   10 Miles

30

3

The Retreat From Caporetto

The summer of 1917 saw the Allied armies in Western and Southern Europe still bogged down in trench warfare. On the Western Front a continuous line of British, French and Belgian troops faced the Germans from the Belgian coast to the Swiss frontier. In the south the Italians confronted the Austro-Hungarian armies from Switzerland to the Adriatic.

At an Inter-Allied conference in Rome on 6th and 7th July Prime Minister Lloyd George had proposed that the main allied effort should be concentrated on the Italian front with the object of finally defeating the Austro-Hungarians. In this he was supported by the Italian Commander-in-Chief General Cadorna. The latter, however, affirmed that to ensure success he would require the assistance of ten British and French divisions and some 400 guns. This did not meet with the approval of the representatives of the other allies. In the end Cadorna was left to carry out an offensive on the Julian front with the assistance of sixteen batteries of British artillery and thirty-five French guns, mainly of heavy calibre. Colonel Buzzard was commanding one of the British artillery brigades.

On 20th September 1917 by coincidence exactly one year to the day since I left for Ypres – another subaltern and I together with a small party of gunners left England. We formed the first draft of reinforcements for the "British Heavy Artillery, Italy". Our journey from Le Havre onwards by slow civilian train occupied four days with overnight stops at Paris, Culoz and Turin. From Paris to Turin we travelled with a major and forty cadets of the USA Army Air Service. The United States had not yet entered the war. These airmen were going to learn to fly the Italian Caproni, a twin-engined biplane, then in the forefront of bomber aircraft. Eventually on the 27th we reached Palmanova, our railhead and ordnance depot.

Next morning I left to join my new battery. Of Palmanova I got but a vague impression of an ancient town, entirely surrounded by high ramparts and a moat, which one entered by a kind of drawbridge through a narrow gateway in the massive walls – in short an exaggerated edition of a medieval castle. Later I learnt that the town had been fortified by Napoleon and that it contained only three exits, all similar in appearance and leading out on to the open plain. Inside the town not far from the east – or Gradisca – gate was a large piazza. From there to either of the other two gates one passed through a maze of narrow streets. To find one's way out, except possibly by the Gradisca gate, was to a stranger a matter of considerable difficulty. This I was to find out to my discomfiture some weeks later.

Three or four miles out of Palmanova we passed the old frontier and entered conquered territory – or *Italia Irredenta* as the Italians called it – for to them the Trieste-Gorizia area was rightfully part of Italy, which had been guaranteed to them by the Treaty of London. Under the secret Treaty of London in April 1915 Italy had been promised by the Allies, in the event of victory possession of the Trentino, the Cis-Alpine Tyrol, Trieste and Istria, so that after the war Italy's frontiers might rest secure upon a mountain barrier.

The country through which I passed was a flat, open plain, highly cultivated, well irrigated, and intersected by numerous roads. On either side of these frequently ran deep dykes, bordered by rows of acacia trees; beyond lay fields of maize, mulberries, and occasionally vineyards. In places one saw well-constructed trenches and machine-gun emplacements, relics no doubt of the former Austrian frontier defence. After crossing the broad expanse of the Izonso by a substantial wooden bridge, built by the Italian engineers, the country entirely changed. The open plain gave place to rocky foothills, some pine covered, others brown and almost bare of vegetation. To the south lay the dreary waste of the Carso, a barren and water-less expanse of broken rock formation, with here and there a high feature, and interspersed with numerous deep ravines. To the north the broad valley of the Izonso wound its way past Gorizia, skirted the western edge of the Bainsizza plateau and faded from view in a deep valley carved sheer out of the massive body of the Julian Alps.

At this time the Italian front line ran due north from the Adriatic at

Monfalcone, across the western extremity of the Carso to San Marco (some four miles east of Gorizia), crossing the Bainsizza plateau; it then followed the east side of the Izonso valley to about Caporetto whence, curving due west, it followed the southern edge of the Alps to the Swiss frontier. The Izonso front was held by two Italian armies. On the right, the Third Army extended from the sea to the Vippacco river; on its left, the Second Army extended northwards to Monte Nero.

Strategically the position of the Italian forces could scarcely have been worse. In the north they clung precariously to the edge of the Alps, where the precipitous nature of the terrain offered no opportunity for offensive action on a large scale with any prospect of decisive results. In the east the terrain was certainly more favourable, but became less so every kilometre they advanced; whilst the danger of their forces on the Izonso being cut off by an Austrian break-through in the north increased proportionately. One advantage was theirs alone. Being on interior lines, with good rail and road communications, they were able to move reinforcements to any threatened point more quickly than were the Austrians, whose lateral communications were longer and inter- rupted by deep valleys in the mountains. At this time the eleventh battle of the Izonso had recently ended. In this battle the Italians had advanced to a depth of five or six miles on the Bainsizza plateau. In doing so they had unintentionally created a dangerous salient for themselves. Opposite Gorizia and on the Carso they had gained some points of comparatively minor tactical advantage. These few square miles of conquered territory had cost them roughly 160,000 casualties. The strategical advantages gained were nil; the moral advantage was doubtful. One cannot blame the *Commando Supremo* who had acted in accordance with the allied plan. Such is trench warfare.

The British batteries were attached to the Italian Third Army. They were spread out between the sea and the Vippacco – a largish tributary which flowed due west through the enemy lines to join the Izonso a mile or two north-east of Gradisca. The battery to which I found myself posted belonged to the northern-most group, called Gruppo B2. It consisted of five British batteries, and itself formed part of an Italian *Raggruppamento*, commanded by an Italian colonel. He was a Sicilian regular officer, short of stature, always well turned out, imperturbable, courteous, considerate and withal highly efficient. Our battery position lay alongside the Vippacco and immediately behind the San Grado di Merna, a conical-shaped hill some 200 feet high, and surmounted by a ruined monastery. Our gun pits were well protected being blasted out of solid rock and covered with camouflage.

A few days after my arrival I had the opportunity to visit the front line trenches, which at this point skirted the forward edge of San Grado di Merna and lay about 500 to 600 yards in front of the battery position. Here, as indeed was the case on nearly all the Italian front, the most valuable weapon of defence was not the spade but the pneumatic drill. By its aid trenches and deep dug-outs had been carved out of solid rock. Incessantly the work went on, and one soon came to regard the sight of a sweating fatigue party laboriously dragging a drilling machine up a steep communication trench, or a bowed figure calmly piercing holes in the front line, with the same complacency that one regarded similar operations in the streets of London. That day I lunched with an Italian infantry brigade headquarters. Their mess was in a hut cleverly concealed in a deep ravine, one side of which had been blasted out to provide cover. Conversation was carried out through an interpreter – always an unsatisfactory medium – and I gathered that all was not well with the Italian Army. Casualties amongst the infantry had been enormous. Reinforcements were of an inferior type. Rations were poor, and equipment, guns and ammunition were short.

The impressions which I gained that day were afterwards confirmed by other sources. Herein undoubtedly lay some of the elements which contributed to the coming disaster. There were others also. Amongst them was a lack of confidence in the high command engendered by the frequency with which divisional, corps and even army commanders were removed from their posts. For this Cadorna was responsible. Although a man of undoubted ability especially as an organiser, his inflexible will and rigid outlook lacked the essential quality of psychological understanding. He made no allowance for human errors. Any commander who made the slightest mistake was immediately replaced, and consequently every major operation was succeeded by a wholesale reshuffling of generals. Then, too, Italian discipline, based on the Prussian model, was harsh in the extreme, and in the opinion of many, ill-suited to the Latin temperament. The death sentence for desertion was frequently and summarily carried out in the fighting area, with little attempt at privacy. There is little wonder then that the Italian soldier, poorly fed, ill-equipped, and called upon time and time again to carry out offensives under the most adverse conditions, had become somewhat demoralised, hated the "embuscati,* and was generally fed up with the war. Not that this state was universal. On the contrary, regiments such as the

*Literally "those in hiding". A term applied abusively by the Italian infantry to those whose duties were carried out behind the lines, ie, staff, supply and transport personnel etc.

Granatieri (roughly equivalent to our Guards), the Alpini and the Bersagleri still worthily maintained their fine traditions and esprit de corps; whilst in the Third Army the magnificent spirit installed by its commander, the Duke D'Aosta, had largely withstood the influences undermining morale, despite the heavy losses it had suffered in the Carso fighting.

The relations between the British and Italian troops could scarcely have been better. The British soldier is collectively the most adaptable and understanding person in the world. Our guns had taken part in the May and September offensives on the Izonso and the assistance which they had rendered the Italians was out of all proportion to their numbers. In the first place, being plentifully supplied with ammunition, they were able to do two or three times the work of the Italian artillery, whose ammunition was strictly rationed. Secondly, their accuracy was such that their effect was very considerable and moreover, enabled them for instance to fire on targets close in front of the advancing infantry without the risk of causing casualties amongst them, whereas many of the Italian guns, being of obsolete pattern and therefore less accurate, were unable to provide such effective and close support.

The British batteries had been sent to Italy without any supply or transport services. For these they relied on the Italians. Although there was much grousing amongst the gunners concerning the rations supplied to them – these were a curious Anglo-Italian mixture, including an unwelcome amount of macaroni, and cheese and bacon unsuited to the British palates – nevertheless the maintenance of these essential services served to bring the British troops into much closer contact with their allies than would have been the case had they been served by their own Army Service Corps.

Possibly too the barrier of foreign tongues was less of an obstacle to mutual understanding between allies than is usually the case. Many Italian soldiers had been domiciled in London and New York before the war, and delighted in airing their knowledge of cockney and yankee whenever they met an Englishman.

Needless to say, their conversation on these occasions was liberally interspersed with swear words. An amusing instance occurred one day when I was superintending the unloading of ammunition from a lorry at the battery. I had occasion to order the driver to back his vehicle nearer to the guns. I gave the order in my halting Italian. To my astonishment he calmly turned to one of my gunners, and in inimitable cockney style addressed him thus, "Oi! Bill. Just shift that .... stone from the .... wheel!"

Life on the whole was pleasant enough during those early days of October 1917. After the battles of September both sides lay back exhausted, whilst reinforcements were brought forward to fill the gaps. Ammunition was conserved for the next round of the great contest. Comparative quietness reigned on the Third Army front. The British batteries alone, being liberally supplied with ammunition, remained fairly active. In consequence they came in for a certain amount of attention from the Austrian artillery. Intermittent shelling of our positions served to keep one alive to the realities of war. The Austrian employed a peculiar type of shell, which we termed "a double event". The head was filled with shrapnel, which was exploded by the usual time fuse. The base was filled with high explosive, and was fitted with a percussion fuse. The effect of shrapnel, followed by a burst of high explosive as the base struck the ground, was alarming, but the physical damage caused was usually slight. The Austrians continued to use these shells up to the Armistice, and in time one came to regard them with complacency.

One day I had occasion to visit Gorizia, which lay about six miles to our north. I found a large and pleasant town, well laid out with broad streets, public gardens and squares, and surrounded by villas. I was amazed to see how little it had been damaged considering that it had been the scene of heavy fighting prior to its capture in the spring of 1916, and since had been continually within range of the enemy's artillery. I learnt that before the war it was the Cheltenham of the Austrian gentry. This probably accounted for their present reluctance to see it destroyed. Despite its proximity to the front line, the streets were by no means deserted, and here and there a shopkeeper continued to ply his trade. On the outskirts I passed an ambulance unit of the British Red Cross. They had been in Italy for a long time and had done yeoman service on the Izonso.

Soon after my arrival two out of the three British artillery groups were ordered to Egypt. Gruppo B2 alone remained in Italy. On 19th October the enemy artillery showed signs of increased activity. That night their infantry carried out an unsuccessful raid on our section of the front. The weather had now turned colder and heavy rain fell. During the next few days rumours of an impending Austrian offensive circulated freely. Their heavy artillery had evidently been reinforced and twelve-inch howitzers started to register on the back areas. On the 23rd I carried out a reconnaisance in the front line, and found the trenches much damaged and water-logged. Next day the enemy attacked Dosso Faiti – a prominent feature on our right front – but was easily repulsed. On the 25th I was on duty in the observation post. All day the Austrians pounded our trenches. Towards evening they again attacked and succeeding in establishing themselves on Faiti, but were promptly driven off by a counter-attack. At 8pm I was informed that my own and another British battery had been ordered to move into position further in rear. On returning to the battery position next morning I found it occupied by an Italian field battery. My own battery had left behind a detachment to look after some stores and a large quantity of ammunition which still remained. We were busy loading these up and sending them back to the guns. At 3pm a heavy bombardment started. Several large aeroplanes appeared flying low, and bombed the trenches and battery positions. The machines were Gothas, which tended to confirm the rumours that the German army had reinforced the Austrians. Very heavy howitzers were shelling our artillery. I saw one very heavy shell score a direct hit on an Italian artillery gruppo headquarters, sending up an enormous shower of rocks and pieces of timber. When the smoke cleared a cloud of paper was seen descending from the sky, like some fantastic snow storm. By a miracle the gruppo commander survived to witness the spectacle.

At 5pm I was relieved and went back to join the battery. The position which it had been ordered to take up was on the reverse slope of a thickly wooded hill some three miles in rear. On the narrow track up this hill I found the guns jammed in a block of traffic – guns, lorries, horses and men. The major told me that a heavy Italian mortar had got ditched and was blocking the way. As there was nothing I could do to assist, and hearing that I had had no food all day, he sent me off to get a meal, and then ordered me to return to the forward position. I arrived back there at 9.30pm, having picked up a motor-cycle en route.

That night the enemy again attacked Faiti and captured it, but of this I knew nothing at the time. All night my small party of gunners loaded up round after round of ammunition and sent it back, whilst the field battery kept up an incessant fire – now *vivace*, now *lento*. Around us the sky flashed with the lightnings of artillery and the hills echoed with the thunder of bursting shells. At intervals the blinding glare of a rocket burst forth over the trenches, throwing into vivid relief the ghostly figures of the gunners as they sweated at their task and casting weird shadows on the hillside as slowly it sank to earth. Gradually our work proceeded. Two light lorries were the only transport available, and these had some eight miles to cover on each trip. In between we smoked, drank tea and snatched what little rest we could. The men chatted cheerfully and joked with one another. To retire a few miles was to them a novel experience, and unfortunate, but in war one takes the rough with the smooth. Little did any of us realise what the future held in store. At daybreak the Italian field gunners fired their last few rounds and retired. The bombardment had now died down. An ominous lull fell. Save for the rumble of traffic, the intermittent roar of artillery, and the staccato tack-tack of a machine gun, all was quiet.

At noon I was recalled to the battery, leaving eleven men behind. The battery had gone into action in the early hours, but had now received orders to cease fire as no one knew where our front line lay. Two hours later I was ordered to return with a lorry and collect the few remaining stores. The battery had been ordered to retire to Gradisca, three miles further to the rear and west of the Izonso. There I was to rejoin them. As I went forward the road was packed with infantry – retiring. Progress was difficult. There was still a large quantity of ammunition in the forward position. Frantically I searched in my mind for some crumb of military knowledge which would enable me to destroy rapidly some 800 hundred-pound shells, but all in vain. Close by flowed the swift waters of the Vippacco. Into them we threw cartridges and firing tubes whilst bundling the few remaining stores into the lorry. Then hastily we departed. As I rode back on my motor-cycle my mind was uneasy. Should I have stayed and risked capture whilst we strove to dump the shells into the river? Should I have waited to erect one vast bonfire of shell and cartridges? Or should I have acted as ingloriously as I had done? I comforted my conscience with the thought that the shells would be of no use to the enemy unless he succeeded in capturing one of our guns, and even if he did he would have to improvise the firing tubes and cartridges to go with them.

Fortunately my mind was quickly diverted from these heart-searching inquiries. On emerging into the main road an amazing sight met my eyes. Converging on to the bridge over the Izonso was a vast confusion of traffic – lorries, men, guns, horses, carts and all the paraphernalia of war. Amidst these I came upon a British war correspondent. He represented as far as I can recall, *The Times* or the *Telegraph*. His car was struggling in the throng. He plied me with many questions. The Austrian attack had apparently succeeded. A retirement had been ordered. That was all I knew. How far the army was to retire I could not say, but undoubtedly the line of the Izonso would be held at all costs. He became swallowed up in the confusion of traffic.

Darkness had now fallen. As we crossed the Izonso a battalion of Granatieri passed in the opposite direction, singing as they marched. I watched them cross the river – fine upstanding men, the pick of the Italian army – and wondered how many of them would come back again. Slowly I threaded my way through the traffic to Gradisca. There I learnt that the battery had been ordered to Versa. Arriving there I found the battery and the battery commander standing shivering in the rain, which was now falling hard. I had out-distanced my lorry so started back to find it and volunteered to try and find the major's coat, which had got left at Gradisca. My mission successfully accomplished, I returned to Versa. All the British had left except an officer of another battery, who told me that the whole group had gone on to Palmanova.

The road was now one seething mass of traffic. Progress was all but impossible. Only those who have experienced an army in retreat can conceive the pathos, the grandeur and the tragedy of that night. For miles on all sides the country flickered with the light of innumerable fires as dumps, stores and depots were systematically destroyed. Yellow tongues of fire suddenly pierced the blackness of the night, and as suddenly died down to glowing balls of red. Clouds of black smoke crept like shadowy monsters across the plain. The air was thick with the pungent smell of burning wood. Acid fumes smote the nostrils. The deep thunder of explosives and the sharp crack of musketry rent the air. Along the road plodded the army in retreat – a ghostly procession in the flickering light. Astride the road, in two's tramped infantry, bowed down with heavy packs, great coats, machine guns, trench mortars and a thousand and one *impedimenta*. In the centre wagons and lorries piled high with ammunition, rations and baggage; here a field gun, its team of horses trampling and chaffing at every halt; there a heavy gun, weirdly draped with coats, helmets, haversacks, etc, cast off by the gunners who sweat and heave at the drag-ropes as slowly it crawls forward, creaking and groaning like some gargantuan chariot drawn by a gang of slaves. Harness jingles, wheels crunch, ropes creak, feet tramp and brakes grind. Now and again over the low murmur of tired men's voices a sharp order rings out as the procession moves jerkily onwards. Phut! Phut! My motor-cycle goes slower and slower. It pulls up with a jerk beneath the tailboard of a stationary lorry. I move to the side to pass round. A solid mass of humanity bars the way. Feet astride, I lean forward on the handlebars and my eyes, weary with the incessant strain of seventy-two hours, close. I fall asleep. Crash! I awake, sprawling in the ditch; motor-cycle on top. Painfully I drag myself and the heavy machine on to the road as the procession crawls slowly forward.

At 5am I reached Palmanova. Our guns lay parked in the piazza. The men lay sprawling beside them, fast asleep. Orders were awaited. Whence they were to arrive no one could tell. All was vague and uncertain. The shops were deserted; owners and stock had vanished as if by magic.

I entered an open doorway and lay down on a pile of sacking beside an empty counter. Hours (or was it minutes?) later I was rudely awakened by someone seizing me by the coat and bundling me unceremoniously into the street. The building was on fire, so we took refuge from the pouring rain in a church close by. The major wanted me. He was down the street. Which street? The orderly could not remember. Together we set out, lost our way and wandered in vain. In the piazza a mass of cavalry were drawn up – Novara and Genoa Lancers. (Within a few hours they were to play a major role in stemming the advancing tide.) Of my battery there was now not a sign except for one lorry.

The NCO in charge had orders to join the battery outside the Gradisca Gate. I climbed in beside him, and off we went. At the rendezvous there was not a sign of British troops. For three miles we proceeded eastwards against the stream of traffic until a side road enabled us to turn. Back we went once more to Palmanova, where the piazza was now empty. Westwards we plunged into a maze of narrow streets, past burning houses and looted shops. In vain we searched for an exit from the doomed city. Eventually we came upon two lorries belonging to another battery. One of the drivers knew the way, and we emerged on to the Latisana road. That was the road taken by our batteries, he said. All three Italian drivers now announced that they were short of petrol, so in search of petrol we went – only to find that the petrol dumps had been burnt. It was now dark, and my driver lost his way – and the other lorries. By luck we regained the main road and proceeded steadily for three miles. The road was strangely deserted, except for an occasional stranded vehicle. In attempting to pass one of these we slid gracefully into a ditch. There remained no alternative but to unload our vehicle. The cause of our misfortune was eventually repaired – and obligingly pulled us out of our predicament. Re-loaded we set out once more. Progress got slower and slower as we caught up with the tail of the retreating column.

Daylight came and revealed a heart-rending sight. The civil population, fleeing terror-stricken before the advancing enemy, had become hopelessly and inextricably mingled in the retreating army. Old men, women and children trudged painfully, bowed down with the weight of heavy bundles. At the entrance to his deserted cottage stands a peasant with his family, cart, cattle, gesticulating, pleading, struggling to join the ever-swelling stream. In vain he pleads. The traffic is halted – jammed vehicle to vehicle. Suddenly and jerkily it starts to move. Willing hands heave and push. A gap is formed and one more family sets out upon this tragic pilgrimage into the unknown. Incongruously behind guns and lorries shuffle patient oxen yoked to clumsy carts piled high with furniture, clothing, poultry, pots, pans and bedding – the sorry remnants of deserted homes.

Towards noon the rain ceased and the sun shone out of a cloudless sky. Soon enemy planes appeared, flying low. Rifles and machine gun opened fire on them, but with little effect. Up and down the road they sailed, dropping their load of bombs and then disappearing. Within the hour they returned with a fresh load. And so at regular intervals until darkness fell their unwelcome visits continued. Mercifully their marksmanship was poor. I only saw two direct hits upon the road. As a demonstration of air power it was unimpressive. Had they swooped down upon the road using their machine guns the havoc would have been ghastly. One likes to think that the desire to avoid hitting the refugees accounted for their bad marksmanship. If so, their chivalry was wasted, for several civilians were killed and wounded.

During one of these raids the traffic was halted, so I took cover in the ditch. Beside me cowered a mother with a whimpering infant clasped to her breast. I tried in vain to calm her fears. Terrified and speechless she gazed at the machines roaring over our heads. I cursed my inability to help her, and the utter cruelty and futility of war. Ashamed I scrambled to my feet. I was powerless, save for a revolver. Where were our aircraft and anti-aircraft guns to drive these devils away?

Twenty-three years later I was to witness similar scenes in the retreat to Dunkirk. The main differences were a preponderance of cars piled with household goods rather than carts, and ruthless enemy air attacks.

Of that night I have but the vaguest memory. At times we halted for an hour or more, then crawled onwards for a few hundred yards, or even a mile. As dawn broke we approached Latisana, where road and rail spanned the Tagliamente River by narrow bridges. I was dozing in the back of the lorry when a terrific hubbub woke me. Outside someone shouted that the Austrian cavalry were upon us. I scrambled out and fell heavily, scraping my shin in the process. As I picked myself up

41

half-a-dozen men dashed past shouting. Panic broke loose, and in a minute I was caught up in a seething mass of soldiers and civilians. Cursing and struggling I was carried forward in the crush. On either side of the road was a wide irrigation ditch filled with water. There was no escape. Soon we reached the high bank of the river and the crowd thinned out. Guarding the railway bridge stood a solitary Carabineri. One moment he was shouting and struggling to quell the rush, the next moment he was gone, trampled to death by the panic-stricken mob as they fought and struggled madly to get on to the narrow bridge. Cursing and shouting they surged across. A man slips on the uneven surface of the track, clutches frantically at the lattice girders and falls with a shriek of terror into the swirling waters beneath. Another follows, and another. Close by, on the approach to the road bridge I find one of our batteries. We collect a few men and prepare to remove the breech blocks from the guns to render them useless. It is impossible to move the guns themselves, so tightly are they wedged in the traffic, and we have no ammunition. Gradually the panic dies down. Across the river a brigade commander had already got his men in position along the bank, and he himself stands with rifle in hand at the bridge threatening the mob. Gradually order is restored.

Already trenches have been dug and reserve formations brought up to defend the line of the Tagliamente. Here it is a formidable obstacle, in full flood, deep and broad. Stragglers cross the bridge and are directed to appointed rendezvous. Units partially reform, command is reasserted. My own battery is across the bridge, but others are not. Another officer and I go back to help them.

For the first time I now appreciated the scarcity of transport in the Italian Third Army. Large quantities had been withdrawn before the retreat to reinforce the Second Army. We British had been allotted a few tractors and a handful of lorries, far below our normal scale. The lorries sufficed to carry stores and equipment, but ammunition had to be abandoned. Many of the tractors were giving trouble due to overloading. One I found hitched to three of our howitzers with a trench cart tacked on behind the third gun. Its engine strained and knocked under the heavy load and steam whistled out of the radiator. Every few yards its stopped, and had to be coaxed into activity again. This little party was in charge of one of our subalterns, named Dalton, who for some reason, was enveloped in a grey Italian army blanket. He was desperately urging the Italian driver to greater efforts. His limited knowledge of the Italian language was freely mixed with the British Tommy's limited repertoire of invective. Little did I realise that my dishevelled companion, Hugh Dalton was, in a few years, to become Chancellor of the Exchequer.

By luck we found a petrol dump intact beside the road and refilled the almost empty tanks. Fresh drivers appeared and later a new tractor. By nightfall all our guns were across the river intact. Shortly afterwards the road and rail bridges were blown up. The rest of the journey to Portogruaro was comparatively rapid, and on arrival we became a united formation again. Billets were found near the station, rations obtained, and everyone was able to get some sleep. Several of us shared a dormitory in the railwaymen's quarters. We exchanged experiences and speculated as to the future. Someone had seen a newspaper. The Austro-German armies had effected a complete breakthrough at Caporetto and were sweeping down on to the plains. The Third Army had been forced to withdraw to preserve its communications. The Second Army was in desperate straits, thousands had been captured, but the remnants were retiring according to plan. The Army would stand on the Tagliamento. Italy would fight to the last man. We argued. Some thought the war was finished. The Italian Army was demoralised; the men would not fight – they would cast away their arms and return to their homes. Should we be interned or sent back to France? Others argued that although the Army was demoralised it was not defeated. Now that their country had been invaded the spirit of the Italian nation would revive.

Early the next morning we were woken by a violent explosion. The enemy planes were busy again. One bomb had fallen on a billet wounding five of our men. The afternoon brought further air raids – and orders to entrain that night for Treviso where Group Headquarters were being established. No one could say why we were being sent there. Rumours in plenty spread around. We were being sent back to refit; we were bound for another part of the front; the Italian Army was not standing on the Tagliamente: it would retreat to the Piave – to the Po? The Government had asked for an armistice? At dusk we started to entrain. I shared a carriage with one of our majors. The windows were broken and it was bitterly cold. He lay wrapped in a blanket shivering. He had received an internal injury the previous day, and was in great pain. Later he recovered, but only temporarily. He died shortly after the war ended.

Next morning we arrived at Treviso. It was now 1st November. The major and several others got out. Suddenly the train started again and went on to Mestre. Some railway official had blundered. There we stayed. I was now in a poor state suffering from dysentery. At night a train alongside us caught fire. It was loaded with shells and grenades. Someone procured a light engine and pulled our train clear. I lay in the carriage too weak to move and listened to the explosions as the trucks went up in flames.

Next morning Colonel Buzzard arrived by car. Seeing my plight he put me in his car and sent me back to Treviso where I was soon between sheets in a comfortable billet. I later learnt that the Colonel had given up his own bed for me. It was typical of him. After a few days I recovered. The group was now split up. Half the guns were sent to Ferrara to refit and await supplies of spares and ammunition from the UK. I went with them. The remainder, as soon as ammunition arrived, rejoined the Army on the Piave.

In the meantime the Allies had reacted to the disaster of Caporetto with surprising promptitude. France despatched seven divisions and the British five to reinforce the battered Italians. The movement of these divisions was, of course, by rail. Considering that there were only two rail routes across the Franco-Italian border, ie, the Mont Cenis and the Riviera, it must feature as one of the most efficient and effective strategic moves of the war. After some weeks on the Piave, where the front eventually stabilised, our gruppo was moved on to the mountains overlooking the Asiago plateau. Here we came under British command as part of the 14th Corps commanded by General the Earl of Cavan, and, of course, reverted to the title of brigade.

The Caporetto retreat was at the time quite naturally regarded as a disaster. But was it really a disaster in the long term? Sometimes defeat in battle becomes a moral victory. Dunkirk was a disaster but it provided that Churchillian rallying cry, "Let us, therefore, brace ourselves to our duty and so bear ourselves that, if the British Commonwealth and Empire last for a thousand years, men will still say 'This was their finest hour'," and the nationwide incentive and determination out of which victory ultimately emerged. The Dieppe raid of 1942 was likewise a disaster, but, according to many, the lessons learned so painfully were amply justified when it came to the Normandy landings in 1944. As a participant in both Caporetto and Dunkirk I believe that defeat in battle is sometimes necessary to provide the drive and incentive which ultimately spells victory.

4

The Asiago Plateau—the Armistice—demobilisation—journey with a coffin

The Asiago plateau lies at the southern extremities of the Dolomites. It is some twenty-five miles north of Vicenza, at that time a strategically important rail and road junction. The plateau itself lay in a deep valley about 3000 feet above sea level. Its width varied from one to two miles across with a river and rail running through the centre. Across this expanse the British and Austrian infantry faced one another in trenches for the most part blasted out of the solid rock. Behind them the mountains rose up to heights of 600 feet or more, and here the gunners on both sides had excellent observation over the whole plateau with the heavier guns well protected just behind the crests of the mountains. The lighter guns with their shorter range were not so lucky and in some places had to occupy positions on the forward slopes facing the enemy.

By this time I had left the battery and rejoined Colonel Buzzard at his headquarters as brigade signal officer. Compared to the Western Front the war was "cushy" to use a contemporary phrase, and for us heavy gunners almost unbelievably so. The fact that we were living and fighting on top of a mountain in no way bothered the Italian army engineers.

They had erected excellent wooden huts out of the timber which afforested the mountain sides; blasted away the hillside, where necessary to site them so that they were practically immune to all except air attacks; and connected the whole area with roads and tracks, camouflaged wherever they emerged from the cover of the pine-clad mountain sides.

With the arrival of British and French fighter squadrons almost complete air superiority was achieved, and for days on end one never saw an

Austrian plane. Moreover, with the supply of ammunition almost unlimited on our side, and obviously limited on the enemy's side, we gunners had every advantage in our favour. Being a counter-battery brigade our normal task was to silence and, if possible, destroy enemy batteries. It was almost a routine task for one of our six inch howitzer batteries to plaster a known target with 400 rounds, the fire being directed on to the enemy battery position by an observer of the RAF in an RE8 plane fitted with wireless telegraphy and using a simple code.

The Austrian artillery had few weapons equivalent to our howitzers, being mainly equipped with high velocity guns which owing to their low trajectory could not drop shells behind the crest of hills where our batteries were sited. They did, however possess one monster howitzer, of about 15 inch calibre, which occasionally came into action. I was at the receiving end twice when its enormous high explosive shell with delayed action fuse buried itself in the solid rock of the mountains throwing up a volcanic-like eruption of fragmented rock over a wide area. On the first occasion I was just returning to brigade headquarters on my motor-bike, when above the engine noise of my single cylinder Triumph I heard a deep rumbling sound. It was not unlike the sound of a tube train approaching a station, except that in this case one felt one was not on the platform but on the line, and the train was a non-stop one. I jumped off and flung myself under the shelter of a rock face bordering the road. A second or two later there was a deafening explosion and time stood still as I cowered under a shower of rocks of all shapes and sizes.

In the deathly silence which followed the last bit of falling debris I got up and ran towards the signal office which lay in a depression just off the road. Within 100 feet or so of it the shell had carved out a vast crater on the edge of which one of my signallers was wandering in a dazed and half-naked condition. He must have been within a few feet of the crater's edge and yet outside the area of upward blast, and at the same time too near the centre of the explosion to be hit by the fallout of rocks and debris. Miraculously he recovered after a night's rest and was able to join the leave party, as was his due, next day. A hasty check showed that only one man was missing – my corporal in charge of despatch riders. It was some hours later that parts of his body were seen to be lodged in neighbouring trees. He too, poor fellow, was due to go on leave. My own injuries were superficial, and our medical officer soon patched them up.

On June 15th, 1918 the Austrians opened their final offensive designed to drive the Allies out of the mountains and into the Lombardy Plain. Here, by forcing crossings of the Piave, they aimed to advance towards

Treviso and Venice, thus cutting the Allied front in two. Everywhere the offensive was a failure and in a few days the Austrians were back where they started having suffered tremendous losses in men and materials from which they never recovered.

In mid-October the British 14th Corps moved down to the Piave front north-east of Treviso. The move was carried out with as much secrecy as practicable, and we were not allowed to fire a round until the final Allied offensive opened on 26th October. By 4th November it was all over and an armistice declared.

British casualties on the Italian front had been comparatively light. In the closing stages Spanish flu had caused the ranks to thin almost as much, if not more than, the enemy's bullets.

The last shot had hardly died away before we received orders to be prepared at very short notice to move to the Innsbruck area, where it was intended to open a new front against Germany. I do not recollect that any of us took this order very seriously. At that time the news from the Western Front was so encouraging, with the Germans in retreat, that the armistice of 11th November came as no surprise.

We moved into comfortable billets south of Padua, where we spent Christmas and the New Year in the peace and tranquility of the Italian country-side. Food and drink were plentiful. Two of us spent a weekend at one of the few hotels open in a sand-bagged Venice. The gondoliere were just returning. Those who were of military age, and I daresay some who were not, had plied their skills with marked bravery and success in those small craft which ferried our assault troops across the Piave. Apart from St Marks and the famous glass works Venice appeared to be a city in mourning with all its attractive features veiled in camouflage or hidden behind piles of sand-bags.

Before the armistice in Italy was declared we had, to everyone's regret, lost Colonel Buzzard who was suddenly whisked away to join the British staff at Versailles gathered there for the peace conference. Another officer of our brigade staff who was recalled at the time of the armistice was Lieutenant Gilbert Ledward RA – the initials in this case denoting Royal Academician. He was later to become well known as the sculptor of the Guards War Memorial on Horse Guards Parade, amongst his many other works. To this day, I cherish a panorama sketch showing the enemy battery positions on the Asiago front signed, G Ledward 2/Lt, and a pencil sketch of myself with the same signature.

47

For a nation which had never previously enforced conscription it was almost inevitable that the demobilisation of massive armed forces would give rise to unprecedented difficulties, delays and injustices – and in consequence popular denunciation of those in authority. It was also inevitable that the needs of the nation should in many cases run counter to those of the individual. The conversion of Great Britain from a peaceful industrial nation relying very largely on overseas trade to a highly organised and tightly regulated war-orientated society was not accomplished in a matter of weeks. In effect it was not until after the introduction of compulsory service in May 1916 that the full resources of the country in both manpower and materials were mobilised. The process had taken nearly two years.

To the men and women in uniform, many of whom had been volunteers and had remained on active service overseas for two or more years without home leave, there appeared no reason, now that the war was over, why they should not be released without delay. They expected to be out of uniform in a matter of weeks. But their expectation was in so many cases to be replaced by frustration at the delays. In a few instances in France and at home this frustration led to sporadic mutinies.

As the end of the war approached the War Office, on which the major responsibility for demobilising some 3.5 million men evolved, drew up plans which gave priority release to those whose pre-war occupations fell into the "reserved" category, eg, miners, railway employees, agricultural workers, etc. Obviously this policy could only lead to hardship and injustice for many of those whose occupations were not "reserved". It was eventually modified to take into account marital status, length of service and other personal factors. Added to this problem which affected the individual was that of disbanding war-time units and reforming those which were required for the peace-time forces and, in particular, the armies of occupation.

As a young and, in one's own estimation, war-experienced officer I must admit that I gave little thought to these problems at the time. I had got a regular commission and was, therefore, not faced with the immediate problem of entering a profession in "civvy street" as so many of my contemporaries were. To this day I do not know in accordance with which policy my unit was disbanded. All I know is that in a matter of weeks after the armistice we were sending parties of men to England, whilst others were detailed to hand in our guns and stores to the nearest ordnance depot. Thus everyone was kept busy and contented. Halfway through this process I found myself on board a troop train bound for Southampton via Le Havre.

In these days when troop movements appear to be carried out mainly by road or by air it may be of interest to recall to mind the long distance troop trains of those days. Other ranks travelled in the supreme discomfort of those famous freight wagons labelled in large letters, "Hommes 32-40 Chevaux en long 8." Since facilities for cooking and sanitary purposes were non-existent frequent stops were essential at stations equipped to meet these requirements. Officers fared considerably better being accommodated in 1st or 2nd class coaches, where at least they could obtain some comfort in a sitting position. On arrival at Southampton I was directed by a staff officer to proceed to a demobilisation centre on the outskirts of London. On stating emphatically that as a regular officer I was not eligible for and certainly did not wish to be demobilised he appeared nonplussed. However, after some delay I was told to take leave for a few days and then report to Bedford.

The few weeks which I spent at the Royal Engineer (Signals) Depot can only be described as the most boring of my Army career. The permanent staff comprised a small nucleus of "regulars". Their task was to process the demobilisation of an endless stream of soldiers whose sole aim was to cast off their uniform and return to "civvy street" as quickly as possible. I have no recollection of being occupied in either the paper work involved or in the replacement of uniform by civilian clothing. Two incidents which occured during those boring days in Bedford do, however, remain firmly embedded in my mind.

On one occasion, as orderly officer I was detailed to march a considerable body of troops through the centre of the town. For what purpose I can't remember, and is at any rate immaterial. On emerging into the main street the men who were supposed to be marching at "attention", that is to say not talking, started to talk loudly and make remarks at passers-by. In endeavouring to maintain order I lost my temper and shouted at them. The result, as I should have known, was fatal. The men went on laughing and talking, and when we eventually arrived at our destination they virtually dismissed themselves leaving me to slink back to my billet. That day I learnt a lesson which I have never forgotten. To lose one's temper in public and in particular with those who are one's subordinates, is to invite their disrespect and contempt.

A few days later through a casual remark by an officer in the mess I learnt that some unfortunate soldier due for "demob" having caught venereal disease had committed suicide rather than face his family in this unfortunate condition. His family lived on a farm outside Aberdeen and had, one surmised, been brought up in the strict Presbyterian faith. The powers-that-be had decided that the body was to be despatched at public expense to his home for burial. In addition they decreed that the coffin was to be accompanied by an escort. This escort was to be an officer whose delicate mission was to express the Army's condolences to the family and, no doubt, to answer any questions which might be asked as to the unfortunate man's demise. My mind was made up in a flash. Here was a chance of getting away from the boredom of demobilisation for a few days, with the possibility of a spot of leave in Aberdeen where my great friend Graham Murphy of the Gordon Highlanders was stationed. Besides, I had never been to Scotland.

A hasty visit to the Adjutant's office followed, and I came away delighted to find myself detailed for the job of escort. It did not occur to me that the imminent threat of a railway strike might have something to do with the lack of volunteers for the job. Two days later in the late evening I duly settled myself in an empty 1st class carriage at Bedford station, having satisfied myself as far as practicable that the luggage van attached to the rear of the express contained the coffin and the corpse entrusted to my care. I slept well, and next morning woke up to find the train stationary at a platform. Nearby on the side of a hill overlooking the railway a church with a curiously distorted spire attracted my attention. It was a little time before I realised that the station was deserted. Eventually I unearthed some railway official who informed me that the whole railway system had been on strike since midnight last night. It was only then I noticed that the train was without an engine. My informant went on to say that it was only by courtesy of the train crew that I had been stranded in so desirable a town as Chesterfield, and that no further movement of the train would take place until the strike was settled.

My first reaction was one of disappointment that my trip to Aberdeen had ended so abruptly. It then dawned on me that I was faced with a situation which called for decisive action – and that fairly promptly. I might add that it was late spring and the weather was already warm. At breakfast at an hotel near the station I learnt there was a Territorial Army Drill Hall in the town. So there I went to seek help and advice. The officer who received me could not have been more helpful. Yes, they would certainly arrange a military funeral. It would take a day or so to collect the necessary volunteers for an escort, and they had no padre. Would I make the necessary arrangements with the vicar and the sexton? I then proceeded to the vicarage. The vicar offered all assistance. Could I arrange for the funeral to take place tomorrow afternoon, as it was the only time he would be free for the next few days? If so there was no need for me to bother about anything, he would make all the necessary arrangements.

On 'phoning the drill hall they obligingly agreed to do their best to meet the new deadline. So all was settled satisfactorily.

By now it was lunch-time, so I returned to the hotel and after telephoning the adjutant at Bedford, who concurred with my arrangements, settled down to a leisurely meal. I had reached the coffee stage when I heard the whistle of a railway engine. Instinctively I went outside and there to my horror saw a locomotive under full steam slowly backing on to my train. Seizing my luggage I arrived breathless at the station and inquired of the engine driver what he proposed to do with the train. "Take it to Leeds" was his reply.

"Leeds? Why Leeds?" I enquired.

"Because me and my mate live there, of course, and like you we got stranded here last night. So if you want a ride jump on board."

It was a lovely sunny afternoon as we steamed slowly out of Chesterfield station. I looked up at the famous church. In the graveyard surrounding it I could clearly see the shirt-sleeved figure of the sexton with spade poised, ready to turn the first sod of a new grave. I only hoped that his labours did not go unrewarded, because by the time we reached Leeds and I had got a message through to Chesterfield, his task must have been completed.

Next day my luck was in. Leeds was the home of a Territorial gunner regiment which by chance was due to bury one of their own men with due military honours including, of course, a gun carriage. The funeral was to be held in four days' time. If I could arrange with an undertaker for a hearse to bring the coffin to the cemetery gates at a certain time they would then arrange to bury it with full military honours after their own funeral. Four days later I arrived at Leeds Central station well before the appointed time. In due course the hearse arrived drawn by two splendid looking black horses. In charge were the driver and one other man. I shall always be grateful to the railwaymen on strike picket duty who helped me with the aid of a trolley to convey the coffin along the station platform and on to the hearse. By the time this was accomplished my carefully arranged programme was well behind schedule. No sooner had the coffin been placed on the hearse than the driver and his mate leapt on the box and with a crack of the whip drove off through the centre of the city at a smart trot leaving me standing on the pavement. Not to be outdone I leapt onto a passing tram and after two changes arrived at the cemetery just as the ceremony was being completed.

51

After the strike had been in progress for about a week a skeleton service of trains was started. The train crews were, of course, all volunteers and many of them amateurs. I returned south in one of these trains. There was no signalling system in operation. At the numerous level crossings crews had to descend and open the gates and then shut them after the train had drawn clear. Needless to say progress was leisurely and what was normally a journey of about 5 hours to London took all day. So far as I recall there were very few, if any, acts of violence or intimidation aimed at stopping these strike-breaking activities. Today under similar circumstances there would inevitably be scenes of violence. Such is progress!

5

Mission to South Russia—Odessa—the Crimea

The armistice with Germany on 11th November 1918 left the Allies with one major problem unsolved – that of Russia. Following the "October Revolution" of 1917 and the signing and ratification of the Treaty of Brest-Litovsk between the Bolsheviks and Germany the Allies were faced with two alternatives. Either they could recognise the Bolshevik regime as the *de facto* rulers of Russia and try to come to terms with them, or they could support the anti-Bolshevik groups, the so-called Whites, who were struggling to defeat Bolshevism and set up a democratic regime. It was the beginnings of a political pattern of conflict which today has become all too familiar in every quarter of the globe.

Unfortunately the Allies could not agree on a common policy and their efforts to come to some agreement with the Bolsheviks, and at the same time support the Whites, were destined to failure. To make confusion worse confounded it was apparent, even at the time, that Whitehall was divided. The Foreign Office under Lord Balfour favoured non-intervention in Russia, whilst Mr Winston Churchill at the War Office was all for supporting the anti-Bolshevik forces. So far as Britain was concerned the outcome took the form of military intervention in four main areas: the expedition to the Caspian under Dunsterville; the Murmansk-Archangel force; and the Trans-Siberian expedition based on Vladivostock in support of Admiral Kolchak. The fourth area, of which little has been written, was South Russia bordering the Black Sea and embracing the Ukraine and the Don Basin. Here the British Military Mission to South Russia was established in support of the White armies commanded by General Denikin.

I first heard of it in the spring of 1919 when the War Office called for volunteers to act as instructors with the Mission in certain arms of the

Service – including Signals. I immediately submitted my application. Some days later I was notified that my application had been accepted and that I was to hold myself in readiness to proceed at short notice. Furthermore I was to be given the acting rank of Captain, whilst employed with the Mission. I was at that time a Lieutenant with less than three years service. I was, needless to say, highly pleased. Here was a chance to see a part of the world where history was in the making, and where the struggle of good against evil was synonymous with the gallant fight being put up by the White Russians against their revolting Red opponents. Promptly I was issued with kit considered suitable for military duties in Russia. This included an attractive and practical headgear made of white canvas lined with fur and fitted with ear flaps which could be secured by a ribbon tied under the chin. This souvenir of my service in Russia I hung on to for many years until finally the moths claimed it. I mention this triviality because judging by its latitude one would assume that the climate of the northern coast of the Black Sea would resemble that of the French Riviera. This is generally the case most of the year round. But in mid-winter north winds sweeping across the Steppes of Central Russia can produce periods of intense cold.

In due course I received orders to proceed in two days' time to Marseilles by sea and rail. Within 48 hours the order was cancelled. At this distance of time it is impossible to remember the number of similar orders and counter-orders I received. I believe it was close on a dozen. On one ocasion I got as far as Le Havre before being recalled. No doubt the conflict in Whitehall between the Foreign Office and the War Office produced the game in which I and other volunteers were involuntarily acting as shuttlecocks. Eventually a small party of us reached Constantinople (Istanbul), and after a few days' delay we sailed to Novorossisk where at that time the Headquarters of the Mission were located.

My stay there was to be short-lived. By now the White forces under General Denikin, which only a few weeks previously had advanced to Orel, 250 miles south of Moscow, were in full retreat. They had reached Rostov, and from all accounts were likely to retreat further. There was now very little the Mission could do on this part of the front. The objects of the Mission, apart from the obvious one of giving moral support to the White Russians, were to supply arms and equipment to Denikin's forces and to help train them in their use. Since our detachment at Rostov reported that the White soldiers were deserting in large numbers and, in the process, disposing of their arms openly, whilst the training establishments were either overrun or broken up, there was nothing to be achieved by sending further supplies or instructors up country.

Further west in the Ukraine the situation was reported to be more stable. So once again I was given orders to embark, this time for Odessa.

My brief stay in Novorossisk (a town which incidentally was to play an important part in World War II, since it marked the limit of the German advance along the Black Sea coast and like Stalingrad never surrendered) left little impression on me. I had no official duties so spent some time exploring the large estuary, which formed a natural harbour, and the town. It did however, enable me to take stock of my fellow "missionaries". Apart from a handful of warrant officers and senior NCO's the personnel of the Mission comprised officers up to the rank of Colonel under the command of Major-General H C Holman. Whilst the majority were "regulars" there was a good sprinkling of "temporaries" ie, those who held war-time commissions. The former had, one gathered, mainly volunteered like myself to gain further experience and to escape the boredom of the demobilisation period. Many of them had served with distinction during the war and others were to rise to high rank in later years. The temporary officers were naturally a minority and it is probably fair to say that of those which I contacted during my stay in Russia, some were pure adventurers and others for various reasons were in no hurry to return home to the bosom of their families.

One, who fell into the adventurer class and was apt to boast of the part he had played in more than one South American revolution, I have reason to remember. I forgot the details of his revolutionary activities beyond that they were always on the winning side. No doubt he regarded the upheaval in Russia as another such episode. But in this case he had unfortunately chosen the losing side. However, he did his best to make up for this error of judgement in other ways. His appointment was administrative and amongst his duties was that of paymaster. In that capacity he had to pay out of an imprest account the five shillings per day overseas allowance due to each officer. I got acquainted with this officer in Odessa, where one of his more endearing characteristics was to hire a droshky after a late night drinking bout and order the driver to speed through the main streets of the city whilst he sat back and took pot shots at the street lamps with his revolver. As a result of such escapades his stay in Odessa was, needless to say, cut short. He was sent home; but not before cheating myself and at least one other officer out of two months' allowances by the use of his glib tongue and some dud cheques. There was an amusing sequel to this. A year or more later the War Office paid me the deficient sum accompanied by extracts from a letter from our adventurer. The War Office had evidently allowed him to slip through their net. On return to England he had quietly demobilised himself after carefully ensuring that any pay and allowances due to him had been credited to his account. He then caught the first boat to South America and in the fullness of time informed the War Office in writing of his opinion of that establishment and all its ways.

I arrived in Odessa in December 1919 and joined a small detachment of the Mission commanded by a colonel. We were billeted in a large house in a square favoured by senior government officials and wealthy businessmen as a residential area. The house was furnished and so we lived in comparative luxury and comfort. So far as I can recall the task of the Mission was hampered and reduced at times to impotence by lack of information as to what was happening at the front. To describe the situation as fluid would be a gross understatement. This was no conventional war between rival armies representing rival states, but an ideological struggle between the old and new regimes. They were supported by such elements of the massive, ill-equipped and ill-led Russian Army as could be coerced, driven or otherwise persuaded to support either the new Bolshevik leaders in Moscow – notably Lenin and Trotsky – or alternatively those representing the old regime who believed that out of the ruins of the past some form of democratic government could be established to revive and remould the glories of their Motherland. Desertion was rife. In some cases men simply deserted one side and joined the other; but in the majority of cases one suspects that they abandoned such military equipment as they possessed and tried to make their way home, even though this involved travelling vast distances shorn of all normal communications and under threat of execution if arrested.

Shortly after Christmas a shipload of arms and equipment arrived from England and I was detailed to take a consignment up to Nikolaiev, and there hand them over to a newly formed unit. This involved a voyage of about 100 miles across the Bay of Odessa and up the River Bug. Looking back on this voyage one is struck by its dream-like quality. Being unable to speak Russian I was given an interpreter. I was told that he would be a Russian officer of aristocratic birth. To my astonishment when we met on the quay at Odessa harbour my interpreter turned out to be a dapper little man dressed in the uniform of a major in the French Army. He answered to the title of Compte which he claimed to have acquired through marrying into the Russian nobility, or, for all I can remember, it may have been through French-Russian parentage. Anyway he spoke Russian, French and English with equal fluency and proved an amiable travelling companion. I never did discover what a major in the French Army was doing in Odessa at this juncture, but by then one's critical faculties were becoming so blunted that one treated the unexpected with nonchalance. We embarked on a small coastal vessel and duly arrived at our destination.

A few days later, after ceremoniously handing over the arms and equipment we boarded a larger ocean going ship and proceeded down the river. By this time the weather had turned bitterly cold.

Our speed declined progessively as ice formed in the river, until by dark, when we reached the open sea, the ship literally ground to a halt in a surface of thick ice. After fruitless and lengthy arguments with the captain my companion assured me that the latter and his crew were quite content to stay where they were until the ice melted; in the meantime their position had the advantage of more or less isolating them from political pressure by either Whites or Reds. Secretly one could not help sympathising with their point of view. However we had no wish to share their predicament so the Compte and I decided to go ashore with the object of contacting Odessa by telephone or telegraph. This we accomplished by the simple expedient of getting the gangway lowered and walking to the nearest habitation. Fortunately I there found another member of the Mission who was due to join our ship and return to Odessa. Eventually we learnt that a small ice-breaker was expected that night to rescue two or three fishing boats which lay ice bound off-shore. We wasted no time and walked out and boarded the nearest of these vessels. By "We" I include only my British companion. On some slight and unconvincing plea the Compte declined to accompany us. His departure from the scene was as sudden and unexpected as his arrival. To this day I still wonder who he really was and what brought him to Odessa.

By the time the ice-breaker arrived and had taken our fishing boat and one other in tow it was the early hours of the morning. As we gradually got under way the noise of the crashing ice against the ship's steel plates made sleep, or indeed speech below deck impossible. So I went on deck despite the freezing temperature. On emerging my ears soon became attuned to a very different sound. Clustered on the stern of the ice-breaker was a group of sailors. Suddenly they started singing. Like the Welsh the Russians are, generally speaking, possessed of fine voices. These sailors were no exception. After all these years I can still recall the scene. It was a moonlit night with occasional low clouds which cast moving shadows across the silvery surface of ice-bound sea. Slowly

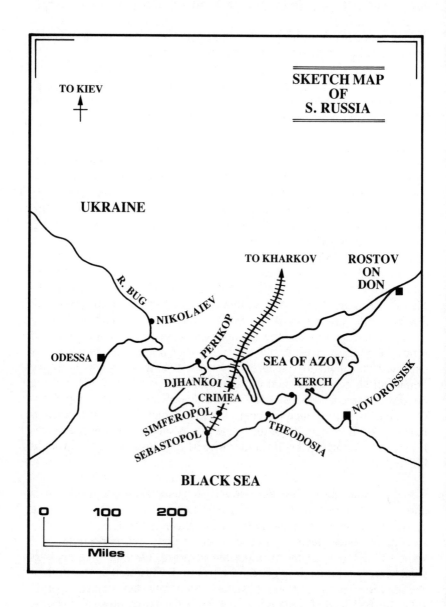

SKETCH MAP
OF
S. RUSSIA

TO KIEV

UKRAINE

TO KHARKOV

ROSTOV
ON
DON

R. BUG

NIKOLAIEV

PERIKOP

SEA OF AZOV

ODESSA

DJHANKOI

KERCH

CRIMEA

NOVOROSSISK

SIMFEROPOL

SEBASTOPOL

THEODOSIA

BLACK SEA

0   100   200

Miles

through the cracking and splintering sheet of ice our little procession crept on across the Bay, whilst over the narrow gap which separated our frail craft from the ice-breaker rang out to the accompaniment of an accordian a magnificent rendering of that haunting song, "The Volga Boatmen". It was an unforgettable experience.

Shortly after my return to Odessa, Denikin's western front in the Ukraine collapsed. After some days of uncertainty the Mission was withdrawn to Constantinople, where the bulk of our detachment sailed for home. I was amongst the few who volunteered to stay, and in due course took passage in a light cruiser of the Royal Navy to join the Mission Headquarters which was now at Theodosia, a port on the south-east coast of the Crimea. At this time General Denikin gave up command of the anti-Bolshevik forces and left the country. He handed over to General Wrangel who had been his commander on the Eastern front.

Although I must have seen and probably met Denikin once or twice, he left no lasting impression on me. On the other hand one has vivid memories of Wrangel. Baron Peter Wrangel was an aristocrat from the Baltic states. His tall slim figure, always impeccably clothed in cossack uniform, alone always commanded respect. Not only was he a leader in the military sphere, but, unlike other White Russian commanders, he had the political sense to realise that without a stable base from which to operate and restore order, both civil and military, his efforts would be in vain. As a base the Crimea was ideal. Virtually an island, some 260 miles from east to west and 100 miles from north to south, jutting out into the Black Sea, its only connections with the mainland are the Perikop peninsular 4-5 miles wide, and a bridge which carries the main railway line from Sevastopol to Kharkov. On its eastern extremity the Kerch peninsular guards the narrow entrance to the Sea of Azov. Through the port of Sevastopol external communications were assured by the presence of British and French Naval forces in the Black Sea.

It was now the spring of 1920 and General Wrangel with driving energy set about the task of reorganising the army and establishing a sound and corruption-free civil administration. To an astonishing extent he was successful, but not without employing methods which at this distance of time seem ruthless, but which, in the chaotic and pitiless atmosphere of revolution, seemed normal. During the war we had come to regard the death and mutilation of human beings in battle with something approaching indifference. Since my arrival in Russia I had witnessed human distress and suffering daily. In particular the huddled bodies of refugees – men, women and children – dying or already dead from typhus were a common feature of railway stations and other centres of travel. In the Crimea things were different. Although the towns were over-crowded with refugees, a semblance of law and order appeared and was gradually reinforced; trains started to run on time, shops and markets operated more or less normally, as did the postal and other services. But when one day I saw a body strung up by the neck from a lampost, I was sharply reminded that one was mixed up in a revolution infinitely more cruel and bloody than the French Revolution.

Throughout the early summer I lived with a detachment of the Mission at Dhanjkoi, a railway junction 60 miles north of Simferopol. Our accommodation consisted of railway goods vans in which we slept, and an open passenger coach which acted as the mess room. Life on the whole was peaceful and interesting, because at last one was able to move about and make contact with the White Army.

Apart from a mobile wireless set mounted in a light van, with which I was responsible for communications with the rest of the Mission, we had no road transport and had to rely on the railway. The only journey which I accomplished by other means was on a visit to a unit guarding the narrow strip of land which lies as a kind of barrier protecting the north-east coast of the Crimea from the Sea of Azov, known as the Tongue of Arabat (Arabataskya). On this occasion I travelled successively in a horse drawn cart and a rowing boat. Apart from these somewhat unusual modes of transport I can only connect the journey in my mind with the enormous dish of fried seagulls eggs with which I was confronted on my arrival at my destination. They were delicious.

I suppose there were occasional exchanges of fire between the Red and White Armies facing one another across the Perikop peninsular, but if so, one heard or saw little of them. There was an airfield at Dhanjkoi occupied by a White squadron of RE8s handed over by the RAF detachment with the Mission. I became friendly with one of the pilots who spoke English, and sometimes used to fly with him as a passenger. On these occasions I never saw any activity over the front.There was no sign of either Red aircraft or anti-aircraft guns. For this I was grateful. The RE8 was designed as an artillery spotting plane. In this role it had done yeoman service during the war, as I was able to testify from my service on the Italian front. It was a biplane capable of flying at low speed and fitted with wireless telegraphy by which the observer directed the fire of a battery on to its target.

In August Whitehall, in its wisdom, decided that enough public money had been wasted in supporting a lost cause. The Mission was ordered to close down, leaving two Russian-speaking officers as observers with Wrangel. Accordingly we assembled at Sevastopol and awaited passage to Constantinople. Several of us took the opportunity thus provided to visit the battlefield of Balaclava. We hired a launch and skirted the cliffs east of the entrance to the harbour of Sevastopol. Unexpectedly a narrow cleft in the cliffs appeared on our port side and turning sharply we found ourselves entering the small harbour of Balaclava, nestling beneath the 'Heights' which overlook the famous 'Valley of Death'. One tried to imagine this placid little sheet of water as it was in the winter of 1854 crowded with shipping and providing the only supply line for the British Army engaged in the siege at Sevastopol. We climbed up on to the 'Heights' and were pleasantly surprised to find, in a neat circular building, a panorama of the battlefield in the charge of an English-speaking Russian guide.

Finally a hospital ship arrived to convey us to Constantinople. As we sailed up the Bosphorous next day we passed an imposing array of British warships, including battleships, with their guns ready trained to deter the forces of Mustafa Kemal from attempting to cross from Turkey in Asia, to Turkey in Europe. Largely due to the firmness and diplomacy of General Sir Charles Harrington, our Commander-in-Chief Constantinople, they never came into action.

Looking back with the benefit of hindsight it is easy to condemn the Allies, and particularly ourselves, for intervening in Russia after the revolution of October 1917. But it must be remembered that until the armistice of November 1918, German troops which had occupied vast areas of Western and Southern Russia were being freely transferred to the Western front. At the same time there was the risk that the Germans might persuade the Soviets to hand over the enormous quantities of military supplies given by the Allies to the Russians, and stored at Murmansk and Vladivostock. This forced the Allies to occupy those ports. Thus, when in the spring and summer of 1919 Kolchak from the east and Denikin from the south were advancing to within striking distance of Moscow, it must have seemed to the British, French and Italian governments – but not apparently to the US government – that there was a reasonable chance, with their support and backing, that the overthrow of the Red regime would be accomplished and some form of democratic government set up in Russia. Furthermore the Allies, having extended a helping hand to the White Russians, could not easily or hastily withdraw it once the tide of battle turned against them.

Writing this account of the British Military Mission to South Russia over sixty years later I am very conscious of the futility of any part which I tried to play in its functions. I appear to have accomplished nothing. Such limited contact as I had with the White Russians were fleeting and largely sterile due to the language problem. I comfort myself with the thought that, through no fault of my own, I arrived at the Black Sea at a time when any influence which the Mission could bring to bear on the White Army was confined to such effect on their declining morale as our actual presence could produce.

It is perhaps presumptuous for one with such superficial contact with the Russians to comment on their characteristics, but the one feature which struck me forcibly was the streak of fatalism ingrained in their make-up. The "Let us eat, drink and be merry, for tomorrow we die", attitude is one which I find hard to comprehend. It must either be a sign of great courage or crass stupidity. In the Russian case I do not think it was either of them. It was an inborn fatalism which prompted the belief that what the Almighty ordered human frailty could not alter, so why worry. The Russians are, or at that time were, a race deeply influenced by religion.

6

Officer and undergraduate—The Birth of Royal Signals—Royal Engineers and Signals Board

I returned home in September 1920. As I was suffering from some form of dysentery, I went into hospital at Colchester for a few days and then got sent to a convalescent home in Brighton run by the Red Cross. I was enjoying myself in most congenial surroundings when I got orders to proceed to Cambridge immediately. I had, the War Office informed me, been selected to undergo a two years' course at the University with the object of reading Engineering, with special emphasis on the comparatively new science of Wireless. I was allotted a vacancy at Clare College.

Prior to 1914 the only officers of the Army who held degrees, apart from medical and veterinary officers, were those few who were granted regular commissions under a system of direct entry from the universities. All other officers had to pass through the Royal Military College, Sandhurst, or the Royal Military Academy, Woolwich, and the majority were posted direct to regimental units on receiving their commissions. In the case of the Royal Engineers the technical qualifications were such that after leaving the "Shop" they underwent further training at the School of Military Engineering at Chatham.

Largely due to one man, Professor F J M Stratton* of Cambridge, who had served with distinction during the war, conversations had been going on between the War Office and the University with the aim of broadening the training of RE officers, and at the same time ensuring that military engineering advanced in step with civil engineering in an age when technical developments were surging ahead largely due to the impetus created by war. A typical example was wireless communication

*The late F J M Stratton, DSO, OBE, ETD, FRS, Professor of Astrophysics.

where the thermionic valve had opened up the vast field of radio-telephony.

When I arrived at Cambridge I found that about fifty junior "sapper" officers were spread among the various colleges plus a few like myself who were seconded to Signals.

It was perhaps fortunate that my experience at school had left me with no enthusiasm for games. Apart from some games of hockey, I found few distractions to drag me away from my books and the wireless lab. Occasionally I attended, purely as a spectator, debates at the Union. On one occasion the Duke of York, later to become King George VI, was asked to open a debate. I have long since forgotten the subject, but the ordeal which it must have entailed for that shy, slight figure, suffering as he was from the appalling stammer, (which in later years he was so successful in conquering), was both embarrassing and painful to behold. When he arose to speak his mouth opened three times before a word passed his lips. His speech of a few minutes appeared endless as he forced the words out of his mouth. His ordeal was made the more poignant by the distinguished guest speakers who followed. These included Winston Churchill who, needless to say, in his speech included some kindly reference to the young Duke.

In these early post-war days the Cambridge 'rag' was at its height. Today the student rag is an organised event in aid of charity. The Cambridge rags were organised hoaxes or pranks on a large scale. So far as I can recall no charity benefitted. One of the most memorable was the Jesus gun raid. After the war the War Office decided to present some captured German guns to the University with the object of distributing them to some or all of the colleges. The idea was that they should adorn prominent architectural features in much the same way as some stately homes are adorned with earlier weapons. It so happened that the gun presented to Jesus' College was larger than that presented to Gonville and Caius. Some of the undergraduates of Caius decided that this injustice should be remedied. Accordingly a night operation was planned with meticulous detail and efficiency.

It was commonly understood that the brains behind the whole operation belonged to an undergraduate by the name of Hopkinson, who had distinguished himself as an infantry officer on the Western front. In passing one must add that he also played a notable role in the retreat to Dunkirk many years later. In the early hours of the morning the Caius party stealthily removed the Jesus gun from the concrete

64

plinth on which it was mounted, leaving behind a miniature toy cannon. They then hauled their trophy through the streets to Caius where next morning it was displayed in a prominent position inside the college.

Those who are familiar with Cambridge will appreciate the major difficulty in carrying out this operation. Firstly, to obtain access to the gun in Jesus' grounds and remove it without being observed must have involved a high degree of skill and cunning. Secondly to trundle it safely and silently through some of the narrowest and busiest streets of the city en route to Caius entailed wrapping the wheels with sacking and detailing parties to divert the attention of any police or Jesus men who might be on or near the route. Thirdly, to obtain entrance to Caius through the only gate wide enough to admit the gun meant unlocking the massive double gateway facing Trinity Street corner. This gate, so far as I am aware, is never opened and remains locked, bolted and barred from year in to year out. At the time one got the impression that the university authorities were secretly amused by this episode. Certainly no serious attempt was made to take action against the ringleaders whose identity was scarcely veiled.

Another rag was inspired by the opening of Tutankhamun's tomb in Egypt by Howard Carter. This was re-enacted one Saturday morning in the crowded market place. The underground 'Gentlemen' acted as the tomb from which the 'treasures' were extracted by means of an aerial pulley leading to an adjacent upper window. Finally there was the 'Pavement Club'. This absurdity was ostensibly inspired by the need for contemplative leisure to ease the strain of modern living. For 3 or 4 consecutive Saturdays between noon and 1pm King's Parade, one of the busiest thoroughfares, was the scene of a mass sit-down by undergraduates of both sexes engaged in chatting, reading, knitting or mere contemplation. Needless to say all traffic was halted and as the police and university proctors approached, the squatters politely rose up and as quietly resumed a sitting posture as the 'Law' passed on.

The university authorities and the police very wisely regarded these expressions of youthful exuberance as harmless and tolerable with the result that, apart from an occasional night in the cells followed by a magisterial caution for the few who overstepped the mark, relations between town and gown were on the whole friendly.

Not all undergraduate escapades received the publicity attendent on the last two instances I have mentioned. On more than one occasion some intrepid spirits somehow or other succeeded by night in scaling the topmost pinnacles of King's College Chapel, leaving as evidence of their feat a flag or preferably an item of feminine underwear.

During my first summer vacation at Cambridge an Irishman, (with whom I had served in South Russia) and I, decided to tour Europe on the cheap. We would travel second or third class and put up at the smaller hotels or boarding houses. In the event we did neither. We travelled mainly first class and stayed in largish and comfortable hotels. The reason for this apparent change of heart was not of our choosing. We wanted to see as much of Germany and Austria as possible. It so happened that we had barely crossed the Channel when the currencies of those two countries plumbed to phenomenal depths. The pound sterling bought marks by the million and schillings by the thousand. We spent a couple of nights in Berlin in a comfortable hotel near the Unter den Linden. The first night we booked seats at the Opera House for a performance of *The Flying Dutchman*. Casually we turned up a minute or two after the curtain rose, and were asked to stand in the corridor until the end of Act 1. The house was packed. The Berliners were determined to derive what pleasure they could before facing bankruptcy. The next night we attended, punctually this time, a performance of *Orpheus in the Underworld*; neither one of us knew a word of German but the musical rendering and the scenery were unforgettable.

From Berlin we travelled down the Rhine Valley and on to Vienna. The scenery in the Rhine Valley must nowadays be familiar to thousands of British tourists. Although I had had my fair share of travel in the last few years, it had all been under war conditions, and so to this day I cherish the memory of this unspoiled scenery with its terraced vineyards, its fairy-like castles poised on hilltops and its picturesque riverside villages.

In Vienna our appreciation of that gay and lovely city was distinctly marred by recent riots, which had forced many shopkeepers in the Ring to board up their windows. However, the open air cafes and restaurants were in full swing, each with their quota of musicians, and the weather being fine we took our meals out of doors.

After two nights we moved on again, this time bound for Graz. Before leaving Vienna I went to a bank and hurriedly changed a £5 note for schillings. In return I was handed a small brown paper parcel containing a large number of 100 schilling notes. These were done up in bundles of ten, each bundle being secured by the usual paper band. The train was due out when we arrived at the station. All seats were taken and it was not until we had stopped at several stations that we were able to get seats. We then checked our bundles of notes. Out of each bundle of ten one note had been extracted. The loss to us was minimal. I recall that our indignation at being cheated was tempered by a feeling of pity for some minor bank employee, who, no doubt driven to distraction by the rapidly fading purchase power of his salary, had resorted to this form of petty theft.

Behind the facade presented by cafes, cinemas and restaurants crowded with foreign tourists and black marketeers lay real poverty amongst the Viennese of all classes. No doubt, the situation outside the capital was not quite so bad, but we were given no opportunity to find out.

The afternoon we arrived a Graz, having taken the precaution of wiring ahead to reserve rooms at an hotel, only to be greeted by the news that all rooms in every hotel in the town were occupied. So back to the station we trudged and caught a train for Munich. En route some fellow travellers strongly advised us not to waste time seeking accommodation in Munich, so we stayed on the train and eventually ended up at Augsberg. It was now nearly midnight. After a frantic and fruitless cab ride round hotels we gave it up and returned to the station. Fortunately the night was warm and railway stations have always fascinated me. Next morning the milk train took us the short journey to Nurenberg. Our stay was brief, since we could only get beds for one night and my only lasting impression was of the museum with its grim collection of instruments of torture, including the notorious iron lady.

It did not fall to my lot to serve in the Armies of Occupation in Germany after the 1914-18 War, so my knowledge of the German people in defeat must be based on second-hand accounts.

In 1918 Germany was defeated not so much by her own military and economic collapse as by that of her Allies. The German Army was not defeated or fatally demoralised. It was still capable of putting up a stiff fight. Since the collapse of Russia it no longer had to fight on two fronts. Although the sea blockade had caused shortages, the country was not living under siege conditions. Rumania and the Ukraine had been occupied by the German Army thus releasing rich supplies of grain, coal and oil. Food was rationed, but the rations were not inadequate. The main reason why Germany capitulated was because the government and the people had ceased to maintain the will to go on fighting. Their Allies, Austria, Bulgaria and Turkey had laid down their arms. The

Allied Powers were gaining in strength as the American war effort got into top gear, the German had passed its peak. The average German felt let down, the tremendous loss of German lives, he argued, could have been avoided with better strategy. And now as a final insult the Allied Powers were demanding colossal reparations, and shouting 'Hang the Kaiser'. In short the German people were wallowing in self-pity, and self-pity blunts judgement. It was, therefore, not surprising when some ten years later they greedily swallowed the promises which Hitler and the Nazi party offered them in regaining their greatness, of wiping out their humiliation, and of proving their invincibility. The cry ' Heil Hitler' stirred the adrenalin, but numbed the brain.

In 1945 the situation was very different. The German nation had been driven to its knees; the large towns and cities lay in ruins; the homeless were numbered in their thousands; food supplies were minimal, and the disruption of communications hampered the distribution of what little remained. There was no Allied demand for reparations and Hitler was dead by his own hands. The occupying Allied forces first task was to restore some semblance of normality by distributing food, controlling and minimising disease and helping to shelter the homeless.

The people of Britain, France and the United States had no thoughts of vengeance. This was left to the politicians, who instigated the trial of war criminals. Had it been left to the Russians, all those who were deemed to have committed war crimes would have been shot without trial. After all this was the way they dealt with their own delinquents. It had the merit of saving time and trouble. Their Allies, however, were unaccustomed to such crude and arbitrary methods. They insisted on invoking the whole panoply of the law with its whirlpool of lawyers, witnesses, testaments etc. Into this the Army was necessarily sucked. Few soldiers can have been more immersed in it than I was to become as I shall narrate in due course.

Back at Cambridge however, it was during my two years there that I met the girl I was eventually to marry. Heather Bulmer, whose family lived at Thirsk in Yorkshire, had trained as a nurse and joined the staff of Saffron Walden Hospital during the latter part of the war. Before I came down from Cambridge we were unofficially engaged, but it was not until four years later that we could afford to get married. At that period officers of the Services were not officially recognised as married under the age of 30, in that entitlement to married allowances only started at that age. As it was I was approaching 29 when we got married, and so 'lived in sin', as it was popularly known, for just over a year.

In 1920 the Royal Corps of Signals was formed, taking over all responsibility for military communications from the Royal Engineers. The new Corps could hardly have got off to a worse start. The main disadvantage it suffered was due to official short-sightedness over the provision of officers. It was laid down that the number of officers who were to be permanently transferred to the Corps was to be restricted to about one-third of the required number. The remaining two thirds were to be provided by a system of secondment from other arms of the Service. To make matters worse it was only after some fourteen years secondment that such officers who so wished, could transfer permanently to the Corps.

Needless to say the scheme was an utter failure. But it was not until 1924 that the system was abolished. From that date officers were commissioned in the normal way direct into the Corps from Woolwich, Sandhurst or the universities. The Headquarters of the Corps, known as the Signal Training Centre, was established at Maresfield Park, a hutted camp outside Uckfield in Sussex. The camp was a war-time creation built on the impounded estate of Count Munster, a German aristocrat. Apart from the house, which formed the officers' mess and limited accommodation for un-married officers, there was no permanent accommodation.

I was ordered to report to the STC in the autumn of 1922 and on arrival found myself posted to a company training wireless operators.

It is not easy to build up a new organisation inside such a conservative body as the Army. It soon became clear to those of us who had been permanently transferred to Signals that we were burdened with a heavy responsibility. On our behaviour and efforts the future standing of the Corps would largely depend. The STC embraced the Army School of Signals, to which junior officers from all regiments and corps of the Army came on short courses. The impression they carried away of Signals would permeate the whole Service.

In order to help build up *esprit de corps* much emphasis was placed on sport, in particular athletics, boxing and cross-country running. For the first time in my life I found myself taking an active interest in games, and to my surprise discovered that I could put up a creditable performance on the running track and across country. Thanks to the efforts of a few far more accomplished than myself, the Royal Signals in the period of three years won the Army team championships in athletics (3 times), boxing (twice) and cross-country (once). Apart from running my other sporting activity was hockey, of which I became secretary and occasional member of the first eleven. I also became a member of the mess committee. In peacetime the formalities of an officers' mess demanded a first class standard of service; a table adorned with shining silver and neatly folded linen napkins; and that officers dined in immaculate and highly colourful mess kit every night except Sundays.

The formation of a new mess required time, patience and money. Apart from a few senior officers who had pre-war experience of regimental life most of us had no such knowledge, having joined the Army in wartime. However, we quickly learnt, as did the staff, thanks to an efficient mess sergeant. Catering was another problem. There was then no Army Catering Corps to provide expert cooks. Eventually after many changes and much grumbling the committee decided to hand the responsibility over to a firm of caterers.

It was whilst at Maresfield that I acquired my first motor car. Hitherto my personal transport had been a Rudge multi motor bike; a splendid machine so called because of its multiple variable gear. My new mount was an ABC horizontally opposed two cylinder car bought for £170 second hand from a brother officer who was going overseas. It was a long low open two-seater with a sporty looking aluminium body. The two large cylinders stuck out on either side of the bonnet.

About this period the first mass-produced British car appeared on the market and some of my brother officers bought the famous bull-nosed Morris Cowley. The cost of a new one was around about £200. It was a two-seater with a dickey seat. The more affluent purchased the Morris Oxford with a four-seater body and a slightly larger engine. Self-starters were a recent innovation, and not very reliable. Such refinements as heaters were unknown. One provided one's female passenger with a travelling rug to wrap around her lower half in cold weather.

I recently found amongst some old papers my bank pass book for 1927 which showed that my net monthly pay was £50 per month. It also showed that I was able to manage quite well without incurring debts or an overdraft. I only wish I could say the same of my financial state in later years when the Services pay, far from increasing with the falling value of the pound, was actually cut on one occasion. I only mention the question of pay to show that post-war conditions did make it just possible for officers to live on their Army pay and allowances. Prior to 1914, generally speaking this was not possible. Indeed even after the war it was, to say the last, unusual to find an officer in the Guards,

Cavalry or the more prestigious county regiments who did not possess private means.

I have never forgotten a conversation I had with an elderly reserve major who was commanding a battery on the Italian front. He asked me what I intended to do after the war. To which I replied, "Well, having got a regular commission I feel I should be well-advised to stay in the Army for a bit to see how things turned out for people with my background."

"Don't be a fool," he said, "unless you have more money than sense, the Army is the occupation for the rich man's imbecile son."

Like many a word spoken in jest this remark contained a germ of truth. Up to the turn of the century the Army did not demand brains. It did demand a private income. Weapons were simple; mobility relied on the horse or shanks' pony; the soldiers were mainly illiterate and servile. The purchase of commissions was not abolished until 1871, and thereafter promotion was based on seniority rather than merit. In peacetime the life was admirably suited to the sons of landed gentry. It afforded ample opportunity for the exercise of their traditional sports of hunting, shooting and fishing; whilst if they were posted to India for a period they could additionally enjoy polo and pig-sticking. Intellectual pursuits were neither demanded nor encouraged. The majority never attained much above the rank of captain because once they were married and with a young family they preferred to settle down and lead the life of a country gentleman. For those who decided to treat the Army as a profession there was the newly instituted Staff College at Camberley, where during a two year course the serious study of war could be pursued.

The 1914-18 war marked a profound change in the military art. This was brought about by two major scientific advances, both attributable to the internal combustion engine, namely mechanisation of the means of transport, and aviation. The former was eventually to lead to the disappearance of the horse from the field of battle and the latter to a completely new dimension in land and sea warfare. My generation, such of us as had survived the 1914-18 war, have been privileged to participate in this evolution and the internal struggles and rivalries which it engendered between the two World Wars.

Largely owing to the failure to exploit the tank as a weapon of offence in its own right (rather than a supporting weapon for infantry on the Western front) and because mobile warfare became a dead letter except in the final stages, those senior officers, who had been brought up to regard the horse as a *sine qua non* for military and recreational purposes, refused to acknowledge the obvious fact that against the machine gun, the unfortunate horse was a sitting target. Moreover in the field of logistics the back-up in the form of fodder, veterinary and remount services – not to mention water in desert areas – required for a mounted force was immense compared with the requirements of a mechanised force of equal firepower in terms of petrol, oil, workshops etc.

Fortunately there was a small number of senior officers who recognised these facts and foresaw the part which mechanisation, and in particular armoured vehicles, were to play in future warfare. Notable amongst these men of vision were Generals Broad,* Pile,** "Boney" Fuller† and Colonel Q Martel‡; whilst outside the Service Basil Liddell Hart by his writings, based on a profound study of military history, probably contributed more than any other single individual in Western Europe. Unfortunately his works created greater impact in Germany than they did in either Britain or France as we were to learn to our cost in 1940. This is not the place to dilate on the struggle between the "horsemen" and the "mechanisers". It has been well covered in Liddell Hart's autobiography. I only mention it because as an ardent mechaniser I endeavoured to bring what little influence I was able to bear through speaking and writing. These endeavours were facilitated in 1924 when I was appointed an instructor at the School of Signals, my main task being to instruct junior officers in the basics of wireless. In this capacity I was able to spend some time on Salisbury Plain following the developments of the experimental Armoured Force – the forerunner of the armoured division. I never had any doubts that the armoured division was the essential formation in which to exploit the tank.

In 1925 the STC left Maresfield and moved into permanent accommodation at Catterick Camp in Yorkshire. A year later Heather and I got married and settled nearby into a rented house in Richmond.

---

*The late Lt-Gen Sir Charles S N F Broad KCB, DSO
**The late Gen Sir Frederick A Pile GCB, DSO, MC, GOC, in C Anti-Aircraft Command 1939-45
†The late Maj-Gen J F C Fuller CB, DSO
‡The late Lt-Gen Sir Giffard Le Q Martel KCB, DSO, MC

Professionally army life was tinged with the bitterness of frustration. Pay was low. The standard of living set by pre-war officers all of whom appeared to have private means, seemed to us impecunious juniors, high. Not that we complained. On the contrary I seem to remember that we rather enjoyed it, and willingly sacrificed such minor luxuries as holidays in an attempt to maintain the required social standards and at the same time balance our fragile bank accounts. The cause of our frustration lay primarily in the shortage of modern equipment. It was inevitable that in the early 20's the Army had to rely on the large stocks of equipment which were left over from World War I, but towards the end of this decade such equipment had not only become obsolete but was largely worn out. Units of the regular army were in consequence getting frustrated by the lack of realism in training, when on manoeuvres. Added to this was the shortage of manpower due to poor recruiting resulting from low rates of pay and antiquated barracks.

In the Territorial Army the manpower position was better and most units had little difficulty in obtaining recruits – in the technical arms at any rate. Unlike many regular officers who regarded the TA at best as something which had to be put up with, and at worst something to be shunned, I held it in high esteem. This was in part due to the friendly relations I tried to establish with local "Terrier" units wherever I was stationed and partly to a genuine belief that, in the event of another major conflagration, the regular army could only act as the spearhead whilst the main body of our defence would rest on the TA. I based this belief on the relevant home strengths of the two bodies, namely five regular divisions as compared with twelve territorial infantry divisions. In my view the regular and territorial armies were the component parts of one and the same structure.

It may be relevant at this point to refer to what actually happened when war became imminent after Munich. The Chamberlain government, acting on the advice of the Secretary of State for War, Mr Hore-Belisha, doubled the territorial army by the simple expedient of ordering each TA division to form another division. This method of increasing our ground forces was much criticised at the time on the pretext that there were insuffcent officers, NCO's and regular army instructors to cope with the new units thus created, and especially that there was not adequate equipment available for such expansion. I had been in India for some years when this radical step was adopted and was not, therefore, in a position to judge the wisdom of it from first-hand knowledge. My inclination at the time was to regard it as a wise and logical step since it meant building on an established foundation with the local loyalties and ties which the territorial system engendered. In the light of subsequent events I have no reason to change that view.

After three years at Catterick I was posted to London as a junior member of the Royal Engineer Board.* This organisation, which was under the control of the War Office, occupied offices in Grosvenor Gardens. It was responsible for research, experiment and design of equipment for Engineers and Signals. The two Signals members of the Board directed the work of the Signals Experimental Establishment, which at that period occupied hutted accommodation on Woolwich Common. Subsequently it moved to Christchurch, Hampshire.

Our main task was to develop a series of radio telephone and telegraph transmitting/receiving sets capable of providing communication between the different echelons of command in the field. So far as the bulk of these sets were concerned the technical problems were mainly confined to overcoming the question of reliability and portability. The latter involved using light-weight materials and often conflicted with the former need for reliable operation under extreme conditions of temperature and humidity – and above all rough handling in transport by manpower, vehicle and even mule pack. The most difficult and at the same time urgent problem in this field was the provision of radio telephone communication between tanks on the move where the limited space available, the vibration and the mechanical noise level presented problems which were not satisfactorily solved until after war was declared in September 1939.

Today, 60 years and another world war later, advances in the science of electronics have made these technical problems fade into insignificance, but at that time, when radio depended on the use of a number of thermionic valves which were in effect fragile glass tubes, they were formidable and time and money consuming. At the same time, one cannot help feeling that had there been full cooperation between the three Services in the field of experiment and research some of the technical problems would have been more quickly and economically solved. As it was both the Admiralty and Air Ministry had their own experimental establishments. I have no recollection of any effective form of cooperation between the three services in the field of technical development.

---

*The title was later changed to RE and Signals Board

I do however recall that my fellow member, Colonel A C Fuller† and myself kept in close touch with the Home Office which was at that time starting to establish a network of police radio communications. At present, when every uniformed police officer carries a walkie-talkie in his pocket, it may be of interest to recall what was, I believe, the first demonstration of personal police radio communication.

The year was 1930. At the invitation of the Home Office, Fuller and I motored down to Esher where we joined a party of some thirty or so others assembled on the verge of the main London-Guildford road. Here was parked a small truck containing a radio telephone transmitter. Alongside it stood a police constable in uniform holding his helmet in his hand. Inside the helmet was crammed a valve receiver and attached to one side of the helmet was an earphone. Fastened to the back of the policeman's belt was a small case containing a battery and rising from the case was a small aerial. With this contraption the constable was able during the demonstration to receive messages up to several hundred yards from the transmitter. He was not, of course, able to reply.

†The late Major-General A C Fuller CBE, inventor of the Fullerphone which was largely used on the Western front in the 1914-18 war.

7

R101 disaster—Staff College, Camberley—Arrival in India—Karachi

From boyhood I had always been keenly interested in aviation. My interest was not confined to aeroplanes. I closely followed the progress of airships and like many others came to believe that for long distance travel the rigid, ie, Zeppelin-type airship, would eventually replace the ocean-going liner as the quickest means of carrying passengers and mail over long distances. The Zeppelins had, of course, failed during the war in a military role. This was due to their vulnerability to incendiary bullets fired from aeroplanes, and to the lack of navigational aids when operating over the North Sea or hostile territory. The success of the British R34 in carrying out the return journey from the UK to New York in July 1919 seemed to augur well for the future of airships: especially as she was the first aircraft to cross the Atlantic from east to west against the prevailing winds, a feat which at that time was well outside the capability of any heavier-than-air machine. However, five years were to pass before the government made up its mind as to the next step in airship development. In October 1924 public funds were allotted for the construction of two prototype ships to explore the possiblity of opening up regular services between the Dominions and the Mother Country. The ships were later designated R100 and R101. In the meantime the Germans forestalled us with their first post-war commercial airship – the Graf Zeppelin. She was the inspiration of Count Eckner, and I vivdly recall being amongst the crowd of several hundred who went to see her land at Hanworth, not far from the site which later was to become Heathrow Airport. The ease with which Eckner brought the giant ship to ground assisted only by a team of Rover Scouts, whom he instructed through a megaphone, was indeed impressive.

In August 1930 the R100 completed a return crossing of the Atlantic to Montreal. A few days after her return my wife and I motored to Cardington to see her as she lay tied to the mooring mast, prior to being hauled into the adjacent hangar for overhaul. On her outward journey she had encountered heavy storms which had caused damage to her fabric. The return flight was uneventful and was accomplished in 57½ hours.

On October 4th, a Saturday, I went down alone to Cardington to see the departure of R101 on her maiden voyage to India. It was a typical autumn evening when I arrived and joined the small number of sightseers gathered on the Hitchin-Bedford road. The airship lay at the mooring mast about 400 yards from the road and a similar distance from the giant twin hangars in which her sister ship R100 now rested. There was a slight breeze which hardly stirred the R101. The scene was almost eerie. One had expected a show of terrific enthusiasm with crowds cheering, bands playing and flags waving in a manner typical of the maiden voyage of a new ocean liner. On the contrary, the tone was subdued.

Inside the vast belly of the ship there was little sign of activity apart from an occasional figure silhouetted against the dimly-lit windows ranged along the underside of the torpedo-shaped structure. At the foot of the mooring mast a few vehicles came and went as the VIP passengers arrived. There followed the whine of the lift conveying them up the tower-like structure. They could then be seen crossing a small gangway into the nose of the ship. Eventually at 6.30pm the five huge diesel engines were started, causing ripples along the smooth fabric-covered sides of the airship. It was as though some monster was rousing from its sleep. Some minutes later a gap appeared between the bow of the ship and the cone of the mast in which it had been nestling. Gradually the gap widened. The ship slowly turned in a south-easterly direction at the same time rising gradually, but so slowly that it appeared reluctant to leave *terra firma*. I watched it for perhaps 15 to 20 minutes as it disappeared over the low ridge of hills north of Hitchin. One could not help heaving a sigh of relief as it passed out of sight, so heavily it appeared to labour in clearing this slight obstacle.

We were living in a flat in Beaufort Street, Chelsea at the time and I was due to meet my wife at Grantham Station next day on her return from Yorkshire. I got up early, considering it was a Sunday, and as I drove down the deserted King's Road a news poster caught my eye. It bore the words 'R101 disaster'. I stopped, and as I read of the disaster at

Beauvais my reaction was one of bitter sorrow tinged with anger. Sorrow that so many brave lives had been lost, including a close friend of my Uncle Capel, Sir Sefton Brancker; and anger that despite its known defects and limitations political expediency had outweighed technical expertise in allowing the airship to undertake the unchartered voyage to India.

For many years I did not have occasion to go anywhere near Cardington. In 1972 I happened to be driving from Norwich to Newport Pagnell. My route took me through Bedford. About 6 miles short of that town I suddenly and instinctively looked in the direction of Cardington. To my utter astonishment there was an airship in flight. It turned out to be a small non-rigid airship built by the Goodyear Corporation for advertising purposes, but it brought back poignant memories of that evening 42 years ago. On my return journey I stopped at Cardington village and there in the churchyard paid tribute at the common grave of those who perished in the cause of aviation – the crew and passengers of R101.

Today the large passenger carrying airship is a thing of the past. The aeroplane has become a common means of transport for millions of people. But it is as well to remind ourselves from time to time that progress, especially scientific progress, entails failures and sacrifice. However, sacrifice is seldom in vain.

Before I left the School of Signals, the Commandant had suggested to me that I should try and get to the Staff College. On due reflection I decided to take his advice. It was generally accepted that if one wanted to climb the promotion ladder in the Army the letters 'psc' after one's name in the Army list were almost essential. The letters stood for 'passed staff course'. Moreover I realised that as a technical officer my chances of reaching senior rank were limited, whereas, if I passed the staff course I was almost certain to be given the opportunity of proving my worth in a staff appointment. The course at the Staff College, Camberley lasted two years, with an entry of some sixty students each year. Generally speaking admission was limited to those under 35 years of age. Students had to be recommended by their commanding officers and were required to pass an entrance examination held annually in London. Competition was considerable. At least three hundred officers sat the examination each year. About half the vacancies were reserved for those who had attained high marks in the exam. The number of such vacancies were spread over the various arms roughly in proportion to their strength. Signals had one such vacancy. The other vacancies were allotted by the War Office, who nominated candidates on their records of service.

The examination took place at the end of February and covered a period of two weeks. It consisted solely of written papers for which three hours were allotted. Frequently one had two such papers a day. I sat the examination three years running and finally got the Signals vacancy. It was during these exams that I first encountered a character who was conspicuous by his monocle, and by the ease or contempt – it was not clear with which – he tackled the papers. He invariably got up and handed in his paper after about an hour whilst the rest of us were scribbling away like mad and fighting against the clock. His name was Wintle. I was to encounter him again later.

In January 1933 my wife and I settled into a rented house at Camberley. Life for students at the Staff College was in many ways similar to that at a university – the main differences being the high proportion of married students, the shorter vacations and the horses. Yes, the horses. Those in high positions in the War Office were still convinced that the horse had an important role to play in war. Consequently whilst the Royal Tank Corps was starved of equipment and reduced to a minimum, officers of all arms were expected to maintain a high standard of horsemanship. With two exceptions which were officially 'experimentally equipped' with armoured cars, the Cavalry regiments were still mounted. And so students at the Staff College were alloted a horse, and those who like myself had not recently served in a mounted unit were given a refresher course at the riding school of the adjacent Royal Military Academy before we were allowed to have a horse of our own. To my mind the ironic part of this waste of public money was that during our two years at Camberley only once were we required to carry out an exercise on horseback, and that exercise could equally well have been carried out in a car or on a bicycle. One surmised that a not inconsiderable excuse for students' chargers was the continued maintenance of the Staff College drag hounds.

In criticising the importance attached to horsemanship at Camberley I must emphasise that this in no way detracted from the value of the course. Any large organisation whether it be in the field of business, government, industry, transport or the armed forces can only function efficiently if the component parts which make up the main body act in unison and with a common purpose. This implies smooth and intelligible two-way communication between those at headquarters or head office and those in the field or branch offices. It is the task of the Managing

Director of a large concern to implement the policy decisions arrived at by the Board; but these decisions must to a large extent depend on information received from lower down the scale, where those responsible for production, sales, personnel, etc, can supply details which are vital to decision-making. Likewise instructions passed down from head office are useless unless framed in such terms that those responsible for their implementation can clearly understand them.

In the Armed Forces, where decisions in war have to be made at very short notice, and the orders implementing those decisions passed rapidly to the front, it is essential that at all levels of command there should be a common language, in the sense that brevity and clarity of expression should be combined to the maximum extent possible. To this end the Staff College course was aimed at teaching one to think logically, to speak and write with brevity and clarity, and above all never to issue an order or instruction without mentally putting oneself in the recipient's shoes and asking oneself, "Will they clearly understand what they have to do?" All this may sound simple and obvious, but in my experience a large part of the ills which befall government departments, large businesses and industrial concerns are due to failure to observe these simple principles; and above all to failure by the leaders of such organisations to maintain contact with their employees.

In the Army such contact is embraced under the term man-management. Its importance is impressed on every officer from the day he first puts on uniform. It may be fairly argued that in a highly disciplined body like the Army it is easy for a general to find time to go round the units under his command and to talk to and make himself known to those serving under him; whereas in a large industrial company this is far more difficult. But it can be done. I have it on the authority of one of their employees that the managing director of one of the largest engineering companies in the country with factories in many areas regularly visits them. On such occasions he spends as much time as possible touring the shop floor and talking to as many people as he can. Many years later I was to find that such practice was common in the USA.

On the other side of the coin one recalls that some time after Dr Beeching was appointed Chairman of British Rail in 1963, a total railway strike was threatened. According to Press reports Beeching was then on a motoring holiday in Italy, and there was some delay before he could be contacted. He returned home, and shortly afterwards appeared in an interview programme on TV with Sidney Green, the General

Secretary of the National Union of Railwaymen. In the introduction to the programme it transpired that this was the first time the two men had met. To many this revelation must have come as a shock. Here was the chairman of a vital and labour-intensive industry who had apparently never made the acquaintance of the leading trade union officials in it. In criticising Beeching, who no doubt was a man of many outstanding qualities, one is really criticising our higher educational system.

Although we are a "nation of shopkeepers" whose economy depends on a healthy balance of trade with the rest of the world, those who control our universities and polytechnics neglect the fact. With one or two exceptions these institutions offer no facilities for the study of business organisation and management. This is probably a hangover from the days, going back to the first half of the century, when the upper classes considered trade to be a somewhat dirty word, and those who succeeded in it were described as the *nouveau riche*. Curiously enough there were exceptions. It was perfectly respectable for the aristocracy to be seated on the board of banks, insurance companies and other white collar industries, whose head offices were preferably situated in the confines of the City of London. I have never found an acceptable explanation for this phenomenon.

In December 1934 I left Camberley and in the new year six of us from the Staff College met again at Southampton where we boarded the troopship *Dorsetshire* bound for India. We were due to join units of the British or Indian Armies for a period of a year after which we could normally expect to be posted to our first staff job. On arrival at Karachi three weeks later I went up by train to Rawalpindi, where I joined a unit of the Indian Signal Corps as a company commander.

It may be of interest to recall that up to the Second World War about one half of the British Army was at any one time serving in overseas stations, of which India absorbed by far the largest number of troops. There, British and Indian units served alongside one another in the same fighting formations and in the same garrison towns. Technical units, notably Engineers and Signals, were exceptional in that they all formed part of the Indian Army and were of mixed Indian and British composition, the British personnel being attached to the Indian Army for a fixed period – usually five years.

The system on the whole worked well. Most young officers of Signals completed a tour in India early in their careers, and thus were able to learn the language and get to know the customs and background of the

Indian soldiers without much difficulty – and at the same time enjoy to the full the opportunities offered in that vast and varied subcontinent for sport and travel whilst still bachelors. I was less fortunate since I was already nearly 37 and married when I first set foot in India; and was to spend only a year in a unit before being posted to a staff apppointment in which one's contact with Indian troops was minimal. Consequently, although I passed the necessary examinations in the Urdu language, I never had sufficient service with Indian troops to acquire fluency of conversation in it. This I was to regret later when during the war I had a large number of Indian units under my command.

No sooner had I settled in Rawalpindi than the unit was ordered to move to Karachi, but not before I had experienced a shock which was to have a profound influence on my attitude to Anglo-Indian relations for the whole of the nine years I was to spend in that fascinating but in some ways tragic country. A country I was to learn to love.

In Rawalpindi, as in most other cantonments, the centre of activity was the European Club – in this case the Gymkhana Club. There had recently been posted to our unit two young Indian Officers who, having passed through the Indian Military Academy at Dehra Dun had been granted the King's Commission. That is to say they held the same commission as myself or any other officer of the British or Indian Armies. One of them, I remember, came from a very aristocratic South Indian family. In conversation in the mess one day I learnt that he had applied to become a member of the Gymkhana Club to which, needless to say, nearly all the British in Rawalpindi belonged. He was politely informed by the Club Secretary that as an Indian he could not be accepted. When I heard this I was horrified and wanted to protest to the Club committee, but was told that as a newcomer to India and comparatively junior (I had not long been promoted captain) it would be useless. Some years later, under different circumstances I was to be more successful. I shall explain how this happened in due course.

It may be argued, as indeed it was by many people, that as temporary inhabitants in a foreign land there was nothing wrong in having a club for Europeans only, where they could relax in an atmosphere in which they had been brought up. The weakness of this argument was to my mind overwhelming. India was not a foreign country: it was part of the British Empire. The policy of successive British governments was to encourage and train Indians to participate in the civil administration and armed forces of India with a view to eventual self-government. Increasingly Indian officials were sharing the same offices and bearing the same responsibilities as British. In the case of the Services they were living in the same quarters and eating in the same messes. Many had been educated in British schools and universities. Therefore, it was at the worst insulting and at the best foolish to prohibit them from membership of clubs in their own country. One would not have felt so strongly about the matter if Indians had been admitted as honorary members, but most clubs went so far as to prohibit their entry even as the guests of club members.

My stay in Rawalpindi was not to last long. At the end of March the unit moved to Karachi – a two days' journey by train.

A few days after our arrival my wife joined me, and we settled into a furnished house on the outskirts. Unlike Rawalpindi, which was then primarily a military cantonment, Karachi was a centre of commerce and the second largest port on the western seaboard of India; Bombay being the number one. Apart from the occasional troopship and a weekly service from Bombay, Karachi was primarily a commercial port handling mixed cargoes, but few passengers. Like almost any other port in the world the harbour was a complex of go-downs (cargo sheds), cranes, rail tracks and offices, whilst the city comprised an agglomeration of shops, office blocks, hotels, etc. On two sides of the city were residential suburbs which housed the European and Indian business and official communities in western type houses and bungalows – although not in the same streets. Outside the city the bulk of the native population lived in squalid and insanitary slums. The more fortunate had what can best be described as concrete or mud huts, whilst the rest had to make do with tin shanties.

A few miles inland lay the airport at Drigh Road under the control of the RAF. As a tragic reminder of the R101 the giant hangar built to house that ill-fated airship dominated a corner of the airfield, whilst not far away stood the mooring mast erected to receive her. The airmail to the East had not long been inaugurated, and it became quite a common habit to search the skies for the weekly Imperial Airways De Haviland "Hannibal" class 4-engine biplane which brought the airmail from home.

In the early hours of 31st May 1935 a violent earthquake struck Quetta, the administrative capital of Baluchistan and a large military centre 400 miles north of Karachi. The bazaar was virtually destroyed and hundreds of natives were killed outright, whilst many died later of their injuries or were crippled for life. Fortunately the bulk of the troops were out of barracks on a night exercise, but many of their families were partially bereaved and practically all buildings destroyed or rendered unsafe. Communications by rail, telegraph and telephone were cut off and the news of the disaster did not reach Karachi until some hours later, when communication by wireless was re-established. The only road to Quetta from the rest of India was virtually an unbridged track in places, so it was not until the rail was repaired nine days later that refugee families started arriving at Karachi where the racecourse had been prepared as a vast tented reception camp. My wife and other ladies were kept busy attending to the needs of these unfortunate people until such time as they could be moved into more permanent accommodation, or, in the case of the British, shipped home.

8

Simla—Quetta—journey by flying boat—war declared—return to UK

In January 1936 I was posted to my first staff appointment – at Army Headquarters, Simla. At that period it was the practice of the Government of India and Army Headquarters to migrate annually between Delhi and Simla. The reasons were climatic ones. Delhi was considered too hot for Europeans in the summer months, so about the end of April from the Viceroy downwards all officialdom packed their bags, their files and their typewriters and proceeded in special trains to Simla 6,000 feet up in the Himalayas. Early in October the process was reversed and Simla became comparatively deserted by officialdom.

The exceptions to these annual migrations were certain sections of the Army HQ for which there was insufficient accommodation in the magnificent pink stone edifice, known as the Secretariat, in New Delhi. It was to one of these sections permanently established in Simla that I found myself posted. My job was a minor one in the Directorate of Military Operations and Intelligence.

For the first time in my career I found myself with time on my hands. My appointment was largely concerned with work of a routine nature and left little scope for initiative. I was therefore delighted when in September I learnt that I was to be promoted major and posted to Quetta early in 1937 in a second grade staff appointment, ie, appropriate to my new rank. Since the appointment would embrace both personnel and supply matters, I felt confident of the outcome. Administration had always appealed to me, and my previous service had not been such as to give me either the experience or the enthusiasm for the operational side of the Army, which in any case I considered was outdated and designed to fight the last war rather than a future war.

Pens more fluent than mine, from Kipling onwards, have described life in Simla during the heyday of the Raj. I have no intention of joining their number. Suffice it to say that, apart from writing, I found a new interest in acting. The famous Simla Amateur Dramatic Club with its Gaiety Theatre, (modelled on its London namesake), was about to celebrate its centenary, and I was lucky enough to take part in three of its productions. According to a fairly recent account the theatre still flourishes in the hands of officers of the Indian Army and their families.

I arrived at Quetta in May 1937. The next three years were to prove one of the happiest and most constructive periods of my life, and an invaluable and instructive prelude to the war years which were to follow. Quetta, the most westerly of the cities and larger towns of what is now Pakistan, was one of the most healthy and popular stations for the Army in pre-war India. It stood astride the southern gateway to Afghanistan, the borders of which lay some 50 miles to the west at the nearest point. Like Peshawar, which guarded the northern approaches to Afghanistan, it was not only a military centre but also the administrative capital of a vast area of hills and desert; in this case the District of Baluchistan. Standing about 3,000 feet above sea level, and in the same latitude as Cairo the climate could hardly be bettered. In the summer the temperature was that of England at its best, but without the vagaries of cold and rain to which we are accustomed. In the winter sunshine and snow abounded. The air was crisp and invigorating, rather like parts of Switzerland. For men it was shorts in the summer and sheepskin coats in winter.

When I arrived reconstruction after the 1935 earthquake was approaching completion. The military cantonment had suffered far less damage than the city with the result that the latter had been given priority in the rebuilding programme. In the cantonment much use had been made of hutted accomodation pending the provision of permanent earthquake-proof buildings. After a few weeks in a hutted hotel I moved into a pre-earthquake married officers bungalow. It was occupied by another member of the staff whose wife was shortly leaving for home. The building, like its neighbours, had suffered little outward damage in the earthquake, but owing to its structure and the continued threat of further heavy shocks it was not considered safe enough to sleep in. As a temporary measure mud walled rooms with tent roofs, called "Wana" hunts, had been erected in the gardens. These were our bedrooms. They were delightful in summer, but in winter, when one had to have a fire to heat them, they became somewhat unbearable.

In the meantime, new buildings made of reinforced concrete were arising fast. They were not architecturally remarkable, but they were safe. One knew that under violent stress they might bend and crumple like a metal biscuit tin, but unlike the pre-earthquake brick and wood bungalows the walls and especially the roof would not collapse and crush the sleeping inmates, as happened in 1935.

With the construction of the cantonment went hand in hand a refinement unknown outside the largest cities of India, such as Delhi and Bombay, namely a central sewage disposal system. To my mind one of the most unattractive features of life in India was related to the loo's. To perform one's natural functions one had to sit on a wooden privy equipped with a bucket. The common name for this primitive contraption was a "thunder box". The word privy is not really apt, because it was the duty of a menial to squat at a respectful distance and, as soon as one left, to remove the bucket and deposit its contents in an incinerator. The latter functioned day and night emitting a stench which lingered in the nostrils. To make the whole procedure more distateful the menial, whether male or female, belonged to the untouchable class, that most depressed and maligned strata of human life in the Indian subcontinent. Even today, despite legislation designed to eliminate untouchability, I understand that this blot on humanity still exists.

My predecessor as deputy to the senior administrative staff officer at Baluchistan District Headquarters – the cumbersome offical title was Deputy Assistant Adjutant and Quartermaster General (DAA and QMG) – was Major Gott. His nickname 'Strafer' well befitted him. As he was essentially a fighting soldier he was naturally quite pleased to vacate an administrative staff job to take over command of a battalion of his own regiment, the Rifle Brigade. His hour of distinction was to come in 1942, when as commander of 13th Corps in North Africa his ability was tested to the full. So successful was he that when in June General Auchinleck found it necessary to replace General Ritchie as commander of the VIIIth Army, 'Strafer' Gott was selected to take his place. Unfortunately the aircraft carrying Gott to his new Headquarters crashed and he was killed. As everyone knows, his replacement was Montgomery. It is idle to speculate what effect Gott's survival would have had on the campaign in the Desert.

Not long after I took over from Gott, a young Indian officer was posted to my small staff in the rank of captain. Cariappa was the first Indian officer to be commissioned from Sandhurst. He was a native of Coorg, a small state in the south west of India. My wife and I quickly became very friendly with him and his charming family. Little did we guess that he was, in a few years, to become the first Indian Commander-in-Chief of the Indian Army.

My new appointment marked the end of a period of twelve years in which I had mainly been an observer of the 'Army game' from the touchlines. Apart from the nine months in Karachi I had remained apart from regimental duties and was merely a chairborne witness of military reorganisation and training. Now I was able to take an active part in a portion of the Army, consisting of British, Indian and Ghurka troops, which was kept in a state of readiness for active service either on the North-West Frontier or outside of India.

Of the combatant units under Baluchistan District about half were stationed in Quetta and the remainder in frontier posts at Chaman, Fort Sandeman and Lorelai. These were organised into two brigades. The commander of the Quetta brigade was a man of remarkable character, whose outstanding services to the country in World War II have never, in my opinion, received the credit they deserve. Brigadier Bernard Paget* came from a distinguished clerical family, his father having been Bishop of Oxford and his mother a daughter of the Dean of St Pauls. In one respect only he resembled that other Bishop's son, Bernard Montgomery. He was a man of high principles to which he rigidly adhered, and expected others to do the same. On the other hand he was the first to acknowledge human failings, and to make allowances for them. He did not seek publicity, and abhorred ostentation. As Commander-in-Chief Home Forces 1941-43 he was responsible for the training of these troops which later formed Monty's 21st Army Group in the reconquest of Europe. And yet his achievements are usually ignored by historians of the period. For part of my time at Baluchistan District the commander was Major-General Hubert Huddleston†, who, after a distinguished career in the Sudan, was in 1940 recalled from retirement to return to Khartoum as Governor-General.

I consider myself lucky to have served under these men, from whom I learnt much, and received many kindnesses.

---

*The late General Sir Bernard Paget GCB, DSO, MC, C-in-C Home Forces 1941-43 and Middle East 1943-46.

† Major-General Sir Hubert Huddleston KCMG, CB, DSO, MC, GOC, Sudan 1924-30, Governor-General, Anglo-Egyptian Sudan 1940-44.

At the end of 1938 my wife and I sailed home on three months' leave. In order to have as long as possible at home, and to satisfy my passion for flying, I booked to return by air on my own, leaving my wife to travel back by sea.

Today, long distance air travel has lost all its glamour, most of its comfort and retains only one advantage, namely speed over other means of transport. If one is travelling, say, from Heathrow to Johannesburg, one arrives at least an hour before the plane is scheduled to leave. You struggle up the stairs, so that even if you can find one on arrival, a luggage trolley is of little use. After checking in and handing over your suitcase, you join the scramble for a seat and/or duty free goods in the departure lounge. Eventually your flight is called and you join a long queue hurrying down a seemingly endless corridor. At last you reach the end and are ushered into a waiting room. When all the passengers are assembled – there may be 350 of them – you are called forward by number, and eventually get on board your aircraft. Inside it looks like an elongated cinema. There is little room to move. If your legs are long (mine are) you know that you are destined for at least 18 hours of cramp and discomfort. The lavatory accommodation is quite inadequate and to reach one you have to negotiate an aisle about 18 inches wide. Really fat people must travel in the small first class cabin or stay at home. You can't see out of the window unless you are lucky enough to occupy a seat by it and once there it is difficult to extricate yourself when you want to go to the loo. The compensation is the food: it is usually good.

When at last you do arrive at your destination, having been confined to your seat, even when the plane stopped en route, your discomfort is not over. You have to stand for what seems like hours on end to claim your luggage as a slowly moving stream of assorted luggage spews out of the bowels of some mechanical monster into a barren hall filled to suffocation with your fellow travellers and a quite inadequate number of luggage trolleys. Eventually you pass through immigration and customs and stagger out into the fresh air and sunshine. You have arrived dazed, dirty and exhausted.

In March 1939 Imperial Airways had not long since opened a regular air service to India using the Short Imperial flying boat, the forerunner of the RAF war-time Sunderland. My journey began at 7.30pm on March 19th when, at Waterloo station I handed myself and my luggage over to the care of an airway's official. He conducted myself and four other passengers to a reserved saloon attached to a Southampton express. During the journey an excellent dinner was served to us in our seats. At Southampton we were met and put up in the South Western Hotel for the night.

Early next morning we took off from Southampton Water and I experienced for the first time the thrill of taking off in a powerful 4-engined flying boat – the *Canopus*. In a land plane the actual moment of becoming airborne is almost indistinguishable above the noise of the engines. Not so in a flying boat. For you are sitting comfortably in a luxury speed boat. As it accelerates the bow wave increases in height, spray spumes upwards obscuring the windows whilst the crescendo of water breaking against the hull drowns the throb of the engines. Suddenly the cascade ceases, the noise dies down, the windows clear and one looks down on a rapidly receding sheet of water.

Our first stop was at Macon where we landed on the River Saone, and were ferried ashore to an estaminet for coffee whilst refuelling took place. After another stop for lunch on a lake outside Marseilles we landed on Lake Bracciano at dusk and were driven the 30 kilometres into Rome. There we were put up in a first class hotel. On, early next day, to Naples, where our pilot gave us a bird's eye view of the crater of Vesuvius, and then on to Brindisi and Athens arriving at Alexandria for the night. Daylight faded as we crossed the western tip of Crete, and so we landed at Alexandria guided by a flare path anchored in the water and supplemented by the searchlights of RN ships in the harbour. The last night stop was at Basra, where the modern air-conditioned hotel proved a welcome haven from the scorching heat of the Persian Gulf.

So far our journey had been quite uneventful – almost leisurely and most comfortable. The passenger accommodation was in the hull of the flying boat, which being a high wing monoplane, afforded an excellent view over a wide range. Compared with modern planes the windows were large and one could stand up and view the scene without craning one's neck. The number of passengers varied from stopping place to stopping place and seldom exceeded a dozen. Few of us were booked for the full journey from the UK to India. On the last stage we were due at Karachi early in the afternoon, so we were called at 3.30am and took off an hour and a half later. After refuelling at Bahrain we landed at Dubai. Here we were given lunch in a building which might have been taken straight out of the film *Beau Geste*. This picturesque fort-like structure was the sole habitation standing in a wasteland of shimmering desert. Adjacent stood a primitive landing stage where lay the launch which had brought us ashore. Apart from a road which ran straight into the obscurity of the horizon, the landscape was featureless.

Our next and final stop should have been Karachi, but on take-off our captain explained that he would be stopping at a place called Jawani on the Baluchistan coast to pick up an Airway's employee. He added that Jawani was being developed as an emergency landing place on the air route. Whether we were expected or our arrival was unheralded I never discovered. As we approached, the inlet, on which the buoyed channel had been laid out, was obviously being cleared of native craft. These we learned later were bringing building materials from Karachi. Our captain circled round for a while until the channel appeared clear. He then did a perfect landing. We were taxiing slowly when the plane swerved and came abruptly to a halt on a sandbank – a boat was still blocking the channel. After some delay we were escorted to the only completed building, which was the bungalow occupied by the station superintendant and his wife. He informed us that as the tide was still on the ebb there was no hope of refloating our plane for 10-12 hours.

During the course of conversation I discovered that the superintendant was a sergeant in R Signals who had recently taken his discharge in India in order to take up this present post. My time was passed pleasantly in his company and he insisted on taking me all round his domain in a jeep – and in the late afternoon to the airstrip to refuel a De Havilland Hannibal en route to Karachi with the Mail. His wife filled us all with admiration and gratitude for the impromptu tea and supper which she conjured up for passengers and crew. Eventually we refloated and took off at 1am, reaching Karachi just over two hours later.

Altogether the journey from London to Karachi had taken 100 hours compared with the scheduled time of 90 hours. By today's Concorde standards I had journeyed in a flying stage coach. Since that day I have flown thousands of miles over many portions of the globe, yet none of these journeys have given me greater pleasure than my slow flying boat passage to India in 1939.

The declaration of war on 3rd September coincided with the termination of my appointment at HQ Baluchistan District. It now appeared likely that I would be kept in India indefinitely as was happening to other British Service officers. It was, therefore, with great relief that on 2nd January 1940 I received a warning order to be prepared to return to the UK early in February.

On 18th February my wife and I together with many other married families set sail from Bombay on the troopship *Dorsetshire*. The voyage was uneventful, uncomfortable and until we entered the Mediterranean, unescorted. A few days later we disembarked at Marseilles. To complete the journey we travelled across France in a troop train and eventually landed at Southampton from Cherbourg on 9th March. That evening we settled into an hotel in Kensington.

Somehow it never occured to either of us that we should see India again. India had been promised independence. Although the war might delay the transference of power for a while, it was unlikely that, once Britain and France had defeated Germany, British troops would be required in India again in any number or for any length of time.

9

Dunkirk—GHQ Home Forces—2nd Division—
Visits of Churchill and King George VI

Within hours of my return to London I was informed by the War Office that I was required to proceed to France to take up an appointment at GHQ. The appointment was GSOI (Signals); in other words principle staff officer to the Signals Officer-in-Chief. The War Office wanted me to cross to France almost immediately. I pointed out that I had been overseas for five years, had no residence in the UK and required time to collect my heavy baggage from Southampton and find somewhere for my wife to live. Eventually I was given three weeks leave, which enabled us to find a flat in Chelsea and get our furniture out of store.

In Quetta, 4,000 miles away, the war had made little difference to the social life of the British community. Food and drink were plentiful, likewise petrol. The usual round of cocktail parties, picnics, dances, etc, continued as in peacetime. There was little reason to change. But in London it came as a revelation to find that, apart from the blackout, life proceeded much as before the war was declared. The theatres, cinemas, restaurants, etc, flourished and there was no shortage of food, drink or petrol. Whether it was a case of the calm before the storm or "eat, drink and be merry for tomorrow we die", I could not fathom. One's inclination was towards the latter.

I reached the GHQ at Arras on 4th April and next day was able to take over my predecessor's comfortable billet outside the railway station and more important, his batman, Private McRoberts. McRoberts was a regular soldier who, having served his time in the Argyle and Sutherland Highlanders, had hardly settled down in civilian life when the war started and he was called up as a reservist. His medical category was such that he was not fit for front line service and so he was posted to the pool of batmen for GHQ then forming at Aldershot. As a batman he could not be bettered.

The staff of GHQ was scattered in and around Arras, the Signals staff being in the town itself. My first task was to familiarise myself with the order of battle of the BEF (British Expeditionary Force) and then to visit the various principal Signal units and meet their commanders.

Much has been written about the un-preparedness of Britain for war in 1939. I can only record the impressions of a soldier, who had been abroad for five years and now found himself at the hub of the BEF.

The first shock I received was the discovery that the BEF had only one tank brigade and that the 1st Armoured Division which had been forming for over three years, was still in the UK and not yet fully equipped for active service. Out of ten infantry divisions in France only one was mobile, ie, fully mechanised. The divisions themselves were well equipped with modern weapons and well-trained. This was amply demonstrated during the retreat to Dunkirk. The signal communications relied on a backbone of telephone and teleprinter circuits carried on the French PTT (*Poste Telegraphes et Telephones*) system, and shared with the French civil population. This entailed our own R Signals personnel manning a portion of the PTT exchanges. Since all the main routes of the PTT system were in buried cables this was considered reasonably safe in the event of active operations. Unfortunately this proved a fallacy since the cables were laid along the sides of the main roads, and these were to be the targets of German 'Stuka' dive-bombers.

The cable system was supplemented by military radio sets, but the number and capacity of these proved inadequate when the cables were cut. Furthermore messages had to be sent in code or cipher which, of course, imposed delays. Radio telephony was provided for forward communications in the fighting zone, but some commanders and staff officers cases were wary of using it, fearing that the Germans would be able to pin-point their headquarters by picking up the signals.

In the early hours of 10th May I was woken by the firing of an anti-aircraft gun in the railway yard adjacent to my billet. A few minutes later a despatch rider arrived with a message summoning me to a conference in the Operations room at 6am. I would not normally have attended such a meeting, but the Signal Officer-in-Chief, Brigadier Chenevix Trench, was away on a tour of the Lines of Communication which extended as far south as Marseilles.

The 'Ops' room was in the basement of the Hotel de Ville at Arras. I arrived early, and so did two others. All three of us by coincidence had been stationed in Quetta not many months previously. Brigadier Charles King had been in charge of the reconstruction of Quetta; he was now Deputy Engineer-in-Chief. Brigadier Oliver Leese had recently been an instructor at the Staff College, Quetta. Leese had only arrived the night before to take up the appointment of Deputy Chief of the General Staff on Lord Gort's staff. The first question he put to King and myself was, "What does the BEF consist of, and where are they?" We did our best to give him a quick run-down before the meeting assembled. I was to work closely with these two during the ensuing hectic days. My admiration for them increased as I got to know them better. After Dunkirk our ways parted.

The next time I saw Oliver Leese years later was under very different circumstances. It was at the annual Chelsea Flower Show. He was presiding over a stand containing cacti and succulents. After the war he and his wife had entered the horticultural world and had become the leading British experts on these plants. King we shall meet again later.

I have no intention of recounting the events of May 1940 leading up to the evacuation of the bulk of the BEF from Dunkirk. But certain individuals and events remain embedded in my memory. Firstly the C-in-C, General Lord Gort VC. It has often been said by military critics that Gort's appointment was a mistake on the grounds that intellectually he was not of sufficient calibre to lead an army in battle. In Montgomery's* view "the job was above his (Gort's) ceiling." Considering the few weeks that I served on his staff I make no pretence of being able to judge whether this criticism is justified or not. What I do contend with conviction is that, when it came to extricating the BEF from a position which at one time looked quite hopeless no commander could have arisen to the occasion more adequately than Gort. Throughout the retreat I saw him almost daily. No matter how gloomy the situation might look he always found time to say a word to members of his staff, however junior. His human touch and the confidence he inspired by his very presence were to me, and I am sure to many others, a tremendous booster to morale.

*Montgomery, *The Memoirs of FM The Viscount Montgomery of Alamein* KG. (Collins)

One example of Gort's leadership is worth recording. The retreat had just started. After a rapid march through Belgium followed by some days of heavy fighting in which our troops had held up the German advance, it became necessary to order a retreat. The necessity arose in order to avoid being cut off by the German armour which, having broken through the French line on the River Meuse, was rapidly becoming a threat to our right flank. Gort called a conference of his corps commanders and senior staff. The venue was a modern children's hospital. The room in which the meeting took place had plain glass walls on three sides separating it from corridors down which a constant flow of doctors, nurses and others passed pausing only to glance at the array of brass hats assembled inside – like goldfish in a bowl. I happened to be present as the Signal Officer-in-Chief was still away.

After the C-in-C had outlined the situation he turned to General Barker, Commander of 2 Corps, and told him that one of his divisions would have to retire a considerable distance that night to conform with the French withdrawal on our right. Barker, who by this time was obviously suffering from the strain from the last few days, stated emphatically that his infantry were too exhausted to carry out such a movement. Gort listened patiently to Barker's protestations. Then he quietly but firmly reminded all of us what endurance and guts our troops had shown in similar circumstances in the retreat from Mons in 1914. Incidentally we were only a few kilometres away from Mons, which to my mind added force to the C-in-C's statement. Gort spoke for perhaps three minutes. The effect was startling. Barker changed his tone and agreed that the movement could be carried out. Gort then turned to General Lindsell, his Quartermaster-General (QMG) and said, "Can you do anything to help Barker with transport for his troops?"

"Yes," replied Lindsell, "I am almost certain I can." He then proceeded to give details of what lorries he hoped to make available. Later I learnt that he had been as good as his word.

When on 10th May the Germans invaded the Low Countries the BEF was about to be reinforced by a fourth corps. GHQ was to become an Army Group. During the nine months' period of the phoney war the staff at GHQ had expanded in proportion to its responsibilities. Not only was the C-in-C operationally in command of three corps, but also of the administration of all British troops and installations in France. This entailed an enormous 'tail' of administrative troops and installations which extended to all the major ports on the Atlantic coast of France as well as Marseilles.

In accordance with the Allied plan the BEF moved forward to the River Dyle – some 80 miles inside Belgium. At the same time the plan allowed for the move of Lord Gort's operational staff so that they would be nearer to the fighting line; leaving the bulk of the administrative staff at and around Arras. However, no sooner had Advanced GHQ been established inside Belgium than Gort decided that he would move nearer to his corps headquarters with a minimum staff and establish a tactical headquarters. This meant that GHQ was now split into three echelons. Indeed for a short period it was actually split into four. Naturally the strain placed on our Signals personnel was immense. They had to ensure that messages addressed to GHQ reached the right echelon; whilst the various echelons were frequently moving from one location to another with little advanced warning. It also meant that he S O-in-C's staff had to be split up. Consequently he and I were separated for most of the battle. It was not until we had been driven nearly back to the coast that I rejoined him.

On 28th May the C-in-C together with the remnants of his staff established themselves in the King of the Belgiums seaside villa on the eastern outskirts of De Panne. By this time all line communication forward had been cut off, but a submarine cable which terminated on the beach provided secure communications with London. GHQ staff was now being reduced to a skeleton so Chenevix Trench ordered me to return to England. After dark, in company with McRoberts and my driver, I set off along the beach in the direction of Dunkirk. Already the beaches were well organised and before long we were instructed to join a queue. The sea was calm, the sky overcast. Further west one could see the inferno which marked Dunkirk, but our section of beach appeared to be of no interest to the Boche. Every fifteen minutes or so a small naval cutter approached the head of the queue and picked up a boat load. Eventually our turn came. Laden with Sam Browne belt, revolver, field glasses, etc, and wearing my best breeches and field boots I struggled to clamber aboard the heaving craft, until an obliging sailor seized me by the seat of my pants and tumbled me headlong over the freeboard. Minutes later on board the Fleet minesweeper HMS *Skipjack*, I was being ushered into the captain's cabin, given a strong drink and invited to help myself to any items of clothing in his wardrobe. There were three or four senior officers in the cabin, but most were content with blankets to wrap round themselves whilst their nether garments were dried.

Of that night I have but vague recollections. I suppose I was too strung up and exhausted to sleep soundly, or even to remove my soaking clothes. I do remember the Captain coming in at some period and saying that it was getting light, and that he would have to up anchor and sail although his own cutter had been unable to pick up as many men as he would have wished. I also vaguely remember looking out of a porthole and seeing the entrance to Dunkirk harbour crowded with ships. Then there was the loud explosion, when a Polish destroyer ahead (or was it astern?) of us hit a mine. Later in mid-Channel, (or was it as we neared Dover?) we passed an extraordinary collection of miscellaneous small craft going in the opposite direction. The "Little Ships" were on their way to Dunkirk – and immortal fame.

Before we landed I was touched to find that McRoberts was clutching my new mackintosh, which I had reluctantly decided to abandon together with the rest of my spare clothes.

I reached London on the afternoon of May 29th and went straight to the War Office before rejoining my wife in our Chelsea flat. Such was the absence of news about the BEF that almost the first question my wife put to me was when was I due to return to France. I assured her that I should not be returning. But I was wrong. On 9th June I was warned to be ready to cross the Channel from Southampton in four days' time. It was proposed to build a new BEF based in Cherbourg and in ports to the south of it in order to reinforce the French. General Sir Alan Brooke had already crossed over with advanced parties of two divisions. I was about to leave for Southampton when France capitulated and all British troops were safely recalled.

In the meantime, on 10th June, Italy had declared war. I remember in some ways feeling relieved, because one felt that perhaps the situation could not get worse. Winston Churchill's famous appeal to the nation a week later, in which he declared the nation's determination to fight on, come what may ("We will fight on the beaches....") seemed to epitomise the true feelings of the nation, which only needed a leader of his calibre to unite them in that determination.

A few days later Chenevix Trench and myself were posted to GHQ Home Forces in the same appointments as we had held in France. The headquarters were soon established in St Pauls School, Hammersmith, the buildings of which have since been pulled down. It then stood a quarter of a mile west of Olympia on the opposite side of the road. A peculiar feature of the school was the dining room. This was on the top floor of the main building, and, when the complete staff assembled there for dinner I could not help wondering what the effect of a judiciously dropped bomb would have been! However, soon after the Luftwaffe became nightly visitors to London, the staff was split up into less vulnerable packets.

On Saturday 7th September I got back to our Chelsea flat late from the office. We had just finished supper when the phone rang, and I was called back to St Pauls by the code-word 'Cromwell'. This was the warning to be prepared for a German invasion. Next day I persuaded my wife to go up to her parents' home in Yorkshire. I was very glad I had done so, because in the early hours of Monday morning several bombs were dropped close to our flat in Beaufort Street, causing considerable damage and some casualties, including a friend of ours who was killed. After two more disturbed nights I decided it was better to sleep on a camp bed in the basement of St Pauls. Not long after I went back to the flat to collect some belongings at the weekend. I found the street outside it blocked off. There was one unexploded bomb in the pavement, and another in the little garden at the back.

Throughout my period at GHQ Home Forces I was mainly concerned in building up the network of communications required for home defences. This entailed close cooperation with the Post Office, who supplied the long distance requirements of the three Services, through circuits in the underground trunk cable system for telephones and teleprinters. The system was known as The Defence Telecommunications Network (DTN). It had been initiated in 1938 but, now that the threat of invasion had become a stark reality, major and rapid expansion was urgently needed.

Relations between the GPO and R Signals had always been good. In peacetime the signal units required for higher military formations in war were provided by Supplementary Reserve units manned by GPO personnel; whilst Territorial Army units of R Signals relied heavily on the same source. It was indeed fortunate that the Engineer in Chief of the Post Office was Sir Stanley Angwin,* who as a TA Officer had served army signals with distinction for 30 years. It certainly made my task easier, and I can only record that I could not have found his staff more cooperative at a time when everyone was working under extreme pressure.

---

*The late Colonel Sir Stanley Angwin KCMG KBE DSO MC TD

Although St Paul's School housed the staff of GHQ Home Forces, it was early established by the Prime Minister that in the event of invasion the C-in-C must be in the same building as himself. This meant that the Operational side of GHQ had to house itself alongside the underground Cabinet War Room (CWR1) in Storey's Gate.* With the ready assistance of the Office of Works we converted a portion of the basement into an elaborate signal office providing communication with all important headquarters and defence centres throughout the British Isles.

CWR1 was, of course, well protected by concrete, sand bags and a stout torpedo net strung flat over the roof, even so being in Whitehall and backing onto St James' Park it was obviously in a prime target area for German bombers. A second Cabinet War Room (CWR2) had therefore been prepared beneath the Post Office Research Establishment at Dollis Hill. Here too we built a duplicate signal office. Being on PO property the Army left it to Research Establishment to look after the CWR2 once it had been completed and to ensure that it was at all times ready for occupation at short notice. One day, knowing that the Cabinet were likely to give it a trial run, so to speak, for a day, I visited it with a PO colleague. Out of curiosity I asked to see the Cabinet Room and the PM's private quarters. In Winston Churchill's bedroom I happened to pick up the phone and found that it was disconnected. Thereafter we arranged for our linemen to test every instrument weekly.

Later, should the Government be forced to vacate London in the event of invasion, a CWR3 was built at Wentworth Golf Club, Virgina Water. Here there were no large buildings to provide top cover, so the simple expedient of burying two sections of tube railway tunnels was resorted to. They were laid side by side and access was provided by inclined slopes at both ends. The space between the two tunnels formed

*Forty-four years later on 4th April, 1984, I was privileged to attend the official opening by the PM (Margaret Thatcher) of CWR1, restored and refurbished as a national museum.

102

a long corridor which in turn gave access to rooms partitioned off inside the tubes. Our own staff manned this unusual set of offices for 24 hours purely for practice purposes, but to my knowledge the Cabinet never followed our example.

Just before Christmas 1940 Chenevix Trench was placed on the retired list. As soon as the new S O-in-C was installed I assumed that I should be relieved, as I knew that he wanted to bring in his own nominee. This did not worry me. I was quite ready for a move. Some weeks previously the Military Secretary's Deputy had told me that I would not be considered for a Brigadier's appointment in Signals. There was a shortage of trained staff officers and I would have to stay in a staff job. At the same time he asked me what type of staff appointment I would prefer. I replied AA and QMG of a Division, ie, senior administrative staff officer. I was, therefore, delighted when in January 1941 I was posted in that capacity to 2nd Division. The Divisional Headquarters was at Pocklington midway between York and Hull. The commander was Major-General Daril Watson, who greeted me with the remark, "I know nothing about Q matters, so I'll leave all that to you." I recalled that remark after the war when the appointment of General Sir Daril Watson as Quartermaster-General to the Forces was announced. Unfortunately I never had the opportunity of reminding him of it. I was in the Far East at the time, but I'm sure he was a great success in that appointment.

A minor advantage in leaving London was the escape from nightly bombings – at least that is what I thought. The first three nights after I arrived at Pocklington, Hull was plastered with resultant heavy damage and casualities including some of our own men who were billeted on the outskirts. I went into the city the morning after one of these raids and was given a vivid account of a German airman bailing out – and parachuting screaming into a department store which was by then a blazing inferno.

In these early days of the war the Lancaster, Halifax and Stirling bombers, which later were to form the backbone of our night bomber offensive, were not yet in squadron service. Daylight raids were the order of the day. At Pocklington there were two Canadian squadrons flying, as far as I remember, Wellingtons. Shortly before I moved there they had been called upon to carry out daylight raids over Germany. Their casualties were so heavy that the squadrons had virtually to be reformed.

Later 2nd Division moved to Gloucestershire. Headquarters were at Moreton-in-the-Marsh, where the staff were billeted in Batsford Park, the home of Lord and Lady Dulverton. We could not have been more comfortable or had a more considerate host and hostess. Here again we were given evidence of the heavy sacrifices of Bomber Command. The local airfield was employed on the training of night bomber crews. The casualty rate from all accounts was ghastly.

The Division was now ready for active service. We had trained and were equipped for the Western Desert. Before we embarked in April 1942 we had two distinguished visitors in the same week. On 28th March Winston Churchill visited the Division. This entailed an amount of detailed planning, which included the provision of a bed and a bottle of liqueur brandy. The PM was due to arrive by car at a pub outside Chipping Norton, where coffee and brandy were laid on. Here the divisional commander and a few of us on his staff were waiting. It was a cold morning and Winston stepped out of his car wrapped up in an enormous coat with an astrakhan collar. He was accompanied by his youngest daughter, Mary, Commander CR Thompson RN, his map room chief, his private detective and, to our surprise the Turkish Ambassador and the Turkish Military Attache. The PM looked strained and pale as he got out of the car and changed his coat for a lighter one. He spoke little as he drank his coffee. He refused the brandy. He was then driven to a field where one of the infantry brigades was drawn up in a semi-circle. In the centre a truck had been parked and equipped with steps, and a microphone feeding a public address system. Winston climbed into the truck and started to address the troops. At first his speech was slow. He appeared to be searching for words. This phase did not last long. Soon he warmed up to a crescendo and words flowed from his lips. To emphasis points he thumped the floor of the truck with his walking stick. The troops cheered him wildly.

Then came lunch in "A" mess. Lord Dulverton, who incidentally provided the brandy, joined us. Before lunch Winston consumed a couple of whisky and sodas, and by the time we went into the dining room he was in a warm-hearted mood and chatting freely. I sat next to Mary, who was dressed as a corporal in the ATS. She was quite charming, and talked freely of her experiences in the anti-aircraft battery in which she was then serving. As lunch progressed Winston became more expansive and brought the whole table into his conversation. Apropos of some remark, as the mess sargeant was refilling his glass, he barked out, "I hear that Hitler has foresworn alcohol for the duration. I suppose they'll be asking me to sign the pledge next."

Lunch over, the PM retired to a bedroom, put at his disposal by Lady Dulverton, for half an hour. He then continued his tour of the Division, and addressed more gatherings of troops. This was the only time I met the great man in person. I was not disappointed.

Our other visitor was HM King George VI. He arrived by train on 1st April and we met him at Bicester station. After all the meticulous preparations for the PM the Royal visit came almost as an anti-climax. Like his father the King was most particular about dress. He wore the uniform of a field-marshal, and I remember thinking that I had never seen anyone better turned out in service dress uniform. His Majesty inspected certain units at their normal training. He was accompanied by one equerry. Lunch in the mess was a quiet and unostentatious meal. Once it got under way the King's shyness and his slight stammer faded. He relaxed and appeared to enjoy himself.

Two weeks later 2nd Division sailed for Egypt via the Cape. For the past two to three weeks it had been my task to arrange for the shipment of the Division. In round figures this meant the movement to Liverpool of close on 18,000 men, and to Newport of some 2,000 vehicles and guns – and their allotment to about twelve ships. This, needless to say, involved a massive exercise in drawing up detailed instructions and tables. I was most fortunate that my senior assistant on the "Q" side was a chartered accountant, Jack Finnis. This work was right up his professional street. Thanks to his efforts the embarkation went without a hitch.

Our voyage in convoy to Freetown, Sierra Leone, (where we stopped for four days for water and fuel), and then on to Cape Town was an experience common to thousands in war-time. Apart from the occasional alert, it passed peacefully, uneventfully and according to plan. But on arrival at Cape Town a surprise awaited us.

Burma was falling to the Japs; the remnants of our Army was retreating through the jungle to India; 2nd Division was to be diverted

105

to Bombay. And so on 2nd June 1942, after an absence of 2¼ years, I set foot on the soil of India once more.

10

GHQ India—Wavell—some administrative problems regarding Prisoners of War, Court-martials and casualties—GOC Madras—amenities for troops —Japan surrenders

On disembarkation the Division moved to the Poona area, some 100 miles south-east of Bombay. Headquarters settled comfortably into the ancient fort of Ahmednagar. Partial re-equipment and training for jungle warfare were now the order of the day. The long voyage from England had been accomplished without a single loss of life. One ship carrying vehicles had been sunk by a mine off the southern-most point of South Africa, but all hands had been saved.

In the meantime the Congress Party had been stirring up unrest and riots broke out in many parts of India. Suddenly the Divisional Headquarters received orders to vacate Ahmednagar Fort at 24 hours notice. Our indignation at losing such comfortable quarters soon gave way to curiosity when we learnt the reason for this hasty move. The Government of India had decided to arrest the leaders of the Congress Party. Pandit Nehru was to be confined in the Fort and Mahatma Gandhi and his entourage occupied a large house outside Poona – and just across the road from the camp occupied by one of our regiments.

I had only been in Ahmednagar a few weeks when I was ordered to take up an appointment at GHQ India. The move did not surprise me, but the appointment did. It was that of Deputy Adjutant-General (DAG) which carried the rank of Major-General. This meant that I was being jumped up from Colonel to Major-General leap frogging the rank of Brigadier; and that at 44 I should be the youngest Major-General in either the British or Indian Armies. I hasten to add that I did not hold that distinction for very long.

At the end of September 1942, I moved to Delhi, and met my future boss – Lieutenant-General William Baker, the Adjutant-General – for the first time. He explained to me that he now had two deputies, partly due to the terrific expansion of the Indian Army since Japan entered the war, and also because, owing to accommodation problems, his staff was split between Delhi and Simla, with even a few at Meerut. More important still, with the influx of British troops since the fall of Burma, a mass of administrative problems were arising which neither he nor either of his deputies felt qualified to deal with, all three being Indian Army and unused to the ways of British troops. Until recently the largest formed body of British troops in India had been the infantry battalion. Now complete British divisions, brigades, etc, were pouring into India raising all sorts of administrative problems. I was to take over from the DAG in Simla. He, "Wully" Baker, expected me to take the full responsibility for sorting out the problems which were arising almost daily, and which had of late necessitated his coming up to Simla, (an overnight journey of 12 hours from Delhi) far too often.

Before leaving for Simla I had my first meeting with the C-in-C, General Sir Archibald Wavell. He received me in his office standing up. He was leaning against a map table, and the first thing I noticed was that it was pitted with minute pin holes. I soon discovered why. The whole time he was talking to me he held in his hand an old-fashioned wooden pen fitted with a relief nib. He spoke slowly, and clearly emphasising points by jabbing the pen on to the map. He must have kept a large supply of these nibs, the tips of which crumpled under the constant pressure.

I only served 10 months on Wavell's staff as, in the summer of 1943 he was appointed Viceroy upon the retirement of Lord Linlithgow. I can, therefore, add little to what others have already written about him. He was a man of immense character, an intellectual, whose whole life was devoted to his profession and his family. Outside these his interests were few, apart from poetry and riding. Socially he could be a most discomforting host, particularly to the opposite sex. I have been at a meal in his house when, with a female guest on either side, he has lapsed into a 'brown study' and hardly addressed a word to either of them during the course of a long dinner. I remember in particular one embarrassing lunch in Delhi when Lady Wavell, next to whom I was sitting, was at pains to get her husband to utter a word of conversation during the whole of the meal.

Without doubt Wavell was one of the outstanding military commanders of World War II. It is, however, debatable whether his appointment as Viceroy of India was a wise move by the British Government. History shows that as a rule distinguished military figures do not make good statesmen. I doubt if Wavell was the exception to prove the rule.

On reaching Simla the first and most urgent problem I had to deal with was that of the system of pay and allowances for British Army personnel. In peacetime the responsibility for this lay in the hands of the Military Accountant General's Department of the Government of India. This was purely a civil organisation with offices in each of the four military commands into which India was divided. The movement of British troops in and out of India took place during the trooping season, ie, in the winter months. There was no secrecy attached to it. The system worked quite smoothly.

But now, since the Japanese invasion of Burma, thousands of British troops were arriving in India. The majority by sea and a few by air. The utmost secrecy was essential if convoys were to escape attack by submarines. Individuals were constantly arriving at (say) Bombay, moving across India from one command to another, and ending up in a unit fighting the Japs on the Indo-Burmese frontier. Needless to say the MAG's department took weeks to catch up with them. In the meantime they were unable to draw a single rupee of the pay and allowances to which they were entitled. The AG's office was being overwhelmed with reports of such cases. For married men the trouble was aggravated by their entitlement to separation allowance. In the UK and all overseas areas where British troops were stationed – with the sole exception of India – their pay and allowances were the responsibility of the Royal Army Pay Corps, a highly efficient professional body. The first task facing me was to get the RAPC to take over the responsibility for British troops in India, including those fighting on the Burmese frontier. Fortunately this had been agreed in principle by the War Office when their AG flew out to Delhi just before I arrived. After a long and bitter struggle with the MAG the Defence Department in Delhi formally agreed to the change. Shortly afterwards a senior RAPC officer flew out from home to discuss details. Within a few weeks the new pay centre was established at Meerut.

Having got the RAPC centre established, with detachments at every port and airport having the task of seeing that all new arrivals were taken on its books, the next problem was to rationalise overseas allowances. Under existing regulations the rates varied in every country where British troops were stationed; the variations reflecting the cost of living in different parts of the world. This was fair and reasonable in peacetime. But now we were faced with the impossible position whereby (say) a British Service officer moving from India to Ceylon for a brief period and then back to India again was entitled to different allowances in each country. The administrative burden involved in implementing such regulations, to my mind, was quite unjustifiable in the case of the Army and totally impracticable in the case of the RAF. The above example illustrates but one facet of the many problems involved. To get the regulations changed required the consent of the Defence Department in Delhi, and both the India Office and the War Office in Whitehall. Correspondence between Delhi and London went on for months without agreement being reached. It was not until I flew to London in August 1944 and was able to talk to those in whose hands decision-making rested, that a workable system of allowances was formally agreed and promptly introduced.

Until I arrived at GHQ I had not realised that the bulk of the 130,000 Italian prisoners of war captured during Wavell's offensive in the desert in the winter of 1940-41 had been shipped to India. I now found myself responsible for their safe-keeping and welfare. They were housed in five large camps scattered between Dehra Dun in the north and Bangalore in the south, the others being at Bikaner, Jaipur and Bhopal in central India. As soon as I could spare the time I visited these camps. They were all hutted, and in view of their size divided by the usual barbed wire fences into sections containing perhaps 1,000 men in each. So far as I could judge from these necessarily brief visits the Italians were being treated well and amply provided with suitable rations, eg, spaghetti and tomato puree.

Generally speaking the Italians caused us little trouble. There was a team of International Red Cross workers in India, who were free to visit the camps at any time. I knew that whenever there were any reasonable complaints the Head of the IRC, a Swiss who lived in Simla, would come straight to me and we would sort them out together. Nor did the security of the camps create anxiety. Attempts at escape were rare, and during my time as DAG I can only recall about six occasions when a prisoner of war succeeded in getting clear of a camp. In all cases, but two, they were recaptured. One Italian managed to gain refuge in neutral territory, namely the tiny Portugese island of Diu, 150 miles NW of Bombay. The other an Austrian, whose courage and ingenuity deserves full admiration, succeeded in entering the wild and little known territory of Tibet. He stayed on there for some time after the war ended, and wrote a book of his experiences.*

Amongst the subjects delegated to me by the AG were those covered by the heading 'discipline'. Soldiers, both British and Indian, were subject to military law (as well as civil law), and the tribunals for trying serious offences against that law were court-martials. Under regulations for both the British and Indian Armies only the highest form of court-martial – the general court-martial – could try officers for any offence against military law, and in the case of other ranks for offences for which the prescribed punishments could be penal servitude or the death sentence. Findings and punishments awarded by GCM's had to be confirmed by the C-in-C or his Deputy.

Much of my time, when not on tour, was occupied in reading the proceedings of GCM's after they had been vetted by the Judge Advocate-General to see whether there were any technical legal irregularities in them.

I had not been in office very long before a case appeared on my desk which caused me considerable anxiety. It concerned what legally amounted to mutiny by some Bengali soldiers of a unit stationed outside Calcutta. The court had found the ring leaders guilty and sentenced them to death.

In France and Italy in the 1914-18 war I had become well aware that deserters were from time to time executed by firing squad behind our lines. I had never been involved in such a case either as a member of a court or as a witness. But the very idea of the death sentence, as practiced, has always repelled me. It is not that I feel it is morally indefensible; on the contrary, it is because of the possible ill-effects it may have on those whose duty it is to take part in the final act. My feelings have not altered over the years, in fact they have hardened.

To revert to the case I have outlined above. I read and re-read the proceedings several times, and consulted the Judge Advocate. Eventually I recommended to the C-in-C that the findings and sentences be confirmed. This he did. The culprits were duly executed by hanging in a civil gaol.

* H Harrer, *Seven Years in Tibet* (Hart Davis MacGibbon 1953.) Strictly speaking, Harrer was not a prisoner of war but an interned alien.

Not all cases were traumatic. I remember one which had all the makings of a drama. It concerned Major X, the commanding officer of a unit stationed at the port of Chittagong. The unit was engaged in forwarding stores destined for XIVth Army in Burma by transferring them from ship to rail for onward transmission. Like all units in India a contractor was engaged to supply the unit's canteen. These contracts were much sought after on the principle that one contract led to another, and that, if one unit commander was satisfied he would provide the valuable 'chit' of recommendation which might lead to further contracts. Knowing this, Major X demanded of his contractor that a 1,000 rupee note should find its way on to the CO's desk every Monday morning. Not content with this he arranged with merchants in the local bazaar that they should relieve him of certain desirable stores, in exchange for which further 1,000 rupee notes were to find their way into his office. Unfortunately for Major X the local base commander got wind of these irregular goings-on and called in the Military Police.

To cut a long story short, when officers of the Special Investigation Branch, uninvited, called upon Major X he was not in his office. Eventually he was run to ground in the officers' mess kitchen stuffing 1,000 rupee notes into the stove. Regrettably he had been unable to operate on his own, and his senior Indian officer and one other had become involved. They all ended up in gaol. During the course of the trial it was revealed that the major's ill-gotten gains were safely deposited in his wife's bank in Calcutta where they could not be touched. Later we managed to get the law changed so that the proceeds of a crime could, on conviction of the criminal, become forfeit.

It is inevitable that with the rapid and vast expansion of the Services in war the number of criminals and the opportunities for criminal acts should greatly increase within the military sphere. Looking back it strikes me as remarkable that the number of court-martial cases which reached my office was not greater than it was. Many of them dealt with the misappropriation of cash or stores. There is after all but a narrow dividing line between occasional 'borrowing' from the quartermaster's stores and making a business of it. On one occasion when visiting a detention centre I was struck with the appearance of one military prisoner. I can best describe his appearance as that of the ideal stage butler. On getting back to Simla I sent for his papers. He was serving a longish sentence for long term misappropriation of stores, a polite word for stealing!

One of the duties of the Adjutant-General is to record casualties to personnel, and to inform their next of kin. In peacetime this duty is negligible, but in war it becomes a very important responsibility, and requires a staff whose watchword must be complete accuracy, if unnecessary suffering is to be avoided. The casualty section at Simla was one of my responsibilities. I was fortunate in that the officer in charge of it was a woman, who apart from being highly efficient was herself a casualty of war. Mrs K G Putnam's husband had been killed in action when commanding an Indian battalion in the Western Desert. She held a commission in the Womens Army Corps (India) and her staff consisted of four junior officers of that Corps together with about 100 clerks. Her section was responsible for recording all casualties occurring in the Indian Army, whether Indian or British. In the case of Indian Other Ranks their Regimental Centres actually informed the next of kin, but in the case of officers the section despatched the appropriate telegram.

All casualties were categorised under one of the following headings:

Killed in action on (date)
Died of wounds
Missing believed killed
Missing believed Prisoner of War
Missing
Wounded

The three 'missing' categories naturally called for the most careful treatment, especially when they occurred in the South-East Asia theatre of war. The Japanese attitude to prisoners of war was simply that they had no right to exist. Their own soldiers were taught that to be captured in battle was an act of the utmost disgrace. To die in battle was the highest honour, to be captured alive was the greatest dishonour. Consequently the number of Japanese prisoners of war captured by our forces was negligible. Up to the time I left GHQ we had no more than a handful to look after. The Japanese attitude was, of course reflected in the manner in which they treated, or perhaps one should say, mistreated our prisoners of war. They gave no information regarding our men who were 'missing' and they would not allow neutral subjects access to their prisoner of war camps.

The result was that, whereas when one of our men was reported 'missing' in the Desert, the chances were that, if he was alive, the Germans or Italians would in due course report the fact through the International Red Cross. In such cases Casualties could inform the next of kin thereby relieving them of much anxiety. But, if the same man was missing in Burma, there was in most cases no means of telling whether he was alive or dead, at any rate until the war ended.

It is to the great credit of Mrs Putnam and her team that during her time in charge of the Section only two 'deaths' were wrongly reported. In neither case was the Section to blame. In one case an officer was reported dead by his unit in Italy, whereas he was badly concussed and after capture by the Germans and medical treatment he recovered. In the other case the casualty reported 'killed' was carrying the wrong identity disc.

One unusual duty which fell to the Casualty Section was what one may term reporting in reverse. It sometimes happened that the next of kin of a man serving in the Indian Army was killed by bombing in (say) London. In this case we were responsible for informing him.

I suppose the most common error which could creep in to the reporting of casualties was due to faulty records. If a young officer got married, (at any rate when I was a junior officer) he was bound to report the matter to his CO, who in turn would have passed the information on to the War Office. Obviously this procedure was occasionally not followed. A friend and contemporary of mine in the Indian Army was killed in Burma. According to the records his next of kin was his father living in Ireland. It so happened that his father had been dead some years, but unaware of this the Casualty Section quite rightly cabled the usual notification to him. His widow heard of his death almost immediately, but received no official report. Consequently she wrote a letter of complaint to the C-in-C.

The advantages of being stationed in Simla, especially in summer when Delhi was unbearably hot, were in my case somewhat outweighed by the necessity to pay frequent visits to the latter in order to confer with other members of GHQ staff, particularly on the AG's side. This was in addition to visits to most of the principal military stations in India. The journeys to and from Delhi became such a burden, due to the time wasted in travelling every few days not to mention the physical strain imposed by the difference in altitude and temperature between the two places, that after the first few months I arranged to divide my time and my office, spending, as far as possible, two weeks in Simla followed by one week in Delhi.

One day during one of my weeks in Delhi, a Lieutenant-Colonel sporting a monocle burst into my office. He was in a highly emotional state of excitement. When I enquired the object of his visit, to my astonishment he replied, "I am Colonel Wintle, I have just arrived. I want you to send a cable to GHQ Cairo ordering them to place their Director of Military Intelligence under close arrest." I had never spoken to Wintle before but I had no difficuty in identifying him as the man who had been so conspicuous during the Staff College entrance examinations. On my asking for his authority and reasons for making this extraordinary request he unfolded a long story, the gist of which was that the officer in question had ordered him to undertake a mission into enemy territory (in this case Vichy, France) knowing full well that he would be arrested and probably shot as a spy. Sure enough he had been arrested and imprisoned. After months of hardship he had eventually escaped and returned to Cairo only to find that all his kit and other belongings had been stolen, no doubt with the connivance of this same unscrupulous officer whose sole object was to get rid of him (Wintle). As soon as Wintle left my office I rang up the Military Secretary who dealt with the posting of officers, as I strongly suspected that Wintle had no authority to be in India. What happened to him after that I had no idea.

It was not until some years after the war that I read somewhere an account of an episode which occurred at the time of Dunkirk. Wintle walked into the Air Ministry unannounced, entered the office of an air commodore, and at revolver point demanded an aircraft to fly him to Bordeaux where he claimed he could persuade the remnants of the French Air Force to fly to Britain rather than surrender to the Boche. For this escapade he was arrested, lodged in the Tower of London, court-martialled and got off with nothing more than a severe reprimand.

In the mid-fifties Wintle really hit the headlines. He accused a solicitor in Brighton of cheating his (Wintle's) sister of a large sum due to her under the will of a relative. The case went to court and Wintle – acting for his sister – lost. Thereupon he lured the solicitor into a friend's flat, removed his trousers and left him to make his way home in his underpants. For this episode Wintle was charged with 'common assault' and sentenced to six months in gaol. Nothing daunted, on his release he again took up his accusation against the solicitor. The case failed. He then took it to the Court of Appeal, acting in person without legal assistance. Again he failed. Finally he got to the House of Lords where, presenting his case personally, he finally won.

In his autobiography*, published after his death, Wintle deals at length with his imprisonment by the Vichy French in Toulouse and subsequent escape, but makes no further reference to his subsequent service in World War II beyond a brief statement that, "I spent the rest of the war most actively in the Middle East, Burma and Italy and – for the second time – in Occupied France." After reading the book it is not easy to assess the worth of this extraordinary character. I suppose history will label him an eccentric. Undoubtedly one of his hallmarks was dogged determination; another showmanship. The former brought him a telegram of congratulations and a jeroboam of champagne from the members of Lincoln's Inn, the latter an appearance on Eamonn Andrews TV programme *This is your Life*.

In September 1944 I left GHQ to take over command of 105 L-of-C Area at Madras. In peacetime Madras District had been considered somewhat of a military sinecure, since few troops were stationed there. It embraced the southern tip of India comprising the Madras Presidency, and the native states of Mysore, Cochin and Travancore. The inhabitants were Hindu by religion and, generally speaking, of smaller stature than the Moslems and Sikhs of the north and west of the Indian subcontinent. The main languages were Tamil and Telegu. These bore no resemblance to the other tongues of India. To overcome the language difficulty the sepoy of the Indian Army was taught to speak Urdu, a mixture of Hindi and Persian. English was the language of the Government.

With the formation of South-East Asia Command (SEAC) and the defeat of the Japanese advance into India in the summer of 1944, the position in South India was one of increasing military importance and activity. When I arrived preparations were well in hand for the day when the Allies would be able to launch combined operations for the recapture of Malaya and the Dutch East Indies. Apart from Calcutta, Madras is the only large port on the east coast of India. These were, therefore, the two centres on which future operations were to be based.

My task was largely administrative, and, therefore much to my liking. In order to convert the area into a base the first thing was to cater for the arrival of reinforcements. These would in the main be arriving from Europe, once Germany was defeated. It was planned that as many as

The Last Englishman (Michael Joseph)

possible would come by air. To this end an air reception centre was to be built at Arkonam, 50 miles west of Madras. Here the troops would arrive in battle dress without personal weapons and with the minimum of clothing. On arrival they would move straight into an air-conditioned building, where they would be fitted out for tropical conditions, and quickly moved out to hutted camps, (several of which were under construction) each capable of holding a complete division. These camps were located so that training in jungle warfare could be carried out in the immediate vicinity.

At a village called Avadi, 20 miles inland from Madras and on the main railway line, a vast area of some 20 square miles was being converted into a supply base, designed to handle every type of commodity required by the Army and RAF, as well as some specialist naval stores. Some idea of its size, when completed in the spring of 1945, may be gathered from the 125 miles of rail track needed to serve the base, and from the 15,000 Indian and 7,000 British troops required to man it, not to mention the 38,000 labourers employed in it. In addition it housed three hospitals for handling the more severe casualties expected to arrive from overseas, until they were fit enough to be moved to hospitals up country.

Other major constructional works involved the expansion of facilities in Madras harbour to meet the needs of amphibious vehicles and the special landing craft required to carry them, as well as other weapons and personnel. Similar works on a smaller scale had to be carried out at Cochin and Vizagapatam.

At the end of 1944 the public at home had become aware of the hardships being suffered by the men of General Slim's XIV Army. It had acquired the title "The Forgotten Army". Thanks to medical science and the excellent services of the Royal Army Medical Corps and its partner the Indian Army Medical Corps the sickness rate in South-East Asia, even under the extreme conditions of physical and mental stress imposed by the jungles of Burma, was kept well under control. Owing to the scarcity of shipping, however, home leave for British troops who had been overseas for long periods was out of the question. After the matter had been frequently raised in Parliament, and a committee of enquiry appointed under the chairmanship of Lord Munster, Under Secretary of State for India, Winston Churchill appointed General Charles King (whom we last met in the cellars of GHQ Arras in the early hours of 10th May 1940) to come out and investigate how the whole question of the welfare of British troops could best be implemented. This was a question which had always been of much concern to me when I was at GHQ, but finance was always the stumbling block. Now at last the British Government was going to release funds. At Madras I found myself in the fortunate position of being able to promote and encourage the welfare of both British and Indian troops to a degree unequalled in other parts of the sub-continent.

Since 1942 the Governor of Madras, Sir Arthur Hope, had instituted an "Amenity for Troops Fund" as part of the province's War Purposes Fund. The latter had been instituted at the outbreak of war, and was used to finance the purchase of military aircraft and other weapons. The "Amenity for Troops Fund" as the name implies, was to provide amenities for the troops pouring into the province after the fall of Burma. Thanks to a Joint War Charities Committee, headed by Lady Hope and two prominent ladies in Madras, Lady Armstrong and Mrs Clubwala, these funds were being used to provide innumerable amenities for both Indian and British troops in the form of mobile canteens and cinemas, furniture and furnishings for clubs and leave centres, to quote but a few examples.

When I arrived, British leave hostels had been established in the Nilgri Hills, that famous tea growing area north of Coimbatore and at Kodaikanal, a less well known planting area in the hills east of Cochin. Now with the imminent arrival of personnel from the voluntary organisations at home, notably the Red Cross and St John's, and the Womens' Voluntary Service (WVS), facilities in which they could best be employed were urgently needed. With the willing cooperation of the local authorities additional clubs, canteens and the like were opened in the main centres such as Madras, Vizagapatam, Coimbatore and Cochin. But my biggest problem was Avadi. The plans drawn up by GHQ completely ignored the amenity side except for an unattractive tin hutted cinema, to reach which men in some parts of the base would have to walk as far as three miles. In the steaming atmosphere of South India, where temperatures up to 100°F were common, this was asking too much of men who had recently arrived from the UK. I, therefore got my staff to draw up plans for two amenity centres in the base. Each was to comprise a large open air swimming bath, a cinema, a dance hall-cum-theatre, playing fields and canteens for British and Indian troops with accommodation for WVS and other female staff to supervise them.

Before the plans for these centres finally came to fruition, an event occurred which led to the building of the first pub in India. A workshop unit comprising some 1500 REME craftsmen arrived from the UK. Their workshops at Avadi were still under construction: huge metal clad hangars. To fit in with shipping schedules, we were told, the arrival of the unit could not be delayed. In order to get the workshops in to operation as soon as possible the unit was put to work on finishing the workshop buildings, and putting some final touches to their own hutted accommodation. A few days after their arrival the Army Commander rang me and said that a senior member of his staff had visited the unit and reported that morale appeared to be very low and discipline poor. I was on tour at the time, so as soon as I returned I visited the unit and got the same impression. Something had to be done. I called the CO and two of his senior officers to Madras and we discussed the situation. From them I learnt that the unit had been quartered comfortably in billets in England, that very few of the men had ever been out of England before and that their departure had been at short notice with consequent disruption of embarkation leave. One of them then added, "Well, after you've been living in comfortable billets and can pop round to the pub when you're off duty, all this is a bit too much of a violent change for some of our lads." This remark gave me an idea. After they had left I sent for my Chief Engineer and said to him, "I want to build a village pub in Avadi. Can you do it? I'll find the money." The date was 7th February, 1945.

To cut a long story short The Wade Inn was built, and officially opened on 6th June 1945. This was followed by a second pub a few weeks later. The original Inn sign of The Wade Inn now hangs in my dining room and the architects' drawings for both pubs adorn the same room.

On reading through some old press cuttings recently I was reminded that the Madras Amenities Fund raised approximately £1,000,000 for troops' welfare. I got most of the money required for the amenities in Avadi, and for many other projects, from this source. I shall always be grateful to the people of Madras province, because it was largely due to their generosity that 105 L-of-C Area got a reputation for the way in which it looked after the welfare of both British and Indian troops.

In May 1945 I took a few days' leave and went up to Simla after a couple of days in Delhi. It was a bit of a busman's holiday, but I needed a change. I had had two short spells in hospital, and was thoroughly tired. The cool air of the Himalayas was just what I needed. However, I

119

had not been there many days when the armistice in Europe was announced. I straightway flew back to Madras in time to attend a thanksgiving service in the Cathedral, a victory parade and other celebrations.

By this time Rangoon had been recaptured and the XIVth Army was making steady progress against the Japs. Already some fighting formations had started to move into 105 L-of-C Area, Avadi Base was stocked and all the intricate machinery for launching 'Zipper' was ready. That was the code word for the combined operation for the reconquest of Malaya.

During the first week in September the troops and transports destined to make the initial landings on the west coast of Malay were at sea. The Japanese had virtually surrendered but our troops were not allowed to land until Mountbatten had formally accepted at Singapore the surrender of all Japanese forces in South-East Asia Command on 12th September.

For some months past we had been making plans for receiving and holding RAPWI. These initials stood for Returned Allied Prisoners of War and Internees. Since the Japs had allowed no outside communication with prisoners of war, little was known as to their locations and numbers. The efficiency with which SEAC tackled this problem was amply demonstrated by the arrival of two ships carrying RAPWI in Madras harbour on 16th September. I went down to meet them. The first ship carried men of the 1st and 9th Gurkha Regiments. I had always admired the Gurkhas, but I think few of us were prepared to witness the sight which greeted us as these tough little men marched down the gangway, formed up on the quay and spurning the offer of transport marched out of the harbour. The second ship was a hospital ship and here one's emotion swung from pride to pity. I shall never forget the spectre of one little Indian, as he was carried ashore on a stretcher with his fleshless bones poking through his skin, his face a mask and one shapeless arm clutching a small paper parcel, presumably containing all that he possessed. The dismal procession continued as ambulance loads, one after the other, carried the sick and maimed on their way to hospitals at Avadi.

That night I invited three of the British Gurkha officers to dine in my mess. My senior medical officer had warned us to be careful of our conversation and on no account to question them about their experiences as prisoners of war. In the event all three behaved perfectly normally and chatted freely about their experiences in Japanese hands. The only sign of abnormality occured when the mess waiter handed round cigarettes and cheroots. I noticed that one of them surreptitiously snatched a cheroot and put it in his pocket – a habit no doubt acquired under the scrutiny of Japanese guards.

For the next four or five weeks I went down to the harbour to meet the RAPWI ships, whenever I could get away. They were arriving almost daily. On these occasions I invited some of the officers to dine. I only hope they enjoyed their first glimpse of civilised life again as much as we enjoyed their company.

Later when I returned to England I realised that the sights I witnessed in Madras harbour were but a reflection of those which greeted our own and Allied troops who overran Belsen and other German concentration camps. Brutality and inhumanity are not the prerogative of any one nation, whether Eastern or Western.

About the second week in October the troopship *Dilwara* arrived at Madras carrying RAPWI from the Nicobars – a small group of islands some 400 miles west of the Malay Peninsular. That night we had three RAF officers and the ship's captain to dine. The RAF officers had a remarkable tale to tell. They were the sole survivors of a plane which had been shot down in the Bay of Bengal. After drifting in a rubber dinghy for many days, they eventually landed on one of the islands, where they received a friendly reception from some of the natives, who housed and fed them: and, moreover, hid them from the occasional Japanese patrol which happened to visit that part of the islands. It was only after they had been there some time that they realised the islands were British.

During 1945 when the focus of Allied attention was being turned progressively towards South-East Asia, the flow of visitors from Delhi and London to 105 L-of-C Area provided the opportunity for meeting many interesting characters. In February, a committee headed by General Wilcox, a New Zealander, was touring the Indian commands. Their task was, as far as I remember, to investigate and recommend measures for the reorganisation of the Army in India. I looked forward to their visit to Madras with pleasure because one of the members was my old friend Cariappa, now a Brigadier. Another member was a Brigadier Powell, whom I was told was an Oxford don and a classical scholar. At the time I was living as a "pg" with Sir Norman Strathie, Adviser to the Governor of Madras, and so was not in a position to entertain parties in my own residence. The committee was staying in an hotel in Madras. I therefore arranged to entertain them, on arrival, to dinner in the Madras Club. Knowing that the club was a venerable and hallowed refuge for senior members of the European community, I told my ADC to mention to the Secretary that one of my guests would be a senior Indian officer. Much to my annoyance the secretary replied that the rules of the club forbade the admission of Indians even as guests. If I insisted on inviting one he would have to call a special meeting of the club committee. My reply was a curt, "Well, kindly do so." In the event the committee agreed to make a special exemption in the case of Cariappa, and I concluded that the matter was ended.

But it was not to be. We were sitting down to drinks in the bar before dinner when the club steward came up to me with a book open in his hand. "The Secretary's compliments, sir, and would you please enter your Indian guest's name in the visitors book."

I said, "Oh, you mean all my guest's names."

"No," he replied, "only this one," indicating Cariappa, who was sitting next to me.

I tried to conceal my embarrassment and anger; beckoning to my ADC, who was sitting opposite, I asked him to attend to the matter – adding audibly that there had obviously been some mistake.

Unfortunately some of the Wilcox Committee went down with what was called 'Madras tummy' as soon as they arrived. Enoch Powell was one of them, so I never had the pleasure of meeting him socially.

Following Charles King's visit to India, ENSA parties started to tour India and SEAC. Whenever possible I made a point of meeting the artistes visiting the Area. One of the most entertaining – both on and off the stage – was Leslie Henson. One night, after the variety show in which he was leading, I invited the whole company to supper. By this time I had moved into a mess. Afterwards we sat in the mess garden until the early hours. Henson's consumption of whisky was equalled by his capacity for amusing conversation. About midnight I realised that our limited supply of scotch had run out. I started to apologise. Whereupon he waived my apologies aside and produced, as if by a conjuring trick, the largest hip flask I have ever seen, from which he proceeded to fill our glasses.

Another visitor was George Formby, the ukelele-playing singer. Both these artistes are now dead. They belonged to the pre-TV era, so their work did not reach the mass media audiences of today. But few of my generation will have forgotten them.

Most of the ENSA companies were from the variety stage, and occasionally we had dramatic performances. One such company was led by Sir John Gielgud and I was able to see two of its productions: *Hamlet* in Madras and Noel Cowards' *Blithe Spirit* in Avadi. Needless to say both were a joy to watch.

Recently I learnt that Gielgud regarded the performance of *Hamlet* which he gave on this ENSA visit amongst the best he ever gave.*

*R Hayman, *Gielgud* (Heinneman) p157

11

Failure of the Cabinet Mission—the Indian Armed Forces Nationalisation Committee—Mountbatten succeeds Wavell as Viceroy—farewell to India—Monty and the Auk

In January 1946 I flew home on leave. BOAC were now operating the Indian air route although the pilots were still in RAF uniform. The homeward flight was in a Dakota; despite frequent stops for refuelling the flight from Karachi to Hurn, Bournemouth took only 70 hours. On the return journey I was delighted to find myself once more in a Sunderland flying boat. The flight from Poole harbour to Karachi lasted 64 hours, including a night stop at Bahrein, where conditions in the rest house had greatly improved since my last visit during the war.

By now demobilisation and reorganisation were in full swing. Hand in hand with the demobilisation of personnel, and the disbandment of war-time units, the process of building up units required for the post-war Armies went on. One was constantly on the move, touring the Area, inspecting units, attending conferences, putting in an appearance at sporting and social events such as athletic meetings, boxing matches, British ranks dances etc, whilst my wife had to compete with a constant flow of official visitors from Delhi and the UK who needed accommodation and entertaining.

By this time Delhi had become the scene of intense political activity. The war-time Coalition Government under Winston Churchill had ended. The July 1945 general election had returned Labour to power with a firm majority under Clement Atlee. No doubt like many others of my upbringing and generation, I had – for the first and only time in my life – voted Labour. My only reason was that I somehow felt that the ageing Churchill, magnificent as he had been as war-time leader of the nation, was not the man to carry the immense burden which post-war problems were bound to impose.

In pursuance of their announced intention of promoting, "In conjunction with the leaders of Indian opinion, the early realisation of full self-government in India,"* the new Cabinet in March 1946 despatched three of their members to India. These were Lord Pethwick Lawrence, Secretary of State for India, Sir Stafford Cripps, President of the Board of Trade and Mr A V Alexander, First Lord of the Admiralty. They remained in India until the end of June. On their return home they announced that their mission had been a success in that the main Indian political parties had agreed to set up a constituent assembly to decide on the form which the future government of India would take.

What this announcment overlooked was the unwelcome fact that the two major policital parties – Congress and the Muslim League – were committed to entirely different aims. The predominantly Hindu Congress led by Pandit Nehru, stood for a United India; the Muslim League led by M A Jinnah, stood for Pakistan, ie, the separation of India into two nations.

Now that the politicians had come out into the open, the extremists on either side got busy and stirred up communal hatred which resulted in riots and wholesale killings in Dacca and Eastern Bengal: followed by even greater bloodshed in Bihar in November. It is to the ever-lasting credit of the Indian Services that these riots were eventually brought under control by Indian troops and armed police – but not before the death role had run into thousands. Here too Mahatma Gandhi's influence was at its best. Moving through the disturbed areas he disclaimed violence and did much to quench inflamed tempers.

On 9th December the Constituent Assembly met for the first time without a single nominee of the Muslim League. The only Muslims in the Assembly were those nominated by the Congress Party. To those in the know in Delhi and Whitehall the writing was on the wall. The chances of a transfer of power from Britain to India on the basis of Dominion status were fading fast; chances of handing over to a government representing all-India interests rested on the ability and willingness of Britain to continue to be responsible for the maintenance

*Extract from the speech from the Throne on the opening of Parliament, 15th August, 1945.

of law and order for an indefinite period, until, and when, Indian politicians settled their differences. To put it bluntly: was Britain to hold the baby whilst Hindus slaughtered Muslims in one part of India and Muslims slaughtered Hindus in another; when the country had been offered self-government either within or without the British Commonwealth; and whilst the political leaders could not agree which form of government they wanted? The answer could only be "No". Britain had neither the manpower nor the money.

In Madras we were fortunate. Events in Delhi – nearly 1500 miles away – seemed remote, as if taking place in another country. Spared the hatred and bloodshed of Northern India one felt secure in the peaceful atmosphere of the Hindu dominated South.

Only once did the possibility of trouble call for swift action on my part. The Governor sent for me one day and informed me that the District Commissioner on the west coast feared that the Moplahs might be out for blood once more. In 1921 the Moplahs, (a section of Muslims said to be descended from Arab traders who had settled on the Malabar. coast), suddenly, under the influence of fanatics, turned on the neighbouring Hindus and inflicted on them murder, rape and in some cases forcible religious conversion.

At the time we had very few troops on the Malabar coast, so I decided to show the flag by moving a British artillery brigade into the area. They were so well received by the locals that they spent most of the time playing football with the Moplahs. After a week I withdrew them.

Apart from that incident the only anxieties we encountered were caused by some West African troops. After the armistice one of the two West African divisions which had been fighting in Burma was withdrawn and stationed in a camp near Madras, so that they could be sent home when shipping became available. Unfortunately weeks and then months went by; but no ships appeared. It was not surprising therefore, that seeing British and Indian units disbanded and the men being demobilised, the African soldiers became disgruntled and their morale sank to a low ebb. In September 1946 there was a state of indiscipline in one particular unit which bordered on a mutiny. Prompt action soon restored order. In consequence Delhi brought further pressure on Whitehall to provide shipping; this time with success. The whole division was shipped to West Africa without further incident.

125

On October I went up to Delhi for two days to attend a conference. The Auk kindly put me up in C-in-C's house. It was then that he warned me that he would almost certainly have to bring me up to Delhi for an indefinite period.

Although a definite date for the transfer of power had not been settled it was generally accepted that the Indianisation of the defence forces, civil service, police, etc, would have to proceed at an accelerated pace to prepare the country for independence. I was not surprised therefore, when just before Christmas I received orders to move to Delhi. I was to be prepared to stay there six months or longer. In the meantime another major-general was being posted to take over my Command.

On 4th January, 1947 I flew to Delhi. The Indian Cabinet had decided to appoint a committee to examine the whole question of Indianisation of the Armed Forces and he wanted a senior British officer on it. I was to be that officer.

In due course the Armed Forces Nationalisation Committee was appointed with Sir N Gopalaswami Ayyanger, CSI, CIE as Chairman. The members were:

>Pandit H N Kunzru (Brahmin)
>Mr Muhammed Ismail Khan (Muslim)
>Sardar Sampuran Singh (Sikh)
>Brigadier K S Thimayya DSO
>Commander H M S Choudri MBE
>Wing-Commander Meer Singh DSO
>and myself,
>with Lieut-Col B M Kaul as secretary.

The terms of reference of the Committee required it to report within six months on:

a) Ways and means within the minimum possible period of replacement of non-Indian personnel by Indians in each branch or service

b) the target date or dates of complete nationalisation for all or each category in the different services if possible

c) the ways and means of retaining, if necessary, non-Indian personnel as advisers or experts in nationalised categories

New cadets (Snookers) at the Shop – RMA Woolwich October 1915.

94th Heavy Artillery Brigade Signal Section Italy December 1918. *(Author front row, centre.)*

Three ton 'Thorneycroft' army lorry. Italy 1918.

Italian gun en route to the Asiago Front 1918.

Reproduced by kind permission of Imperial War Museum

H M Destroyer. Off Odessa Harbour February 1920.

British sailors marching along Nicolaivsky Boulevard. Odessa 6th February 1920.

Scene on the quay at Theodosia after the evacuation of Novorossiysk.

Picnic Party on tug on their way to Balaclava June 1920.

H M King George VI with HQ Staff of 2nd Infantry Division, Moreton-in-the-Marsh 1st April 1941. *(Author fourth from left, second row.)*

Sir Winston Churchill inspecting troops of 2nd Infantry Division 28th March 1941.

Reproduced by kind permission of Imperial War Museum

FM von Manstein in the dock.
Copyright Conti Press, Hamburg

Trial of FM von Manstein at Hamburg. Members of the court *(left to right)*: Brig Dixon, Judge Collingwood, Lt-Gen Simpson, Self, Brig Lambe, Col Liddell.

Public Relations HQ, Hamburg District

Some of the thousands of prisoners of war disembarking at Madras September 1945.

Indian Armed Forces Nationalisation Committee New Delhi 1947. *(Clockwise from bottom left)* W/Cmdr Meer Singh, Sardar Sampuran Singh, Sir N Gopalaswami Ayyanger (Chairman), Lt-Col B M Kaul (Secretary), Muhammed Ismail Khan, shorthand writer, Self, Cmdr H M S Choudri, Witness, Pandit H N Kunzru, Brig K S Thimayya.

Public Relations Directorate, GHQ New Delhi

1st Battalion The Royal Inniskillen Fusiliers. Final Parade of British troops in Fort St George Madras, 4th August 1947.

British Military Cemetery Dunkirk – annual pilgrimage of Dunkirk Veterans Association. M Claude Provoyeur Mayor (Patron) and the author (Chairman).

All photographs, unless otherwise stated, are reproduced by kind permission of the author.

d) the enumeration of those departments, categories or personnel where non-Indian personnel can be replaced by Indians immediately.

The problems facing the Committee were mainly concerned with the replacement of British by Indian officers. It was estimated that the Army of 230,000 would require 7-8,000 officers. There were about 500 Indians with pre-war regular commissions. The majority were in the infantry, armoured corps and army service corps: their highest rank was brigadier and there were eleven holding this rank. In the other arms there were very few Indians and the highest rank in the artillery was major. In the RIN the problem was much the same; whilst in the RIAF there was no similar problem since it was, and always had been, an all-Indian Service.

The Committee met for the first time on 6th January 1947. The only material which the Committee had before it was a paper prepared by the Chiefs of Staff which contemplated complete nationalisation of the Army and Navy within a period of 10 years, and in the case of the Air Force a longer period than 10 years because their technical side was so weak.

From the start it was obvious that the Committee was likely to sit for the full period of six months, since the civilian members were all far too occupied with political activities to be able to devote much time to problems on a subject of which at least two of them had little knowledge and no experience. In addition it was quite clear that the Chief of Staff's paper was out of date.

The political situation was such that complete nationalisation would have to be completed in a much shorter time than 10 years. Consequently after consulting the C-in-C and General Sir Arthur Smith, the Chairman of the Chief of Staff's Commmittee, I drew up a paper outlining a phased plan for nationalisation of the Army by 1st July 1949 in stages of six monthly intervals, after which a small number of advisers or instructors might be required in the technical arms. I submitted it to the Committee at its fifth meeting on 4th February. They decided to send it to the Chiefs of Staff for their comments. Before these comments could be received Attlee announced in the House of Commons the British Government's "definite intention to take the necessary steps to effect the transfer of power into responsible Indian hands by a date not later than June 1948." At the same time he made it quite clear that, if the Indians could not by that date have decided on the form of the Central Government, Britain would hand over power in such a way as

127

seemed "most reasonable and in the best interests of the Indian people." Here was a clear indication that Britain was prepared, if need be, to accept the formation of a separate Muslim state, ie, Pakistan. This would of course, entail the Services being split into two.

The Committee decided, despite the Moslem's members' objection, that it must stick to its terms of reference which were based on united India, but that it would base its recommendations on the new date of June 1948 as the latest date for the completion of nationalisation. At the same time the Chiefs of Staff agreed to submit new proposals based on that same date.

On 24th March, Lord Mountbatten took over as Viceroy from Lord Wavell. It soon became an almost certainty that the date of transfer of power would be brought forward to some time much earlier than June 1948, but the question of Pakistan still remained unsolved.

I was present at what was officially described as "the ceremony of the assumption of office of Viceroy and Governor-General of India by Rear Admiral the Viscount Mountbatten." I only wish I had kept a proper diary in those days in which to describe that historic scene. As it is, I must fall back on the impression which has remained stamped on my memory after the passage of years.

Inside the magnificent marble setting of the Durbar Hall at Viceroy's House (why this vast palace was so called I have never discovered) were seated two or three hundred people facing the dais on which stood the two Viceregal Thrones. The setting resembled that in the House of Lords when the Sovereign opens Parliament. The stark whiteness of the hall was relieved by the scarlet draperies hung as a background to the thrones, and the varied and colourful attire of those present: Indian princes ablaze in resplendent uniforms with gold braiding and plumed headgear; Indian ladies in elegant and delicate coloured saris; European ladies in all shades and varieties of gowns; members of the Congress Party, headed by the familiar figure of Pandit Nehru, in their simple Gandhi-inspired dress of white cotton tunic and tightly fitting trousers surmounted by the plain white cap; bemedalled sailors in white tropical kit; airmen in blue. Alone amongst this scintillating pastiche the soldiers in plain khaki presented a sombre note.

As the appointed hour of 10am struck, a fanfare of trumpets announced the arrival of the new Viceregal couple. Lord Mountbatten in white uniform surmounted by a glittering array of orders marched

128

slowly forward in procession accompanied by his wife, who, dressed also in white, relieved only by the pale blue sash of the Order of the Star of India, appeared the personification of regal dignity.

After the swearing in by the Chief Justice of India had been completed, Mountbatten casting precedent aside delivered a brief speech. His clear message was that he had come to preside over the Government of India with the sole object of its transfer to Indian hands. The guests were then ushered past their Excellencies and presented to them.

Mountbatten was not, of course, a stranger to India by virtue of his war-time experience as Supreme Commander, South-East Asia Command. Nor was Lady Mountbatten. As head of St John's Ambulance she had during the war travelled widely in India visiting military hospitals, displaying that indefatigable sense of duty, which was shortly to reach its climax in the chaos and slaughter resulting from Pakistan.

On the day that the Japanese surrendered she was on a tour of hospitals in northern India. That night she landed at Vizagapatam on the east coast. Brigadier Charles Ford, my sub-area commander there, had but a few minutes notice of her arrival. He and his wife put her up for the night in their bungalow. She announced that she would fly to Singapore at dawn in the morning to attend to the welfare of our men who were prisoners of war on the island. The pilot of her RAF Dakota said that he could not go there without first getting approval from air headquarters in Colombo. He must know whether it was safe to land there, and whether he could refuel en route. All this would take time. Lady Mountbatten demanded that he fly her to Singapore at first light. He did so and they landed safely. It was some years later that she died suddenly in Malaysia, whilst on a somewhat similar mission.

By 11th April the Chief of Staff's paper containing proposals for the nationalisation of the Army had been circulated to the Committee. They were in principle similar to the proposals contained in my paper, except that the interval between the four phases had been reduced to three months. Like my proposals they included provision for a small military mission of an advisory and instructional nature to be retained for a short period after the transfer of power. Proposals on similar lines were submitted by the RIN and RIAF staff.

Our Committee considered these three papers in detail calling as witnesses Sir Arthur Smith and the C-in-C's of the RIN and RIAF to explain various aspects. As regards the Army, one of the modifications affected the medical service. After hearing many witnesses on the subject we, quite rightly in my opinion, recommended that it should be Indianised at the earliest possible date.

On 12th May the Committee signed their final report and I was fortunate enough to be allowed to resume my command at Madras. – On 3rd June Mountbatten made the historic announcement that the transfer of power would take place on 15th August 1947, ie, in 10 weeks time; that India would be divided into two States – India and Pakistan – and that each state would have its own defence Services formed by partition of the three existing Indian Services (the Indian Army, the Royal India Navy and the Royal Indian Air Force).

Thus at a stroke, but not unexpectedly, the whole purpose of the Committee was nullified. On the other hand I am sure that the work of the Committee was not wasted. In the event the final plans for the partition of the armed forces was left in the hands of an Armed Forces Reconstruction Committee with Sir Chandulai Trivedi as chairman. Trivedi had been Secretary of the War Department up to 1946. He was well qualified through his intimate knowledge of the Services and their senior officers. His Committee did not start work till early July. They were, therefore, given barely five weeks in which to produce their plans, get them accepted and for their implementation to commence.

Without the detailed work done by the AFNC I doubt whether this would have been possible. Our Committee had laid down the principles on which nationalisation was to operate, after examining evidence from 177 officers, of whom 45 appeared in person before us. Once the division of resources in terms of ships, regiments, battalions, squadrons of aircraft, etc, had been decided it was not too complex a task to detail the timed phases of nationalisation for the six new Services.

Our Committee had not visualised a united India remaining within the British Commonwealth, consequently we had to base our plans on British officers ceasing to hold executive commands after the transfer of power, since it would not be possible for them to hold commissions in the Services of what would become a foreign power. They could only be attached as advisers or instructors, whilst retaining their commissions granted by the British Crown.

In the event however, both India and Pakistan opted to stay within the Commonwealth. Thus the final nationalisation and partition plans allowed for British to hold executive appointments for one year, renewable thereafter if need be.

Pakistan, whose shortage of senior officers was greater than that of India actually retained a British Commander-in-Chief of the Army and some other senior officers until 1951. India on the other hand dispensed with a British C-in-C in less than one year, his successor being General Cariappa. The Indian Army was in fact virtually 100 per cent national-ised within six months of partition.

Looking back over the four months I spent in Delhi during the crucial events of 1947, one realises that they should have proved a most exciting experience. In fact they did not. Frequently one was inwardly fuming at the waste of time, waiting for the civil members of the AFNC to arrange meetings. On the comparatively few occasions when they did meet – twenty-seven in all – much time was wasted in idle and futile arguments. The Chairman was a charming man, soft spoken and courteous with a long political background as a leading member of the Congress Party, and a future cabinet minister. He was not a particularly good Chairman. On at least one occasion he almost completely lost control of the proceedings. The Muslim and Sikh members were lightweights, only interested in the political aspects of self-government. Pandit Kunzru, the Brahmin, on the other hand was a great character. He struck one as a man of high principles and standards which he adhered to without thought of personal gain. He had a keen brain, had travelled widely and showed a remarkable knowledge of matters military.

As for my three Indian Service colleagues and Kaul, the Secretary of the Committee, I could not have asked for pleasanter and more understanding companions. They were solely interested in the future efficiency of the Services which they represented. It is to the ever-lasting credit of them and their brother officers that the Armed Forces of India and Pakistan have today gained the reputation of being amongst the most efficient and respected in the world, despite the political upheavals through which their countries have passed, and from which regrettably they appear to continue to suffer today.

Two of my colleagues were destined for high rank and distinguished careers in the not too distant future. 'Timmy' Thimayya after a period as C-in-C of the Indian Army ended up commanding the UN troops in Cyprus, where unfortunately he died of a sudden heart attack. Kaul rose to become Chief of the General Staff of the Indian Army in the early sixties.

131

For the last six weeks of my stay in Delhi the Auk invited me to live in his house. The C-in-Cu51s house, which is now the Prime Minister's residence, has been described as "probably the most elegant, distinguished and civilised house in that strange, sprawling city (Delhi)."* It resembles a fair-sized English country house standing in a well land-scaped garden with large lawns, herbaceous borders and shrubberies. The entrance and exit are through large wrought iron gates each guarded by a sentry. On my humble personal transport of a hired bicycle I always felt slightly inadequate passing through these stately portals.

During the period I was staying in C-in-C's house, the Auk's widowed sister, Mrs Jackson, was acting as hostess. Apart from the retinue of servants which long-standing custom had made an essential part of officialdom, the atmosphere was homely and the meals unelaborate, despite the constant stream of guests.

Soon after I moved in, the author Compton Mackenzie arrived to stay accompanied by his secretary 'Chrissie', a middle aged lady who kept as far as possible discreetly in the background. He had been invited to write a book covering the exploits of the Indian Army during the war. This necessitated his travelling all over India and beyond its borders where Indian troops were stationed.

It was Mrs Jackson's habit to retire to her own quarters immediately after dinner, (being normally the only lady in the house), whilst the Auk usually retired to his study to work or to talk to the frequent visitors from Mountbatten's staff: in particular Lord Ismay, who had been Churchill's link with the Chiefs of Staff throughout his premiership. He had now been persuaded to perform a somewhat similar function for Mountbatten. As a former officer of the Indian Army he was a friend and contemporary of Auchinleck. Consequently, I more than once found myself, after dinner, in the company of Mackenzie, who like most writers liked to talk. I must confess that after a short time I found him a rather boring companion, very self-opinionated and who preferred the sound of his own voice to those of his companions. One particular habit he had was to carry a small pocket book wherever he went. He called it his birthday book. Everyone he met was invited to disclose their birthdate, which was then entered into the book. The object of this exercise escapes me, if ever I did fathom it.

One Sunday at lunch he turned to the Auk and said, "You've got a lovely lawn in the garden. It's as good as an English lawn. Why don't you use it?"

"What for?" replied the Auk.

"Why for tennis, or better still croquet. It's ideal for croquet. Just the game when you're getting on a bit, and don't feel like chasing a tennis ball. I'll show you how to play."

Whereupon one of the ADC's chipped in and said, "I'm sure the lawn has been used for croquet. I found a box of croquet things the other day."

In due course the croquet lawn was marked out, and the hoops planted. Thereafter, much to the amusement of the ADC's and myself, who usually made up a foursome with Compton Mackenzie, we discovered that he was not a good loser. Indeed until we jokingly pointed it out to him, he was not above making his own rules to stave off defeat.

After the charged atmosphere of Delhi, it was quite a change to return to the peaceful climate of Madras. The next few months were taken up with the somewhat dismal task of inspecting units to say farewell on their departure or disbandment; with saying goodbye to members of my staff who were leaving, (in many cases without replacement as the headquarters establishment was being cut down); and with making secret plans for the evacuation of Europeans in the unlikely event of very serious communical disturbances.

Before leaving Delhi I had briefly met Pandit Nehru at a dinner party given by Sir G Ayyanger. Although in effect he was Prime Minister of all India at the time, I was not impressed. He looked, and no doubt was, a very tired man. His manner of speech lacked the incisive quality one would expect in a leading statesman. His appearance, despite his immaculate dress, was somehow limp. I suppose history will judge him as an intelligent aristocrat, whose background of wealth and British education coupled with his inherited talents enabled him to create a popular image and to outwit his political rivals. A distinguished Indian journalist had described him as a superb performer whom the people loved. "Nehru", he wrote, "knew India was still feudal and needed to identify itself with a leader and a family. He used his British-oriented education for intellectual flights, based on Fabian Socialism; he used his social upbringing to play the gentleman; he used his inborn talent as a Kashmiri Brahmin to outmanoeuvre his detractors and rivals. He excelled his contemporaries in statecraft."*

*D Das, *India from Curson to Nehru and After*. (Collins) p383

133

Another distinguished Indian politician whom I met on more than one occasion was Sir C P Ramaswamy Aiya, Dewan (Prime Minister) of Travancore State. In contrast to Nehru, C P – as he was invariably known – was an extrovert Madrassi with a brilliant academic record at Oxford behind him. He was to hit the headlines in 1947 when he publicly announced that, rather than join the new predominantly Hindu Indian nation, Travancore would declare itself an independent state and sign a trade agreement with Pakistan. However, after several interviews with Mountbatten and his advisers in Delhi, C P was persuaded to change his mind with the result that Travancore acceded to India. Unfortunately shortly after his return to the state he was violently attacked in the street and nearly lost his life.

The last time I met him was just prior to these events. I was staying with Cosmo Edwards, the British Resident in Travancore, at Trivandrum, the state capital. One day C P called in a state of elation having just received assurance from Jinnah that Pakistan would recognise an independent Travancore. At the same time he complained bitterly that the Indian States had been shabbily treated by the British Government in that they received no forewarning of Attlee's statement of 20th February 1947 regarding the granting of self-government to India by June 1948 at the latest. Next night he came to dinner at the Residency and had us all in fits of laughter with tales of Gandhi's visit to London for the Round Table Conference in 1931. Apparently accommodation for Gandhi was booked at the Savoy Hotel. On his arrival it was found that his entourage included a goat, the purpose of which was to provide the Mahatma with his daily intake of goats' milk. Needless say that the Savoy did not normally cater for goats amongst its guests. Eventually the problem was solved by the hasty erection of a hut suitable for goats on the roof of the hotel. It must surely have been the only recorded instance of a goat occupying penthouse accommodation.

On 1st August the 1st Battalion, the Essex Regiment marked the formal end of an era which had lasted 193 years, when that evening their drums beat tattoo in Fort St George. To mark the occasion I subsequently presented them with the Union Jack which flew over the Fort and was lowered for the last time two weeks later.

It was in 1754 that the first Regiment of the British Army to arrive in India marched into Fort St George. They were the 39th Regiment of Foot, later better known as the 1st Battalion, the Dorsetshire Regiment, whose motto is *Primus in Indus*.

Three days later the CO of the 1st Battalion, the Royal Inniskilling Fusilliers asked if his battalion, which was in Madras awaiting shipment to Hong Kong, could hold a formal parade in the Fort. I readily agreed on learning that their 2nd Battalion had started life in Madras as a regiment of Europeans raised by the East India Company.

On 15th August 1947 British rule in India ended. What had been the Indian Empire, since Queen Victoria assumed the title of Empress in 1877, was partitioned into the Dominion of India and the Dominion of Pakistan. To mark the occasion I had arranged with the Governor of Madras, Sir Archibald Nye,* to lay on a large parade of all arms and services, Indian and British, on the road leading from the city to Fort St George. At the saluting base two flagstaffs had been erected; one flying the Union Jack, the other the new flag of India hoisted but furled ready to be flown by a pull on the rope carrying it.

My wife and I arrived at the saluting base together with the local naval and air force commanders and their wives well before noon, when the Governor and the Indian Prime Minister of Madras Province were due to arrive to take the salute. Sir Archie and Lady Nye arrived dead on time; but there was no sign of the PM. We waited anxiously. To have started without him would have been unthinkable. In the meantime the crowd, which must have numbered at least 100,000 was getting restive. The police and troops, who were endeavouring to keep open the route down which the parade was to march, were obviously losing control. After 25 minutes the PM arrived having taken the wrong approach to the saluting base. The Union Jack was hauled down. Archie Nye and the PM then both tugged at the rope to unfurl the national flag of India. Nothing happened. They pulled again and again. The knot which should have released the flag failed to untie: it only got tighter. In desperation I ordered an NCO to climb the pole and undo the knot. At last the flag flew.

By this time the crowd were quite out of control. The first few units in the parade managed to squeeze their way past the saluting base, whilst the band struggled to maintain control of their instruments. In the end I had to send a message to cancel the remainder of the parade. The Governor and the PM drove off in their respective cars through cheering throngs shouting, *Jai Hind* (Long Live India). My wife and I reached our car with some difficulty. By that time it looked as though we should be mobbed, and so we were, but in the most friendly fashion. As our

*The late Lieut-Gen. Sir Archibald Nye KCSI, KCIE, KBE, CB, MC.

driver crawled along we each sat with one arm out of the window shaking hands till our arms ached. It was a fantastic and heartwarming experience which brought a lump to the throat.

That afternoon I sent my apologies to Archie Nye and the PM over the flag incident. The arrangements at the saluting base had been in the hands of the Madras Guards – an Auxiliary Force (India) unit of Anglo-Indians and incidentally the oldest surviving volunteer unit in India.

Although it could not be proved there is little doubt in my mind that the flag had been deliberately rigged so that it would not unfurl. Archie Nye and the PM were most understanding. In any case in the confusion and excitement of the occasion the incident was soon forgotten.

The Anglo-Indian Community were, of course, the people whose future after partition was most shrouded in uncertainty. Being neither fish, flesh nor good 'red herring, they fitted into neither the British nor Indian social strata. The bulk were employed in the Post and Telegraph Department and on the railways. In the cities and towns they lived in separate enclaves. As the transfer of power approached there were reports of attempts at mass immigration – Africa and Central America were mentioned as possible destinations. Needless to say nothing on these lines materialised. The bulk stayed put and carried on their jobs. Without them the systems of communication in both of the new Dominions would have been severely handicapped.

Shortly after Independence Day I received a telegram from Delhi to say that I had been appointed General Officer Commanding (GOC), Malaya. Having been overseas for six and a half years my wife and I had been hoping that I should be posted to an appointment at home, or possibly in Germany. Our daughter, Suzanne, had reached the age where it was important that she received some continuity in her education. This had not been possible in India.

Since 1935 I had served nearly 10 years in India, had come to love the country and its peoples and had made many Indian friends. The last three years in Madras had been the most enjoyable period of my career, but the constant travelling coupled with the high heat and humidity of the climate had taken it out of me. I was very tired and still plagued with recurrent stomach trouble following my second attack of amoebic dysentery. It was, therefore, with mixed feelings that on 1st September 1947 I drove to the airport at St Thomas's Mount en route to Kuala

Lumpur. There to my astonishment I was greeted by a guard of honour from the Indian Army and Air Force together with 60 of my officers who had come to bid me farewell. I had hoped to hand over to my Indian successor, but this was not possible as he was then commanding a brigade in Japan, and did not reach Madras until some weeks after my departure.

For the past four years I had been privileged to serve under Field-Marshal Sir Claude Auchinleck, C-in-C India, one of the great men who emerged in the war and in the handing over of power to the two new Dominions. Largely thanks to Montgomery his reputation was somewhat tarnished in the immediate post-war years. It was perhaps characteristic of Montgomery, who according to his own account held a low opinion of the officers of the Indian Army,* that he should put on record for all to read, "In the 5th Corps I first served under Auchinleck, who had Southern Command; I cannot recall that we ever agreed on anything"† and that later when he took over command of the VIIIth Army in the Desert he should imply that Auchinleck was preparing to retreat to the Nile Delta and beyond.

History does not record what prompted Montgomery to partly retract this false accusation in a BBC broadcast on 20th November 1958 in which he went so far as to express his, "gratitude to General Sir Claude Auchinleck and the VIIIth Army for stabilising the British front on the Alamein position, thus enabling him (Montgomery) to conduct his successful offensive known to the world as the Battle of Alamein, in October 1942."‡ I only met Montgomery twice. The first time was at GHQ Home Forces shortly after Dunkirk. He was then commanding the 3rd Division as a major-general. One day the Chief of General Staff, General Sir Bernard Paget sent for me. When I entered his office I found Montgomery there. Paget explained that he (Montgomery) had come to ask for some additional telephone connections to his headquarters in Somerset. I explained that so far we had met every request for additional communications requested by Southern Command (3rd Division was under that Command) but I would get on to the Command and see what could be arranged. At the mention of Southern Command, Monty retorted that the matter was urgent and that he could not be bothered to deal with them. He wanted a direct line to GHQ.

*The Memoirs of FM Viscount Montgomery of Alamein (Collins) p25

†Ibid p62

‡Ibid Publishers note in later editions. p10

Whereupon Paget replied, "Really, Monty, you always were an insubordinate officer." I need hardly add that 3rd Division got its extra telephone circuit and that the Auk was commanding Southern Command at the time.

On 23rd June, 1947, with less than two months to go before the partition of India, and the break-up of the Indian Army into two new armies for India and Pakistan, Montgomery – recently appointed Chief of the Imperial General Staff – arrived in Delhi for a brief visit of 3 days. Of this visit he recorded, "It seemed to me that Auchinleck was wrapped up entirely in the Indian Army and appeared to be paying little heed to the welfare of the British soldiers in India." *Fortunately John Connell in his biography of Auchinleck, in which he described these words of Montgomery as 'inaccurate' and 'grossly offensive',† puts the record straight as to the Auk's high achievements and place in history.

Personally I find it deplorably sad that a man of Field-Marshal Montgomery's moral stature and outstanding service to the nation should have allowed himself to lower his standards by attempting to denigrate a brother Field-Marshal, whose place in history is comparable to his own.

*Ibid p390

†J Connell, *Auchinleck. A critical Biography* (Cassell) p848

12

GOC Malaya—the new Constitutions—outbreak of terrorism—departure and death of Sir Edward Gent

My journey to Malaya was not as straightforward as I had anticipated. On 25th August I had received a cable instructing me to arrive in Kuala Lumpur not later than 1st September. There was no direct air service from Madras to Malaya and sailings were infrequent. In the end I arranged to travel by air via Burma, leaving my family to proceed to Singapore by ship.

The first day I flew to Calcutta, stopping en route at Vizagapatam, where more of my officers turned up at the airport to say farewell. On arrival in Calcutta I learnt that in certain parts of the city riots – with the inevitable violence and killings – were taking place. I did not witness these events, which were, I gathered, already largely under control when I drove in from Dum Dum airport. However it made me realise how lucky we had been in the peaceful south. Not that Calcutta was to feature largely in the appalling massacres of the summer of 1947 in which, it is estimated, up to 600,000 men, women and children were slaughtered in the orgy of communal hatred which inflamed Hindus, Moslems and Sikhs alike.

In Bengal, General Tuker – commanding Eastern Command – had made adequate preparations in full co-operation with the civil authorities to quell rioting the minute it started. Furthermore Mahatma Gandhi's continual presence in that potentially explosive area was having a profound effect in easing tension.

In the Punjab no such mitigating factors existed. By the time troops

139

had been sent into the area it was too late. The situation was completely out of control. Whether this could have been avoided must remain a matter of conjecture. Certainly the Governor of the Punjab, Sir Evan Jenkins, had more than once warned Mountbatten that the partition of the province into two would be liable to ignite an explosion, since the population was roughly 55 per cent Muslim, 25 per cent Hindu and 20 per cent Sikh. To draw a boundary which would satisfy all three communities was an impossible task, especially when it had to be done in a matter of a few weeks.

It is interesting to speculate whether the British Government, on the recommendation of Lord Mountbatten (their representative on the spot), were right to announce on the 3rd June 1947 that British rule in India would cease on 15th August, and that by this date the boundaries between India and Pakistan would have to be decided. This, together with the vast and complicated administrative problems involved in the creation of two new nations make it a matter on which there is marked diversity of opinion amongst those best able to judge, notably senior officers of the Indian civil and military services. Much has been written on the subject. My own view is that by delaying partition until the end of the year some of the bloodshed and misery could have been reduced, since it might have been possible to bring some measure of control over the massive migration of people through the Punjab. In the event the authorities were caught unprepared and unable to control the panic movements which followed partition.

On the other hand in the cold light of susbsequent events in Asia and Africa involving the granting of independence to former colonies, a cynical conclusion may reasonably be drawn that the death role of 600,000 was not an abnormally high price to pay where a total population of some 450,000,000 was involved. In conceding this, one has to recognise that the age of savagery is still with us.

The following morning I flew to Rangoon and went straight to Government House, where I was due to stay the night. I have never discovered who the architect was of this remarkable building, but one can only suppose that he was inspired by St Pancras Station. The resemblance between the two is marked. The incongruity of its setting in Rangoon is equally remarkable.

My object in stopping at Rangoon was two-fold. Firstly it enabled me to meet once again my old friends, Hubert* and Noel Rance. The

*The late Major-General Sir Hubert Rance, GCMG GBE CB Governor of Burma 1946-48, Governor of Trinidad and Tobago 1950-55.

former and I were contemporaries in Royal Signals. Our paths had last crossed when I succeeded him at GHQ Arras just prior to Dunkirk. Towards the end of the war he had come out East as head of the civil affairs staff for Burma. Their task was to administer the country during the period of military occupation and until such time as a normal system of government could be re-established. His success in this task was such that eventually he was appointed Governor of Burma with the task of preparing the country for self-rule. This he accomplished with notable distinction.

Secondly, it enabled me to meet, albeit briefly, General Briggs and his senior staff officer, with whom I was able to discuss the secondary duty which the War Office wanted me to perform in addition to commanding the troops in Malaya. Before leaving Madras I had been informed by Delhi in somewhat cryptic phraseology that the War office intended to appoint me, "as a general officer sitting on a civil tribunal for investigation of the recent troubles in Burma." The 'troubles' presumably were those which followed the assassination of the Prime Minister, Aung San, and six members of his cabinet a few weeks previously. By the time I reached Rangoon it was made clear to me that neither Rance nor Briggs had been consulted; that the tribunal, if and when it sat, would be purely civilian in composition; and that if any military representation was required Burma Command were quite capable of providing it. It so happened that Lord Listowel, Secretary of State for India and Burma, was also staying at Government House that night. By the time I reached Malaya the proposed appointment had been dropped. Someone in Whitehall had blundered.

Next morning I caught an RAF scheduled Dakota flight bound for Singapore. As we flew down the coast of Southern Burma I sat in the cockpit alongside the pilot. I noticed that there were certain gaps in the instrument panel. The pilot explained that there was an acute shortage of spare parts for this famous work-horse of the air, hundreds of which had been in service during the Burma campaign. I though of the vast stores of aircraft spares left behind in the RAF Maintenance Unit at Avadi, now awaiting distribution to the Air Forces of India and Pakistan, and hoped that we should complete the journey without mishap. My hope was not to be fulfilled. We landed at Butterworth for lunch and had become airborne for a few minutes when the pilot informed me that he would have to turn back with a faulty undercarriage. After a couple of circuits and bumps to ensure the undercarriage was safe, we landed. I was informed that the aircraft might be there for days before spares could be obtained, so I caught the

141

night mail train and reached Kuala Lumpur next morning. My predecessor was due to leave in two days' time so we had little time to hand over; to make matters worse I had to retire to bed next day with a recurrence of my tummy trouble. Hardly an auspicious start for a new post in a new country.

I must confess that up to the time of my arrival in Kuala Lumpur my knowledge of Malaya was strictly limited – apart from the defence aspects of Singapore which one had studied at the Staff College vis-a-vis the possibility of attack from the sea. – As a schoolboy stamp collector I knew that the country comprised the Straits Settlements, the Federated Malay States and the UnFederated Malay States. I also, of course, knew that the main products were tin and rubber – raw materials which were in worldwide demand, although the latter was already being threatened by synthetics. What I had once learnt (but since forgotten) was that all three constituents of this complicated set-up were in effect British dependencies, with varying degrees of autonomy, under the watchful eye of a British High Commissioner in Singapore. This official not only governed that island but also the Districts of Malacca and Penang (including Province Wellesley, a strip on the mainland opposite Penang) as colonies. In addition he kept a masterly eye on the FM States of Perak, Selangor, Negri Sembilan and Pahang through a Resident-General in Kuala Lumpur; and on the UFM States through an Adviser in each of the states of Johore, Kedah, Kelantan, Perlis and Trengganu. All nine states were in effect minor Kingdoms with an hereditary ruler – the Sultan – at the head. Of these the Sultan of Johore was the most colourful character. Like the rulers of the larger native states of India he was permitted to maintain a small private army. By virtue of this distinction he turned out in the uniform of a major-general on all possible occasions. Before the war his marital affairs had caused him to incur the displeasure of the British High Commissioner, who at one time tried to ban him from the bright lights of Singapore. He was, I understand, part owner of Grosvenor House, Park Lane, where he spent long periods during the latter years of his life.

Before the war the British Government had made various attempts to simplify and co-ordinate the administrative and political complications of Malaya by proposing some form of federal constitution, whereby power would, as far as practicable, be decentralised to the various states. The war intervened before any firm conclusions could be arrived at.

During the war the Colonial Office drew up a new constitution, without, of course, being able to consult the Sultans. The main features of this constitution disclosed a complete reversal of their pre-war policy. It was called the Union of Malaya and virtually made all the states subordinate to a central government in Kuala Lumpur. The power of the rulers were radically reduced. The Union was to include Malacca and Penang, but not Singapore which was to become a separate Crown Colony.

In April 1946 Sir Edward Gent* was sent out as Governor of the new Union of Malaya with the task of setting the new machinery to work. However, such was the feeling against this new constitution that the Malayan rulers, with one exception, boycotted the installation ceremony of the new Governor and the inauguration of the new Constitution. Nor were anti-Union feelings confined to the Malays. There was considerable opposition to the change in Westminster. To make confusion worse confounded the British officials and businessmen in Malaya were at loggerheads. Senior civil servants and other Government officials who had stuck to their posts and been interned by the Japanese in Changi Gaol felt bitterly against those who had escaped and spent the war in England. Unfortunately the early withdrawal of the military administration on Mountbatten's insistence had meant that the former category, who had suffered severe hardships at the hands of the Japanese, had not had adequate home leave in which to recuperate from their harsh experiences.

This disunity amongst the senior British even extended to the Chief Secretary, who on one occasion at a dinner party expressed views critical of the Governor in my wife's hearing. After the happy atmosphere of Madras I found the whole climate amongst the Europeans distateful and disquietening.

For Sir Edward Gent I had nothing but admiration. After a distinguished military record in World War I he had joined the Colonial Service and spent most of his time between the wars in Whitehall. He was then sent to Malaya with no previous experience of the country to put into effect a new constitution drawn up in Whitehall which few people in that country, whether British, Malay, Chinese or Indian wanted, and to which many were actively opposed.

*The late Lt-Col Sir Edward Gent KCMG, OBE, DSO, MC.

The union of Malaya was to be short-lived. By the time I arrived the Colonial Office had decided to recognise the error of its ways. On 1st February 1948 the Union of Malaya ceased to exist. The same day the Federation of Malaya was born. Under this constitution decentralisation, generally speaking, replaced centralisation. Gent became High Commissioner and the Federal Government became responsible for certain reserved subjects of which defence and finance were probably the most important. Since the field of finance covers practically all aspects of Government the freedom of the States to control their own affairs was more apparent than real.

The machinery at the centre comprised a small Executive Council made up of seven officials and seven unofficial members; and a Legislative Council of 76 official and nominated unofficial members, the latter representing the States as well as communal, industrial and other interests.

As GOC Malaya I was directly under General Sir Neil Ritchie, GOC-in-C at Singapore, whose command also included Hong kong, Singapore and Borneo.

It did not take me long to realise that militarily as well as politically Malaya was in a state of flux. Before the war the military garrisons of the Straits Settlements had virtually all been concentrated on Singapore Island. Thus, apart from a small Malay Regiment the mainland was devoid of regular troops.

Now the post-war policy was to maintain a considerable garrison in Malaya (as well as in Singapore). This garrison at present comprised some Indian units and three British battalions and a field artillery regiment. The Indian units were now being withdrawn and in due course the British units were also to go. To replace them four battalions from those Gurkha regiments which were being transferred from the Indian to the British Army were to form the backbone of the post-war garrison together with the Malay Regiment which was in the process of being expanded. To replace British personnel in the technical and administrative services local personnel (Malays, Chinese and Indians) were being recruited.

To cater for this post-war garrison the War Office had drawn up plans for the building of barracks, workshops, hospitals, offices, etc, required to accommodate them. To implement these plans two things were essential – time and money. Unfortunately the latter was only made available in small annual allotments, so that the building programme was falling behind schedule much to the annoyance of the local authorities who not unnaturally wanted the release of accommodation seized by the Japanese during the war and subsequently retained by our own troops.

In particular the Army was occupying as military hospitals two buildings – one in Kuala Lumpur and the other in Ipoh – badly needed for civilian purposes. To aggravate the accommodation situation, under agreement with the Government of Nepal, accommodation had to be provided for the families of the incoming Gurkha units. Since they were due to arrive early in 1948, and since neither money nor time was available to produce permanent accommodation, temporary hutted camps had to be erected. To assist in this and other constructional work someone in the War Office had had a bright idea. Why not form units of the Royal Pioneer Corps in Ceylon, where labour was cheap and unemployment reported to be high?

After much correspondence the scheme finally received official sanction by the governments concerned. The necessary orders were issued to form the units and despatch them as soon as possible to Malaya. They arrived post haste and before reasonable accommodation could be found for them. Apart from a few British officers of low category and still fewer Ceylonese officers, plus some British NCO's, none of whom could speak Singalese, the units were made up of men who had been taken straight off the streets or out of their villages. With no more than a few basic days training and with the minimum of uniform and equipment they had been sent overseas. They now found themselves in a foreign country, where they were unable to converse with the local inhabitants.

Within days of their arrival one unit broke out of camp and rampaged through the suburbs of Kuala Lumpur causing alarm and some slight damage. It was only after weeding out the unsuitable officers that order was restored. Thereafter morale gradually rose and in a few weeks the units settled down and were doing good work. The truth of the old saying, 'There are no bad troops, only bad officers' was seldom better demonstrated.

My arrival coincided with the departure of the last of the Japanese troops, who unarmed and under their own officers had carried out much useful work in helping to restore the country to normal, by clearing communications and similar tasks. There were, however, a few Japs left

145

– in gaol awaiting trial as war criminals. To deal with these the War Office had formed two permanent military courts. I, as GOC, was the confirming officer. For some reason this was contrary to the policy in Europe, where similar courts were dealing with German and Italian war crimes and where, certainly in the case of the death sentence, not even the GOC-in-C had the final decision. Such cases were invariably referred to the War Office where in the long run powers of confirmation rested with the Secretary of State for War. But in the Far East the power of life and death over the Japanese was left in the hands of the District Commander – a mere major-general.

In this way I found myself in the unenviable position of signing the death warrant on half a dozen occasions. The sentence by hanging was normally carried out in the civil prison at Kuala Lumpur. The military were not required to attend the execution. However in one case there was an exception. As happened from time to time during the Jap occupation the main railway was sabotaged by the Resistance Movement, known as the Malayan Peoples Anti-Japanese Army (MPAJA). On the occasion in question as a reprisal the local Japanese regimental commander ordered one of his subordinate commanders to round up the inhabitants of the village nearest to the act of sabotage, including women and children, force them into the largest building, set fire to it and shoot any who tried to escape. This atrocity was duly carried out.

After the surrender some fugitives in the jungle were able to give evidence and the culprits were duly brought to trial as war criminals. The regimental commander, his subordinate commander and one other were sentenced to death, but, because the regimental commander was not actually present when the mass murder took place, the court decided that he should be sentenced to death by the traditionally more honourable method of the firing squad rather than the gallows. On receiving the proceedings of the court I sent for its President and ordered him to reconvene the court to reconsider this sentence. This he duly carried out. The court confirmed their previous sentence. After taking legal advice I found that I had no option but to confirm the sentences or reduce all three of them to terms of imprisonment. I decided to confirm the sentences as they stood.

It was now the duty of the Army to carry out the sentence of death by firing squad. I sent for my Provost Martial and after explaining the position to him instructed him to make the necessary arrangements. Next day he reported to me that he had selected a deserted quarry as a suitable site and had carried out a dummy run with a squad of selected

146

military police, after eliminating one or two who appeared 'unsuitable' as he put it. He assured me that they would carry out their distasteful task efficiently. They did so.

Later, after leaving Malaya, I was to become much involved in British war criminal trials, but I never heard of another case where the death sentence was carried out by shooting.

No sooner had I arrived at Kuala Lumpur than it was made known to me that my period of command was to be a short one. My successor had already been chosen. The bulk of the permanent garrisons in the Far East were to be found from the Gurkhas. Of their eight battalions four were to be stationed in Malaya. Major-General Charles Boucher was a highly experienced Gurkha officer of the old Indian Army. He had for some months been travelling between London, Delhi and Katmandu arranging with the Indian and Nepalese governments for the transfer of the four selected Gurkha regiments from the Indian to the British Army, and for the movement of the men and their families through India, en route to and from the Far East. As soon as these arrangements were completed he was to take over from me.

By the end of November 1947 the last units of the old Indian Army had left. Amongst them was the Second Royal Lancers – the famous Bengal Lancers – which like so many other Indian units found itself split into two parts; the Hindus going to India and the Moslems to Pakistan. Early in the new year the Gurkhas started to arrive. The battalions were much under strength as many of these tough little Nepalese warriors had taken their discharge after the armistice and recruiting had only recently reopened.

On 24th February 1948 the new Federal Legislative Council was opened marking the formal inauguration of the Federation of Malaya. For the first and last time in my life I became involved in politics. As GOC I was an official member of both the Executive and Legislative Councils. In the former capacity I acted as an adviser to the High Commissioner. In the latter I was in effect Minister of Defence without a ministry. My responsibilities were mainly confined to answering questions affecting the continued occupation by the military of civil premises urgently required for other purposes. Since due notice of such questions was given in advance I only attended the Council when such matters were on the agenda; so attendance did not take up much of my time. The Executive Council was a different matter. It met frequently, often twice a week. It was at these meetings that I first got an inkling of the trouble which lay ahead – not that any of us, I believe, had any idea of its magnitude.

The official attitude was that reports of armed Communists and stocks of weapons hidden in the jungle were grossly exaggerated.

From the military point of view, now that we had the Gurkhas in addition to two British infantry battalions and three newly trained Malay battalions, I reckoned that I was in a position to meet any demand for military aid asked for by the police to assist them in keeping law and order. In the meantime I had decided that it was time the people of Malaya – unused as they had been to the presence of troops in peacetime – got to know more about the purpose and workings of the Defence Services. In June, therefore, I arranged in conjunction with the Royal Navy and Royal Air Force a series of Services weeks, starting at Kuala Lumpur with a tattoo, and various exhibits which would tour the main towns. Before the month was out some of these activities had to be cancelled.

The first indication I had of the task facing the security forces in combatting guerilla tactics was the result of a sudden summons to King's House – the High Commissioner's residence – where the Commissioner of Police gave an account of a recent incident in North Perak. An isolated village had been found to be succouring a band of armed communists who periodically emerged from the jungle and forced the inhabitants to supply them with food and money. A party of police was consequently sent into the jungle to track down the hideout of these men and arrest them.

The party set out one night with a local Chinese guide who had volunteered to guide them to their quarry. As soon as they were well into the jungle the guide suddenly disappeared and the party came under fire, the senior policeman being killed instantly. I immediately offered assistance to the police which the Commissioner accepted. Shortly afterwards a company of Gurkhas found the hideout in the jungle, but by the time they arrived the guerillas had left and were probably miles deeper into the jungle. Later I visited the area and with a Gurkha escort climbed into the jungle, which here rose steeply from the road and visited the now deserted hideout. It consisted of two or three well built huts constructed of bamboo and palm fronds and sited in a cleared area of jungle in which sufficient trees had been left to give cover from aircraft and with lookout posts covering the few routes of access.

This single incident gave one a foretaste of the conditions and immense difficulties which were to face the security forces during the so-called 'Emergency' which was to last twelve years. To find the guerillas was like looking for the proverbial needle in a haystack: a needle which had legs!

By mid-June it had become apparent from incidents of murder and sabotage in various areas that the Malayan Communist Party (MCP) was highly organised, well armed and determined, under guidance from Moscow, to destroy the economy of the country by intimidating the villages and bringing the tin and rubber industries to a halt. On the 16th three British planters were brutally murdered on their plantations. Next day in the Executive Council I appealed successfully for emergency powers to be extended over the whole country. Under these the military would have the same powers of arrest as the police.

It was obvious that the Malayan police were faced with an almost impossible task. The uniformed police were all Malays (although the Chinese and Indians formed over half of the population) in a country where there was no common language. The force was deficient in modern equipment in the way of transport and communications. They had no radio. Their contact with isolated police stations relied upon overhead telephone wires, which anyone ill-disposed to, could cut.

Next day Neil Ritchie flew up from Singapore with Charles Boucher who had just arrived to take over from me. Ritchie asked me for my estimate of the threat posed by the MCP armed bands. By this time we had a much clearer picture of the situation from reports coming in from all over the country. I replied that the present forces were quite inadequate. It was essential to bring in reinforcements. These I estimated would amount to two infantry divisions, excluding their artillery. The numbers including engineers, signals, medical and transport would amount to some 20,000 men. Ritchie's response was immediate, "I can't possibly ask Monty for anything like that. He's hard put enough as it is with events in Germany and elsewhere."

Montgomery was at that time Chief of the Imperial General Staff (CIGS) and the Russians were threatening to cut off Berlin. This threat they carried out and the city was only saved from starvation by the airlift. In passing, it is of interest to note that a few years later at the height of the Emergency there were 40,000 regular troops employed in Malaya.

149

From thereon the wires between Singapore and London must have been kept busy. On 25th June events reached a climax. In the morning I was in conference at King's House where by now we had daily meetings. About mid-day an ADC came into the conference room and announced that Mr Malcolm Macdonald* had flown up from Singapore. Gent immediately left the conference saying he hoped to be back soon. After lunch we met again with the Chief Secretary in the chair. I never saw Gent again.

Four days later my wife and I, with our daughter Suzanne, left Kuala Lumpur and flew to Singapore. Lady Gent came to see us off at the airport and apologised for her husband's absence. It transpired that Gent had left and was on his way by air to London. The object of Macdonald's sudden flight to Kuala Lumpur on the 25th had been to break the news to Gent that he was sacked. To soften the blow he was given the option of sending in his resignation on the grounds of ill-health. Gent being a man of courage and honour refused this soft option and decided to fly home and confront the Colonial Secretary. His flight from Singapore was delayed en route.It was not until 5th July that he reached England, where on his arrival at Northolt his RAF plane crashed. Gent was killed.

We were in the Indian Ocean when we heard the news of his death over the ship's radio. My wife and I were profoundly shocked. Gent had been a good friend and had supported the Services wholeheartedly at a time when their role was not appreciated by the general populous, the majority of whom, quite naturally, wanted to settle down to a peaceful life after seven years of upheaval and bloodshed.

Some writers, notably Noel Barber in his book *War of the Running Dogs*, have blamed Sir Edward Gent for not forestalling, or at any rate, foreseeing the danger which lay ahead; claiming that the planters and miners had warned him, only to be received with scepticism and misbelief. In passing judgement it is only fair to take into account the difficulties with which the High Commissioner was faced.

---

*The late Rt Hon Malcolm Macdonald was Commissioner-General for South-East Asia and as such had a supervisory role over British dependencies in that area.

As already stated he was new to the country and found himself faced with a heavy burden of constitutional and economic problems. The British in Malaya – in particular the official classes were divided between those who had suffered internment in Changi gaol and those who had escaped before the Japanese overran the country. Consequently jealousy was all too prevalent. This human weakness scarcely provides the best climate for co-operation. Under the circumstances it is hardly surprising that reports reaching the capital from up country were apt to be contradictory and, therefore, difficult to assess. In addition many junior officials were inexperienced and still in the process of finding their feet. During the war there had been no recruitment to government services, so that the middle ranks of officialdom hardly existed. Above all the members of the predominantly Chinese Malayan Communist Party, having formed the backbone of the anti-Japanese resistance movement during the war, were regarded as most respectable citizens. Indeed some of their leaders had been awarded cash as well as honours for their services. Few realised that, now the hated Japanese had been defeated and driven out of China, the Chinese Communist Party's main aim under the inspiration of Mao-tse Tung, was to drive out the Nationalist Party, under the pro-western leadership of General Chiang Kai-shek, and at the same time to destroy British and American influence in the Far East. The Cold War was just starting.

Moscow and Mao-tse Tung were still partners – but partners of convenience in their aim to destroy capitalism, which within South-East Asia, was nowhere more predominant than in Malaya and Singapore. Now, it seemed, was the right time for the Communists to strike a blow to destroy the whole system of Government in those countries: whilst they were still struggling to restore their war shattered economics. The jungle was to be their base; the weapons dropped to them by the British during the war their armoury; and intimidation of the common people their means of supply.

13

Further involvement in war crimes—Chairman of review of Sentences (Europe) Board—visits to prisoners in Germany and Austria—meetings with Field- Marshal Kesselring in gaol.

We reached Southampton on 31st July 1948 aboard the troop ship *Dilwara*. The voyage home had been uneventful except for one incident, which I can only describe as a modern miracle. On the 28th the ship was passing through the Bay of Biscay, which contrary to its reputation was comparatively calm. It was a warm sunny day, and by mid-morning many of the passengers, including myself, were sunbathing. Suddenly there was a shout from the stern and the ship's alarm bells rang. We had some naval ratings aboard and I saw one or two of them throw their caps into the sea. The news soon spread that someone was overboard, but it was not until much later that the true sequence of events became known.

Attracted by a school of porpoises cavorting alongside the ship many passengers were leaning on the rails watching these entertaining creatures. Amongst them was a young mother carrying her little girl in one arm and some knitting in the other. Accidentally she let the knitting fall to the deck and in a reflexive movement to recover it evidently let her grasp of the child relax, with the result that the poor little infant fell some 30 feet into the sea. It was a good 20 minutes before the ship could slow down, launch a life boat and turn round to the point where the sailor's caps marked the spot. Through field glasses I could make out the doll-like figure of the child floating motionless on her back with arms outstretched. Just as the lifeboat approached her the little figure suddenly started to struggle. In a flash one of the crew dived overboard and rescued her as she was about to go under.

I learnt later from the captain and the ship's doctor that the prompt action of the sailors in throwing their white tropical caps overboard had been of the greatest assistance in marking the spot where the tragedy took place. I also learnt that in falling the child must have been concussed by the violent contact with the surface of the sea and consequently did not struggle until she regained consciousness within seconds of her rescue; and the fact that the child landed and remained on her back enabled her to breath without swallowing water. Next morning the child was running about on deck, whilst in the saloon the ship's chaplain held a service of thanksgiving for this incredible act of Providence.

A few days later after returning home I rang the War Office for an appointment to see the Military Secretary – the official responsible for carrying out the posting of officers. Before leaving Malaya I had received no intimation as to what lay in store for me. It, therefore, came as a great shock when this official bluntly informed me that I was to be placed on the retired list on completion of the leave to which I was entitled. He had only recently taken over his appointment, and was under the impression that his predecessor had written to Malaya to inform me.

I walked out of the War Office in a daze. I was 50 years old – a time of life when most people are professionally in their prime and on the crest of whatever wave lies beneath them. I had joined the Army when I was 17; it had been my life for 33 years. I was entitled to a modest army pension on which we could just manage, but such was my financial state that in the event of my death my wife would be left practically destitute, since military widow's pensions had not then been introduced.

I went straight from the War Office to that department of the Ministry of Labour and National Service set up to deal with ex-Services personnel. The official in charge told me quite frankly that with my age, rank and experience the chances of my being offered a job were quite negligible.

For the next three months I went through that most dismal and demoralising routine, which in the present era of high unemployment is the fate of thousands, namely the scanning of the jobs vacant columns in the Press; writing out applications; occasionally getting as far as an interview; rarely reaching a short list and then only to be pipped at the post in the final selection.

However, on 1st December my gloom was lifted by a letter from the Military Secretary offering to postpone my retirement, if I would accept the appointment of chairman of a board to review all war crimes cases tried in Europe by British military courts. The object of the review was to 'ensure uniformity of punishment for similar offences'. The proceedings of these courts had not received much publicity, being overshadowed by the Nuremberg trial in which a panel of eminent jurists appointed by the Allied Powers sat in judgement on the civil and military leaders of Germany. This trial opened on 20th November 1945 and concluded on 1st October 1946.

In January 1949 No 1 War Crimes Sentences Review Board (Europe) assembled in London having been allotted offices in the former Metropole Hotel, Northumberland Avenue. It consisted of two members beside myself, and a small administrative staff. The members were both lieutenant-colonels named Wilson, but unrelated to one another. One of them, Harry Wilson of the London Scottish, was a great character and a most amusing person with a fund of good anecdotes. On what was by nature a somewhat depressing assignment he proved an invaluable companion.

Briefly, our task was to review the sentences imposed on all those German, Italian and Austrian war criminals, who having been tried and convicted by British military courts were still in prisons in Germany, Italy and Austria. Of the 900 individuals tried, just over 750 had been convicted and sentenced to punishments varying between death and short-term imprisonment; of these, 152 had been executed and a number released on completion of their short sentences. In round figures our 'clients' numbered about 560. They ranged from Field-Marshal Kesselring, the former German Commander-in-Chief in Italy and ten other generals down to a handful of the junior staff of the Auschwitz and Belsen Concentration Camps, who had for various reasons escaped the death penalty imposed on eleven of their superiors.

The Board spent the first six weeks in London studying the full proceedings of the trials and also the report of a similar Board who had just completed a review of all Japanese cases. Broadly speaking the charges fell into three main categories:

1 The murder and ill-treatment of civilian internees and civil labour forcibly recruited for war work from the occupied territories.

155

2   The murder and ill-treatment of civilians by way of reprisals.

3   The murder and ill-treatment of prisoners of war.

The first category, of course, covered the ghastly massacres by gas chamber, shooting and starvation which characterised the concentration camps. The second and third categories in the main resulted from the carrying out of orders issued by Hitler and his henchman Himmler, which authorised local authorities to shoot civilians, and in certain cases prisoners of war, without any form or trial. It may be of interest to note that of the Germans, Austrians and Italians convicted by British courts, only 20 per cent were members of the armed forces proper, whilst 80 per cent were members of other government services, notably the Gestapo, the SS and SD – all of which were civil or semi-military security services under the overall control of Himmler. It should also be noted that in those cases where SS personnel were organised into military units and formations, they were only placed under the command of the Army for operational purposes. Their administration and discipline remained under Himmler's control.

From the beginning I had got the War Office to agree that we would be allowed to visit our clients in gaol, not only to form our own opinion of them, but also to consult those in whose hands their custody lay. Consequently in the second half of February we spent two weeks in Germany. The bulk of the prisoners, including eight of the generals, were held in Werl prison, a few miles from GHQ British Army of the Rhine. It was here that we interviewed FM Kesselring on two occasions. He was courteous and dignified. On the first occasion the prison governor ushered us into a map-lined room, where to our astonishment Kesselring sat at the head of a long table around which six or seven German generals were seated holding a conference. We were informed that under an agreement between the US and British governments the Field-Marshal and his fellow prisoners were engaged in research for the British and American Military Historical Sections.

Undoubtedly Kesselring and the other generals were being treated as humanely as conditions permitted. Just prior to our visit the Field-Marshal had been allowed out on a weekend visit to his wife. His case was probably the most difficult one which faced us. We read through the entire and bulky proceedings of the trial, which took place in Vienna in 1947 and lasted 2½ months, three times. The main charge against him concerned the massacre which took place at the Ardentine Caves outside Rome in June 1944, when 335 Italians and Jews were brutally shot as a reprisal for the deaths of 32 German military police at the instigation of the partisans. Under the direct orders of Hitler this act of retaliation was to be carried out within 24 hours of the bomb explosion which killed the Germans. When Kesselring was informed of this order he protested to Field-Marshal Keitel, Commander-in-Chief of the German Army. His protest was in vain. On Hitler's orders the massacre was carried out by the SD and the caves subsequently blown up.

Kesselring, unlike most of the other generals charged with war crimes, made no attempt to defend himself on the grounds that he was merely carrying out the order of his superiors. On the contrary he stated in court, "If these things took place within the area of my Command, I must, as Commander-in-Chief, accept full responsibility." He was sentenced to death by shooting. The War Office subsequently commuted the sentence to life imprisonment. I was pleased to read in the Press some years later that he had been released from prison on, I think, the grounds of ill health.

On our second interview I asked Kesselring for his views on war crime trials. He replied, "The times demanded them," then added, "but now we should forget the past and all act as friends." On my return to England I received a letter from him through the prison governor in which he wrote,

You had the kindness to ask me as 'General to General' about my views concerning the War Crimes trials. The question surprised me causing me to merely hint at some things which had better be expressed for the sake of complete understanding. While maintaining what I have stated verbally, I sum up as follows:

a Concerning the 'genuine' War Crime trials which brought about the conviction as criminals of the genuine perpetrators, no words need be lost.

b The 'not so genuine' War Crime trials which unfortunately showed to the public more or less considerable defects in procedure have shaken confidence in the justice meted out.

c Legally and humanly correct preliminary proceedings would have prevented many trials from taking place and would have avoided unfavourable psychological effects.

d I consider the review of War Crime trials proposed by the English on their own initiative to be particularly suitable to have a calming effect and to forestall undesirable German reactions which are, however, bound to occur.

In addition to the 300 male prisoners Werl held 27 females, formerly staff of concentration camps. We had assumed, as was popularly accepted at the time, that the junior staff of these camps were found from the criminal classes and other dregs of society. We found no evidence of this and were surprised to see apparently normal young women living in clean and comfortably furnished cells, whom the prisoner governor assured us had had clear records until they were drafted into the camps.

The Belsen trial lasted two months. Of the 45 men and women arraigned before it, 30 were found guilty. Of the latter 11 (including three women) were sentenced to death by hanging; the remainder to terms of imprisonment varying from 15 years to one year. It is of interest that a number of the accused were originally sent to one of the concentration camps as prisoners for offences mainly political, such as expressing anti-Nazi feelings. They were subsequently promoted by the camp authorities to positions of minor authority over the other internees. Four of the women we interviewed fell into this category.

The other prison holding war criminals was at Hamelin, legendary scene of the Pied Piper's exploits. Here we interviewed General von Falkenhorst, former Commander-in-Chief in Norway, who had been tried on nine charges – all connected with the shooting out of hand of prisoners of war. After a trial lasting five days he had been convicted on eight of the charges and sentenced to death. As in the case of Kesselring the sentence had been commuted by the War Office to one of life imprisonment. Apart from two other generals, the prison held only 27 prisoners.

The Governor of Hamelin Prison, who before the war had been Commissioner of Prisons in one of the African Colonies (Uganda, if I remember rightly) had had the unenviable task of supervising the execution of all those condemned to death by British courts. These, as already stated, numbered 152. I imagine he had been present at nearly all of them. He insisted on showing us round the wing of the prison in which the condemned cells and execution chamber were situated. The latter contained two gallows side by side, which he explained had been installed to cope with the rush of victims, the last minutes of some of

whom, in particular the females, he described in detail. We were also shown the plot in which some of their corpses were buried. I well remember being given liquid refreshment in a gloomy room, in which, we were told, all those whose duty it was to witness executions assembled before (or was it after?) the event to fortify themselves with coffee and rum.

There are limits to any human being's powers of endurance. I was not surprised, therefore, to hear some weeks later from a friend of mine on the penal staff of the Control Commission, Germany, that this prison governor had suffered a complete mental breakdown and was in hospital in England.

On our return to London we spent some weeks deciding on the cases of those individuals we had interviewed in Germany. Then at the end of April we took a train to Austria to interview the comparatively few numbers of Austrians and Italians held in the British zone of that country. Fortunately this entailed staying two nights in Vienna, where we had to meet various officials, and where we were accommodated in the famous Sacher's Hotel. I had visited Vienna briefly once before when it was recovering from the aftermath of World War I. Then as a young officer on leave I had not dared venture into the historic portals of Sacher's. Now on duty and in uniform I found myself allotted one of the best rooms in the hotel, and an enormous bathroom, which could have comfortably housed a double bed as well as the bath.

Madame Sacher was still in command and very kindly invited us into her 'holy of holies'; in other words the office in which she sat surrounded by relics of the past displayed on all four walls. These consisted largely of menus of banquets held to mark the numerous occasions when crowned heads of Europe had honoured her board. One of her most treasured possessions was a table cloth on which her guests on one particular occasion had all written their signatures. Edward Prince of Wales (later Edward VII) featured prominently amongst the guests on that, and other occasions. As also did the Kaiser and the Tsar.

From Vienna we moved on to Graz, where we interviewed nine Austrians and 25 Italians who were housed in the prison of Karlau outside the town. We should have moved on to Italy where a further 26 Italians were still being held. However, for reasons, which after this lapse of time escapes me, agreement had been reached with the Italian Government that they would be completely responsible for the custody of these men. They agreed that we were responsible for the review of their sentences, since these had been imposed by British Courts. They would not, however, agree to my Board visiting the men in prison. We, therefore, reviewed their cases in London and sent our recommendations to the Foreign Office. In our report we recommended immediate release in four cases. A few weeks later I read in the press that these men had been released from prison, so the Italians had wasted little time.

Before I pass on to the most publicised of the British military war crime trials, namely that of Field-Marshal von Manstein in 1949, I feel that this is the point, both logically and chronologically to consider the legal and moral ethics of the Allied war crimes trials.

Under the Moscow Declaration of October 1943 the principal Allied Powers affirmed their intention to try war criminals. They divided them into two classes – major war criminals and minor war criminals.

Major war criminals were defined as those persons and organisations whose crimes had no geographical location. They were to be tried, and, if found guilty, punished by joint decision of the governments of the Allies. The International Tribunal at Nuremberg tried the Nazi leaders, and a similar tribunal in Tokyo dealt with the Japanese leaders. Minor war criminals were defined as those individuals accused of offences against the laws and usages of war (as set out in the Hague and Geneva Conventions) and whose offences could be ascribed to a particular location. The bulk of war criminals fell into this class. They numbered around 3,000 and were tried by special courts established by the various allies. The number tried by British Courts was just under 1,800, of whom half were Japanese.

I have little doubt that the majority of people will agree that the decision to try major war criminals was correct. Those responsible for the murder of millions of innocent men, women and children, for barbaric so-called scientific medical experiments, and the murder of prisoners of war could not on any count be allowed to escape the just punishment for their crimes. To have allowed them to do so would have been to cast all ideas of human rights on to the rubbish heap. It may reasonably be argued that the form of the international tribunals, at Nuremberg and Tokyo was open to the accusation that it was trial of the vanquished by their victors. My answer to this is, "Had the panels of judges included Germans and Japanese, I doubt if the findings and sentences would have varied." Even as I write the West German Government has refused to grant immunity to those of its nationals accused of war crimes committed up to 40 years ago.

It is sometimes forgotten that the matter of war crimes was not something which arose as the result of the war of 1939-45. The decision by the Allies to set up their own courts under the Declaration of 1943 was undoubtedly influenced by the precedent of World War I. Then, war crimes though on a scale vastly smaller than in 1939-45 were also committed. One has only to tour some areas of Northern France and Belgium to be reminded of the fact by memorials in villages to those of its inhabitants who were shot without trial by way of reprisals. After that war the Allies decided to leave it to the German government to bring to trial their own war criminals. The result was what I have seen referred to in an official document as "The Leipsig Farce".*

After Nuremberg Field-Marshal Lord Montgomery is reported to have said, "The Nuremberg trials have made the waging of unsuccessful war a crime, for which generals of the defeated side would be tried and then hanged."* Whether Montgomery meant this observation to be taken seriously or not I do not know. For my part I am firmly of the opinion that the trial of major war criminals was not only essential but just.

When we turn to the trial of the so-called minor war criminals, we enter upon an area of controversy, which in the immediate post-war years exercised the minds of many of our countrymen on both legal and moral grounds. These minor war criminals, as I have already indicated, extended from Commanders-in-Chief in the field down to the lowest ranks in the complex Nazi web of security police, and, more particularly in the cases of the Japanese, down to junior officers and men in the armed forces proper. The point at issue is whether justice should be confined to the leaders of a nation alone, or extended down the chain of responsibility to those in subordinate position. There are many arguments to support both views.

---

*The Germans eventually set up a tribunal at Leipsig in May 1921. By this time the number of accused had dwindled to 12. Of these six were convicted – two men sentenced for homicide were given four years' imprisonment, and allowed to 'escape' from prison before they had completed six months – one man convicted for 'refusal of quarter' was sentenced to two years and treated by the German people as a hero.

*R T Paget (Collins) p67

It has frequently been stated that in war subordinates must obey orders; that failure to do so may weaken the structure of the State and its services and thereby lead to defeat. Some people have argued that in war all means are justified to ensure victory and stave off defeat; that the use of the atomic bomb against Japanese civilians was just as much a criminal act as mass reprisals against civilians by the German security services and the Japanese Army. It was, therefore, hypocritical of the Allies to institute proceedings against their former enemies. Others argued that the air arm and total warfare had rendered the Hague and Geneva Conventions obsolete, and thereby nullified the hitherto accepted laws and usages of war; an argument on which the prosecution in many of these trials leaned heavily. Then there were the legal aspects, upon which, as a layman, I do not feel qualified to comment, beyond pointing out that the various allied countries differed in their approach to the legislation convening the trials, and here I quote,

> As they evolved in various countries, the laws concerning the punishment of war crimes, generally speaking, took two different lines of approach. One was followed by some continental countries, such as France and Norway, and consisted in treating war crimes as offences of common penal law which were not, at the same time, justified by the laws and customs of war. There the approach was made through the system of the Penal Codes concerned. The other was followed by countries such as Great Britain, USA, Canada and Australia, that is by countries in which common law is not codified and consists largely of customary rules and judicial precedents. There the approach was made by taking as a direct source of the rule relevant for the punishment of war crimes, those contained in international laws and customs of War.*

On the other hand it may be argued that the laws and usages of war having been accepted by the belligerent nations, non-enforcement of them would have been a serious retrograde step, and an affront to civilisation; that International Law, to be effective, must not only apply to States but also reach out to cover the individual members of a State. Furthermore there is the straightforward common sense argument that the individual must be held responsible for his own behaviour and, if he oversteps the accepted standards of common decency and humanity, he must be prepared to take the consequences. Here lies the crux of the matter. I ask myself, "Would you or any of your companions obey an

*Law Reports of Trials of War Criminals, Vol XI (HMSO) 1949. P 87

163

order, even it is purported to emanate from Whitehall, to shoot prisoners on capture without any form of trial, or to herd old men, women and children in a gas chamber to die?" The answer is, of course, an emphatic, "No", even if it meant that you yourself would be punished for disobeying the orders of your superiors. With the honourable exception of Kesselring, the defence plea that, "I was only obeying superior orders," ran through practically all the German cases which I and my Board reviewed. In British law such a pleas does not exonerate the accused from breaches of the law and it is of interest to note that the German tribunal at Leipsig held that the same plea was no defence in the case of the U-Boat commander, who having sunk the *Llandovery Castle* deliberately left the survivors to drown.

By June our review was finished. It would be improper to give details of those cases in which we recommended remission or reduction of sentences; in any case it would be of little interest without giving details of the charges and defence; suffice it to say that in all cases where we felt that we could recommend remission, we did so; whether our recommendations were accepted by the War Office I am not certain, but I have reason to believe that with the possible exception of one case, they were.

Hardly had the ink had time to dry on the Review Board's report when I received an official letter from the Military Secretary, the War Office 'detailing' me as a member of the Military War Crimes Court about to assemble in Hamburg for the trial of Field-Marshal von Manstein. The mandatory terms of this communication naturally raised doubts in my mind as to whether I was still considered to be on the active list, and as such eligible for future employment after the trial ended, or was it simply another case of suspended compulsory retirement. The Military Secretary confirmed that it was the latter. Nevertheless I agreed to sit on the court, which was estimated to last three to four months.

My main reason for doing so was because, despite continuous efforts to obtain employment in civil life, I had failed. I confess that I gave little thought to the implications of the trial. I had had over the past two years much experience of trials for war crimes – on paper, both as confirming officer in Malaya and reviewing officer in Europe. It would at least be a change to sit on a court and experience a trial at first hand. This was my only chance, as the Manstein trial was to be the last by a British court.

14

The trial of Field-Marshal von Manstein—the ethics of War Crime Trials—meetings with Liddell Hart and Lord Hankey

In the House of Lords on 5th May, 1949 Lord Henderson, the Under-Secretary of State, the Foreign Office, "announced that the Government had decided in the light of medical evidence that Field-Marshal von Runstedt and Colonel-General Strauss were unfit to stand trial – proceedings against them would be dropped and they would be released. The medical evidence regarding Field-Marshal von Manstein was that he was fit to stand trial, and accordingly he was to be tried".* He added that this would be the last trial of anyone accused of war crimes and held in the British occupation zone of Germany.

It was now just on four years since these three senior German generals had surrendered to the British forces and consequently been detained in custody in the British zone. The war crimes alleged to have been committed by Manstein took place in the Polish and Russian theatres of war, and both those countries had asked for him to be handed over to them. The Government had refused both requests – not that they regarded the Polish trials to be unfairly conducted. The inference was obvious. As the Lord Chancellor is reported to have stated in the same debate, "It was only fair to say in regard to Polish trials that they had been fairly conducted. There was no doubt about it." He was not saying it about any other trials.

There can be little doubt that had Manstein been handed over to the Russians, nothing would have been heard of him thereafter. As it was, his home being in the Soviet zone of occupation, all his property had

*The Times – 6th May, 1949.

165

been confiscated by the Russians, and it was with difficulty that he and his friends raised sufficient funds to engage two leading German counsel for his defence. Following a visit by the junior of these two, Dr Paul Leverkuehn, to London in July to seek the aid of British counsel, in view of the difference between German and British Court procedure, Major-General Viscount Bridgeman and Lord De L'Isle and Dudley VC launched an appeal for funds. The sum of about £1,500 was quickly raised. Consequently Mr R T Paget, QC MP (now Lord Paget) agreed to lead the defence together with two juniors, one of whom Mr Sam Silkin has since made his name in politics. I understand that Paget generously waived any fee for his services. The decision to try Manstein after four years of captivity had naturally raised some opposition in both Houses of Parliament and occupied some space in the correspondence column of *The Times*.

On 21st August 1949 the members of the Court assembled at Hamburg. They were Lieutenant-General Sir Frank Simpson, myself, Brigadiers C A Dixon and R B Lambe, and Colonels E T Heslop, L A Liddle and R E Wilson. We were joined by Judge C A Collingwood a county court judge who was to be Judge Advocate, in other words legal advisor to the Court. Simpson, I had known previously, and Wilson had been a member of my Review Board; the others I had not met before. Collingwood was a delightful companion, of whom we all became very fond. His task was formidable and towards the end of the trial we feared that his health would collapse under the strain. He subsequently was promoted to the high court, but died a few years later.

The arrangements for our welfare in Hamburg were all that one could have desired. We were put up in the Four Seasons Hotel, one of the few large buildings which had escaped destruction and provided with our own mess. The defence and prosecution teams of lawyers were each accommodated in separate hotels, the idea being that outside the court the three bodies should not meet socially. We soon put a stop to that, and it was not long before Simpson and I were entertaining the two German defence lawyers to dinner. Thereafter, we all mixed freely out of court.

The trial opened on 23rd August in the Curio House, Hamburg. This was not a museum but a concert hall named in honour of a man named Curio. The only curious feature of the layout, designed to turn the hall into a court, was that counsel were not able to address the court from their seats. Instead they had to move into the well of the court and stand at a lectern-like podium equipped with a single microphone. This was necessary because the hall had been equipped with a simultaneous translation system for English and German. Relays of translators sat in a box overlooking the court and all concerned were provided with headphones. Needless to say the fact that counsel for the prosecution and defence could not address the court without rising from their seats and walking forward a few feet to the podium led to some highly undignified pushing and shoving; so much so that on one occasion at least the President had to adjourn the court for a short interval to allow tempers to cool off.

The prosecution was led by Sir Arthur Comyns Carr KC with Mr Elwyn Jones MP* as his junior, both of whom had had experience of the international war crime trials – the former at Tokyo and the latter at Nuremberg. Comyns Carr was a highly successful barrister, with political leanings. He had for a short period in the 20's been a Liberal MP. Now at the age of 67 years he was at the summit of his legal career. His urbane and quiet demeanour were in contrast to his opposite number – Paget. The latter was one of those seemingly contradictory personalities who despite their comfortable background – he was a fox-hunting squire in the Shires – had joined the Labour Party after the war, stood for Parliament, and was elected. His defence of Manstein was conducted with a fervour and a passion, which at times one could not help feeling exceeded the limits of discretion. Apart from the opening and closing stages of the defence he left much to his junior, Sam Silkin, and the two German lawyers.

Of the British barristers Elwyn Jones impressed me most. He, like so many budding politicians, had been President of the Cambridge Union. He was now the Labour MP for an East London Constituency and obviously destined for preferment. Out of court he was a most engaging personality with a ready wit and a fund of good anecdotes. His opposite number, Sam Silkin, also a product of the Cambridge law faculty had served during the war and risen to the rank of lieutenant-colonel. He had served in the Far East as President of a war crimes court. It says much for the British sense of impartiality and justice that Sam, a Jew, should be part of the defence team in a case where the accused was charged with the mass extermination of Jews. I got to know Sam quite well during the trial, and enjoyed his company; and also that of the third British member of the defence team, Bill Croome, whom I was to get to know still better in later years.

*Lord Elwyn Jones QC. Lord Chancellor 1974-79.

The first day of the trial opened with the submission by Paget that the Royal Warrant of the 18th June 1945, under which the Court was convened, was itself illegal, and that, therefore, the Court had no jurisdiction. This being the case, he argued that under the Geneva Convention the only tribunal which could try Manstein was a general court-martial. The court was not, of course, a GCM. After this plea had been overruled by the Judge Advocate, the prosecution introduced the charges. There were 17 of them, and they covered 39 pages of foolscap. Two of the charges were alternative to one another. It took until lunch time on the second day to complete the introduction of these lenghty charges. They were all concerned with Manstein's conduct in the Polish and Russian campaigns. The number of witnesses was comparatively small; the documentary evidence was massive amounting to no less than 689 documents.

The first three charges related to the Polish campaign, at a time when Manstein was Chief of Staff and not a Commanding General. He was accused of 'authorising and permitting the killing and maltreatment of Polish citizens' by German troops, and of 'deliberately and recklessly disregarding his duty' to take steps to prevent the killing and maltreatment of Polish citizens and Polish prisoners of war. At the close of the prosecution's case on these charges, I personally felt that they could not be sustained. In the end the accused was acquitted on all of them. One can only conclude that they were allowed to stand for political reasons, namely to satisfy the Poles.

The remaining 14 charges dealt with the period September 1941 to April 1944 during which Manstein was successively Commander-in-Chief of 11th Army, Army Group Don and Army Group South. Many of the incidents referred to in the charge sheets took place in the Crimea, and at times I could not help reflecting that Manstein and I were probably the only two people in that court room who had first-hand knowledge of the area involved.

Charges 4-7 all related to the treatment of prisoners of war. They alleged that large numbers died or were shot, or were handed over to the Security Police (SS and SD) to be killed; that under orders issued from the German Supreme Command and an order issued by Manstein himself, Russian soldiers, when captured as stragglers, were to be shot without trial; that Russian prisoners of war were to be recruited forcibly into the German Army; and that others were to be employed on dangerous work. The defence pleaded that under the extremely difficult conditions in the Crimea due to lack of communications, shortage of supplies, etc, Manstein did his best for prisoners of war; that, if there were shot, he did not know about it, and, in any case, they were probably shot when trying to escape. In the witness box the defendant attempted to justify the shooting of stragglers by saying, "The order that dispersed soldiers had to report by a certain date or would otherwise be shot, I consider, in view of the partisan warfare, to be absolutely justified." As regards the employment of prisoners of war on prohibited and dangerous work, the defence maintained that Manstein was acting under superior orders; that in any case it was not contrary to the Hague Convention; that the Allies themselves used prisoners of war labour to clear minefields. The Court found Manstein not guilty of the charge relating to the shooting without trial of stragglers, but guilty on the other counts with certain exceptions (the reader will recall that the charges covered 39 pages of foolscap, quoting innumerable incidents to support each charge).

Charge 8 referred to the notorious Hitler Commissar Order, under which all civil and military Commissars captured were to be summarily executed. The defence maintained that civil Commissars were not covered by the Hague Convention, and that military Commissars were not entitled to be treated as prisoners of war, although they wore military uniform with distinguishing badges. The Court found Manstein guilty on this charge.

Charge 9 was the gravest indictment. Under it the accused was charged with ordering, authorising and permitting the mass extermination of Jews, Gipsies and others by special units of the SD within the area of his (Manstein's) Command. It was not questioned whether these special units (*Einsatzgruppe*) were charged with the horrible task, or that, when operating in the Army area, the Army Commander had power to issue orders to them if operational necessity demanded it. But Manstein and one of his divisional commanders maintained under cross-examination that they knew nothing of these mass shootings at the time, and only heard of them after the war. On the other hand more than one senior member of Manstein's staff, called for the defence, admitted that they knew of these slaughters, but kept the knowledge to themselves. The Court acquitted Manstein on this charge, but found him guilty under the alternative charge 10 of disregarding his duty as a commander in consequence of which these atrocities were permitted to take place within the area of his command. This was, of course, tantamount to saying that he knew what was going on but turned a blind eye to it.

Charges 11 and 12 dealt with the handing over by the Army of Jews and others to the SD for extermination, and with the ill-treatment and killing of the same people by the Army itself. On these two charges the court retured a verdict of not guilty.

The remaining charges 13-17 all dealt with alleged offences against civilians by way of reprisal killings, employment on work directly connected with military operations, eg, trench digging and deporting men and women for labour work in Germany and other purposes. The prosecution produced German documents to show that the killing of civilians as reprisals was carried out by formations and units of the Army; in one case a division reported killing all the inhabitants of four localities as an act of reprisal. The defence maintained that reprisals were in certain circumstances justified in view of the partisan warfare carried on by the Soviets; that in some of the instances quoted in the charge sheet Manstein was ignorant of the events; or that he was acting under superior orders. In one case where 1,300 civilians were shot en masse after a Russian landing at Eupatoria on the west coast of the Crimea, and in which without doubt civilians took up arms, Manstein's attitude was revealed under cross-examination when he stated, "It was immaterial to me whether they were shot during the action or afterwards. Our situation was far too serious for me to bother about it."

One charge (No.14) relating to the executing of civilians was, in my opinion so complicated in its wording, and not without an element of ambiguity, that I felt it should not be upheld. The Court agreed on a verdict of 'Not Guilty'. The last three charges all concerned offences against the civilian population. The accused was found guilty of compulsorily employing men and women on work directly connected with military operations. He was likewise found guilty of forcibly deporting masses of men, women and children as his armies retreated before the Russian advance in the autumn of 1943. The last charge, No.17, also embraced the mass destruction of houses and other objects of economic value, but on this count the court accepted the defence plea of military necessity and acquitted the accused. Regarding the compulsory employment of civilians on works connected with military operations, the defence maintained that all the works were well in rear of the fighting zone and, therefore, not illegal under the Hague Convention, Article 52 of which states, "The work must be of such a nature as not to involve the inhabitants in taking part in operations against their own Country." The compulsory aspect of the work, be it noted, is not *per se* illegal. Bearing in mind that the Hague Convention was drawn up in 1907 its application to the total warfare of the 1940's where even the growing of crops may assist indirectly the prosecution of military operations, the court was faced with a difficult decision. In the event their decision established that in a mass retreat the security of the retreating army may under certain circumstances justify the wholesale destruction of buildings and goods, such as crops, which are of economic value to their pursuers, but not the mass deportation of the inhabitants of an occupied country.

On 30th November the Court adjourned after listening to the closing addresses of the defence and prosecution which occupied seven days. On Monday 12th December Collingwood started his mammoth task of summing up. It occupied the whole week, leaving the weekend in which the members of the court, in the manner of a jury, had to decide their findings on each charge. On the following Monday the court reassembled and the President read out the findings and the sentence. As the President read out the sentence of 18 years imprisonment, Manstein snatched off his earphones and flung them down in a fit of anger.

Manstein who celebrated his 62nd birthday during the trial came from the ancient military stock of Prussia. His uncle was General von Hindenburg of World War I fame, who later became President of the German Reich. Undoubtedly the Field-Marshal was one of the ablest German Commanders to emerge from the Second World War. His appearance in the dock, dressed in a sober suit, during the early stages of the trial was that of a middle-aged successful doctor, lawyer or academic. He displayed little emotion and made copious notes. When it came to his examination by the senior German Counsel, Dr Laternser – Paget being in England – Manstein made a long speech outlining the campaigns in which he had taken part. On the first day I noted in my diary, "Manstein in the box. He lectured under L's examination in impressive but Prussian style. Obviously it was his great day and he. made the most of it." On his fourth day "in the box", it was Comyns Carr's turn to start the cross-examination. To start with Manstein continued to give long and voluble answers to every question, and it was not until the seventh day under gruelling examination on the question of the maltreatment of prisoners that he started to stumble in his replies and appeared to lose a measure of self confidence. Later the defence brought in 16 witnesses, of whom two were heard *in camera* for their own interests. At least one witness, a senior engineer officer, was most unimpressive and certainly did nothing to strengthen the case for the defence.

Somewhat to my surprise, Colonel Scotland, the officer in charge of the London Centre for the interrogation of prisoners of war, was called by the defence to give evidence as to the total number of alleged war crimes committed by the Russians. The figure given me was 3250.

By the end of the cross-examination any feelings I had of sympathy towards Manstein had been replaced by disgust at the manner in which he appeared to be hiding behind his subordinates and relying on the plea of superior orders. I could not help comparing his attitude with that taken by Kesselring at his trial. As already related the latter never attempted to evade responsibility for events which took place in the area of his Command.

Of the two German Counsel employed in the case, Dr Laternser had had considerable experience of war crime trials, having appeared at Nuremberg and also for Field-Marshal Kesselring at the British military court which tried him in Venice in 1947. His proficiency in the English language was limited. Dr Leverkuehn on the other hand spoke English fluently. He had visited England frequently and spoke without a trace of German accent. We all enjoyed his company out of court. On one occasion he arranged for the members of the court to see in private the film depicting the trial and execution of those involved in the plot against Hitler on 20th July, 1944. I have never seen a more horrifying sequence. I understood that Leverkuehn himself narrowly escaped being one of Hitler's hapless victims on that occasion.

Towards the end of the trial, my wife and daughter had joined me in Hamburg. We decided to spend Christmas in Germany, returning home the first week in January. On my return I found waiting for me a letter from the War Office finally retiring me from the Army, thus ending a career of just over 34 years. Shortly afterwards a long letter by Captain Liddell Hart appeared in *The Times* in which he condemned the 'Savage Sentence' inflicted on Manstein, and ending, "His condemnation appears a glaring example either of gross ignorance or gross hypocrisy." Coming from a man whose writings I had always admired, and whose judgements I had respected in the past I found this criticism of the Court quite astonishing and offensive. Indeed I considered it cowardly, since he knew quite well that as serving officers the Court were debarred from contributions to the Press or other publications without special permission from the War Office, which in this case would almost certainly be denied. I therefore wrote to Liddell Hart suggesting that we meet.

As a result he invited me to meet him in a London hotel on 20th January. Our conversation lasted two hours during which I pointed out the seriousness of the charges upon which the Court had found Manstein guilty; the evidence upon which the findings of the Court were based; the nature of which had not been made evident through the meagre accounts of the trial which appeared in the English Press; and that the only yardstick open to the court in pronouncing sentence was that based on previous war crime trials. I added that I could well appreciate and respect the views of anyone who disagreed in principle with the trial of war criminals, but not when they attacked the integrity of the court in a particular case. After a cup of tea we parted amicably.

I do not know whether it was a result of this meeting or not, but a few days later I received a telephone call asking me to visit Lord Hankey. He was then aged 73 and semi-retired. He had been one of the eminent people (Winston Churchill was another) who had subscribed towards the cost of British defence counsel for Manstein. Our meeting lasted about half an hour at the end of which he expressed no opinion of what I had said, and merely thanked me for coming to see him. The findings and the sentences in the Manstein case were subsequently confirmed by the GOC-in-C British Army of the Rhine, but later the Secretary of State for War as the final confirming authority remitted the term of imprisonment to 12 years. In 1953 he was released having spent some time in hospital. He received a pension from the West German Government and in 1955-56 was Chairman of a military committee appointed to advise the Bundestag Defence Committee on the organisation and operational doctrine of the new German Forces of the Federal Republic.

In October – some 9 months after our previous meeting – Liddell Hart rang me up and asked me if I would be prepared to meet General Westphal, who had come to London to intercede for the release of FM Kesselring. I replied that I would be delighted to do so.

Westphal, who spoke good English had been at various time Chief of Staff to von Rundstedt and Rommel, as well as Kesselring. We met at a hotel in London. He had already been or was proposing to see Mr Hore Belisha, the Bishop of Chichester and Lord Hankey; presumably with the idea of getting the matter raised in Parliament. Whether the advice I gave to General Westphal in any small way contributed to the subsequent release of Kesselring, I do not know. I like to think that it did. Many of those who criticised the decision to try von Manstein, and they included men distinguished in many walks of life, based their objections on the delay in instituting the proceedings, and not on the justice of the trial itself. There was no justification for this criticism. Those senior German commanders who were tried for war crimes had to wait for long periods whilst their cases were examined and evidence produced from many sources. For instance General von Falkenhorst, the C-in-C in Norway was tried in 1946 and FM Kesselring, the C-in-C in Italy in 1947. They were both sentenced to death. Later this was commuted to life imprisonment, which was defined as 21 years. Manstein's sentence of 18 years did, therefore, clearly reflect the delay of 2-3 years in bringing him to trial. The documentary evidence in his case amounted, we were told by the Judge Advocates staff to no less than 4 tons in weight, all of which had to be examined, selected and then shipped from the Pentagon in Washington to which building all documents seized by the Western Allies had been transferred for safe custody. Having visited the document room on the first floor of the Curio House I can well imagine that this figure was not exaggerated. Bearing this in mind and also that the British Government was under considerable pressure from both the Russians and the Poles to hand Manstein over to themselves for trial, it is understandable that the preparations for the trial took a matter of many months, and that the charges embraced such multitudinous and specific details.

Now that part of the former German people are our friends and allies, I have often wondered how it was that under Hitler the nation could so degrade itself to perform, or in some cases acquiesce in the most bestial and massive acts of homicide the world has ever seen. I sometimes think that an incident which I witnessed in Hamburg may provide a clue. It was a fine autumn morning and the streets and pavements were thronged with people enjoying the sunshine. My route took me through one of the large squares of this city, on which some of the main thoroughfares with their tram routes converged. As I entered the square a tram with two trailers – all three vehicles crowded with passengers – was just moving off, when a middle-aged man attempting to board the first car, slipped and fell on the street. He lay with his legs towards the rails and from where I was it looked as though his feet would be run over by the trailers. Fortunately this was not so and the train of trams passed without damaging him. In the meantime the driver and many of the passengers leant out of the moving vehicles and laughed at the man lying prostrate on the street. There were plenty of pedestrians about, but not one attempted to go to his help.

I stopped and found that the man was apparently only suffering from shock. After helping him to his feet, my driver and I put him in our car and were proceeding to take him to hospital, when he suddenly addressed me in fluent English and asked me to take him to his flat, which was not far away. This I did, and by the time we arrived he had completely recovered his composure and was prolific in his gratitude. He told me he had been employed as English interpreter on the staff of a German Army corps in Belgium in 1940 and had worked in London before the war.

I puzzled over this incident. Had it occured in Birmingham or Glasgow people would have rushed to the man's aid, the tram would have stopped and the driver and conductor got out and a policeman would have appeared from nowhere. Here in Hamburg it was treated with complete indifference and even jocularity. What was the explanation? Was it that the people of Hamburg were so indifferent to suffering, after the terrifying bombing they had endured, that they treated it with contempt? Or was it that their conduct reflected a streak of cruelty indigenous to the German race? To this day I do not know the answer, but I regret that I incline towards the latter explanation.

15

Appointed Telecoms Attache in USA—involvement in civil aviation—the Queen's trans-Atlantic flight 1955

On my return from Hamburg in December 1950 I was finally placed on the retired list of the Army and granted the modest pension to which Service personnel were then enlisted. I was 51 and had no intention of leading an inactive life, even if my finances had enabled me to do so. I, therefore, set about the depressing task once more of seeking employment. In June my hopes were fulfilled.

The War office were asked by the Post Office to find a retired Signals Officer to fill the appointment of Telecommunications Attache at Washington. They rang up to inquire if I would be interested. Without hesitation and with but the barest outline of the job I replied "Yes. Most certainly I would be interested. I could be free to go to Washington in a month's time." A few days later I was summoned to St Martin's-le-Grand for an interview. I was ushered into an office, where to my relief I found three senior Post Office officials and a decanter of sherry and glasses prominently displayed. I had imagined that I was in for yet another of those formidable short list interviews, when one was ushered to a seat facing a row of eager inquisitors across a table. Nothing could have been further from the truth. One of the officials was my old friend Howard Read, whom I had last met as Lieutenant-Colonel commanding a signal unit in France at the time of Dunkirk. After an explanation of what the appointment involved, I was asked if I would accept it. My liaison work with the telecommunications side of the Post Office during 1940 had stood me in good stead.

In mid-August 1951 the International Telecommunications Union

(ITU) was due to hold its bi-annual conference on radio frequencies at Geneva. The purpose of this conference was to decide the allocation of radio frequencies to various services, eg, aviation, broadcasting, shipping, telephones and telegraphs, and to assign them to the various countries of the world according to their needs and geographical locations.

Howard Read suggested that it would be a good move if, before going to Washington, I accompanied the British delegation to Geneva for a week or so. In this way I should gain experience of how these matters were settled on the international scale, and at the same time get to know some of the USA and Dominion delegates.

The ITU is one of the technical agencies of the United Nations Organisation. It is much older than the latter having been founded in 1865 under the title of International Telegraph Union. Like the United Nations Assembly it conducts it's proceedings in four languages, English, French, Russian and Spanish, simultaneously translated and picked up by delegates through earphones. The first two days of the conference were largely taken up by the delaying tactics of the Soviet delegation. They objected to China being represented by the Nationalist Government of Chiang Kai-shek in Formosa and not by the Communist Government of mainland China. They were bitterly opposed by the US delegates. Once the wrangling was over the conference split up into various committees and got down to work.

At the end of September, I crossed the Atlantic on the *Queen Elizabeth I*. Our arrival at New York was to me, as I imagine it was to most passengers at that time, an anti-climax. One stepped off the luxury liner to find oneself propelled into the midst of a large gloomy shed where chaos reigned supreme. Coloured porters struggled with piles of baggage which were dumped at the sides of the shed beneath the initial letter of the owners name. In kiosk-like offices in the centre stood, or sat, bored looking white men chewing gum or smoking. Had it not been that the Consul-General's office in New York had sent someone to meet me, it would probably have been hours before I discovered that these bored gentlemen were Customs officials, whom one was expected to cajole from their cubby holes to inspect one's baggage before one was allowed to proceed on one's way.

As Telecommunications Attache, my duties were twofold. Firstly, to act as technical adviser to the Ambassador and his staff. Secondly, to keep the Post Office informed on technical developments and to act as their representative with the telecommunications industry. The first task involved close liaison with the appropriate officials in the State Department. In the USA all means of communication were then in the hands of private industry. There were hundreds of telephone companies, half a dozen or so telegraph companies and in the transport field innumerable railways, airlines, etc. Of public utilities the postal service alone was nationalised. I was not concerned with that service, which in those days was considered far less efficient than our own.

The British Embassy is a neo-Georgian building constructed between the wars. It combines the Ambassador's residence with Chancery, ie, the Embassy proper. During the war a temporary building had been built in the grounds to cater for the increase in staff. All the attache's offices together with some of the junior staff of the Embassy proper were in this annexe. This physical separation of the senior Foreign Office from the Civil Service staff (with certain exceptions all attaches were members of the Civil Service) to my mind only emphasised the perceptible social barriers which existed between the members of the two Services.

During three years at the Embassy, with two or three exceptions, I cannot recall ever being entertained by or for that much entertaining any member of Branch A of the Foreign Service. Branch A embraced those members of the service who held senior posts and from whose ranks ambassadorial posts were filled. It would be no exaggeration to say that it was the exception rather than the rule to find these posts occupied by those whose education had not embraced Eton, Harrow or Winchester, followed by Oxbridge. Today the situation has changed and an examination of the Diplomatic List will show that our ambassadors are derived from a much larger social strata.

Luckily for me, my official contact with Chancery was through one of the few female members of Branch A. Miss Barbara Salt was charming, unassuming and efficient. She had, I understood, joined the Foreign Service rather later in life than was normal and by sheer ability and personality rose rapidly. In fact it was only a serious illness, from which she eventually died, that prevented her from becoming our first lady ambassador.

The Ambassador, Sir Oliver Franks, was not a career diplomat. It had long been the practice for the two most important foreign diplomatic posts, namely Paris and Washington to be held from time to time by

179

persons outside the Foreign Service. They are usually chosen by the government in office for, amongst other qualities, their political affiliations. This has the disadvantage that, in the event of a change of government, the ambassador has to be recalled or tender his resignation to give way for someone acceptable to the new party in power. The most recent example was the replacement of Peter Jay after the Conservative Party returned to power in 1979.

Franks, exceptionally, had no political affiliation. He was educated at Bristol Grammar School and Oxford, where he became a distinguished academic. At the beginning of the 1939-45 war he joined the civil service and rose rapidly to the top. When appointed Ambassador in Washington he was Permanent Secretary at the Ministry of Supply. In manner mild and unassuming there is no doubt that his sheer ability and personality made a deep impression on all who met him. I was credibly informed that, before he left Washington in 1953 to return to Oxford, he had visited and made speeches in every State of the Union. As a speaker he was outstanding. He was one of those rare orators who could speak for an hour or so without a note and without hesitant pauses.

His successor, Sir Roger Makins, was a career diplomat with a Winchester and Christchurch background. I can only remember meeting him once during the eighteen months I served on his staff. The occasion was the visit of Sir Ben Barnett,* Deputy Director-General of the GPO, who had come over to settle details of the laying of the first trans-Atlantic telephone cable – a joint venture by Britain, Canada and USA. Barnett and I were invited to lunch at the Residence. Lady Makins was a daughter of a former American Secretary for War, Dwight F Davis who is best remembered for the tennis cup which bears his name.

My appointment as Telecoms Attache involved a considerable amount of travelling mainly to report on new equipment being produced by various firms throughout the country. I also had to act as a link with the various international cable and radio companies which provided services to and from the UK. In this way I was able to obtain a fairly clear picture as to how industry was conducted in the USA. One thing which struck me forcibly was the close relationship between management and what is usually referred to as the shop floor. In British industry at that time (and regrettably the tendency still persists) it was

*The late Sir Ben L Barnett KBE CB MC

quite common to find men, whose influence was derived from upbringing or wealth rather than ability, occupying seats on the boards of large numbers of companies engaged in activities of which these fortunate few could have little practical knowledge. In the USA this was exceptional. I cannot recall any such case to mind, though probably some did exist. On the other hand I well remember a remark made to me by a Vice-President of the Company the first time I visited Bell Telephone, a subsidiary of the giant American Telegraph and Telephone Corporation, at their New York offices. In reply to some question I raised regarding the Company President,* he said, "In this organisation no-one who reaches board room level has not started at the bottom." He went on to explain that all of the 'top brass' had at one time served in a telephone exchange or out in the field. This did not surprise me. Whenever I visited large and medium-sized firms I was struck by the close links between management and the shop floor. Whether I was conducted round the works by a Vice-President or the President of a company it was obvious from the way in which we were received that my host was no stranger to the employees, many of whom he addressed by name.

Another characteristic of American industry was what might be called the mobility of manpower. Men with young families seemed to have no hesitation in giving up a job in (say) Baltimore and moving right across the continent to (say) Seattle. How they solved the housing problem I never discovered, but since, with the exception of the poor blacks, most people bought, rather than leased, their houses, the problem was nothing like as complicated as in this country, where the majority of employees were living in rented accommodation, and the scarcity of council houses was acute. This mobility is understandable in a country where the majority of people have no deep roots in any one locality, they or their forebears having emigrated from Europe. In addition the pioneering spirit which opened up the West in the last century has left its mark.

I am old enough to remember the pre-nationalisation era of what are commonly called public utilities; when such utilities were run by private enterprise. I still have feelings of nostalgia for the various railway companies which flourished in my youth – the old GWR, GER, LBSCR and the much derided SECR.* But one realised that the economic facts

*In the USA the President of a Corporation is equivalent to the Chairman in Britain.

*Great Western, Great Eastern, London Brighton and South Coast, South Eastern and Chatham Railways.

of modern life required the change to one system under public ownership and control. The same applies to gas and electricity. But when it comes to transmission of the spoken word, I never could see how any nation could leave this most intimate and in some ways most essential utility in the hands of a variety of private enterprises. And yet that is exactly what the USA has done and still continues to do. When I was first shown a list of the American telephone companies I could hardly believe my eyes. There were hundreds of them,. ranging from the vast Bell Telephone System, which covered three quarters of the country (and incidentally parts of Canada) down to tiny little companies in rural areas with 100 susbscribers or less. In USA there is a sacred dogma called 'antimonopoly' enshrined in an act of Congress. In order to keep within this act and at the same time provide a nationwide telephone service the Bell Corporation was allowed to provide all the trunk facilities connecting the multitude of individual telephone companies in order to provide a viable system.

The telegraph system had started with a number of competing companies, but gradually the Western Union had swallowed up or forced into bankruptcy all its competitors. It had obtained a *de facto* monopoly of the internal telegraph system. For years Congress had been engaged in the task of sueing it for operating in defiance of the Monopolies Act. The issue was never settled and probably is not to this day. The only beneficiaries of this legal wrangle were, of course, the lawyers.

As my family were in England, I arranged to take leave and join them for Christmas 1952. I flew both ways by BOAC. It is interesting to look back on those flights across the Atlantic and compare them with today's long distance air travel. Now 350 or more passengers are jammed into a cinema-like structure with barely room to move, and left to struggle with their own luggage on departure and arrival. In the early 50's trans-Atlantic air travel even in the ordinary, as opposed to first class, was still luxurious. The aircraft were comparatively slow petrol-engine driven machines; one had reasonable room to move about; and one type included a downstairs bar lounge. The number of passengers carried never exceeded 50. The first class accommodation included sleeping berths, and the ordinary class had fully reclining chairs. Food and service were exemplary. One's baggage was handled by porters. The flying time varied from about 10-15 hours according to weather conditions and especially on the west-bound journey refuelling stops were often necessary at Gander in Newfoundland or Goose Bay in Labrador.

Whilst I was at home the Post Office asked me if I would represent the Ministry of Civil Aviation (MCA) on the telecommunications side in Washington. The Civil Air Attache, Ronald Dickinson* was a close friend of mine. He had one assistant, who was an expert on aircraft engines. Neither of them were versed in telecommunications, which at that period were becoming of increasing importance with the expansion of air routes all over the world. The science of aerial navigation by means of various radio aids and radar, which had originally taken shape under the compelling urgency of war conditions, was now entering a most interesting phase. Hitherto high speed transport on a bulk scale had been confined to the railway. Now three dimensional air corridors were being defined along which the regular air services were being made to run.

Unlike railway lines these corridors were intangible and invisible. Radio communication was the only means whereby the air traffic controllers on the ground could pass information and instructions to airline crews in flight, and also the only means whereby the latter could, in poor visibility, inform the ground of their position at any time. The early radio and radar systems which had assisted bombers and fighters during the war and enabled vast numbers of new military aircraft to be ferried across the North and South Atlantic, were fast becoming obsolete, and a new generation of more sophisticated instruments was now on offer. Needless to say the competition for this valuable worldwide market was intense. The Americans and ourselves were the main contenders.

In order that I might gain insight into this new field of telecommunications, my stay in England was prolonged by three weeks. During this time I underwent an intensive briefing by MCA officials in London, and made visits to their principal establishments throughout the country. These included Heathrow Airport which was just coming into operation, with the opening of terminal No 1.

Shortly after my return to Washington I became involved in setting up a conference between representatives of our MCA and their Civil Aviation Authority (CAA) – the controlling body in Washington. The object of the conference was to try and reach agreement on a new type of navigational aid for worldwide use. The subject was to be discussed at a forthcoming meeting of the International Civil Aviation Organisation

*The late R S S Dickinson, CMG

183

(ICAO) in Montreal. Two systems were involved – one American, the other British. Whichever was accepted by the majority of ICAO members would reap a rich reward for the country of origin. The American system depended on the establishment of a large number of radio beacons (the electronic equivalent of lighthouses) along air routes. From these the navigator of an airliner could measure the bearing and distance of his aircaft, and thus establish his position at any time. The British system required a much smaller number of ground radio stations, widely separated, which provided the same information continuously in the form of a tracing of the track followed by the aircraft displayed on a map in the cockpit.

Since the American system necessitated the establishment and maintenance of a large number of ground beacons, the British argued that the system would hardly be suitable for the underdeveloped countries of Africa and Asia. It would, they argued, entail the siting of many beacons in isolated parts of desert and jungle, where access would be difficult and costly. The British system on the other hand was already in use in Europe for ship's navigation and required no modification; thus killing the proverbial two birds with one stone. The Americans, having already spent large sums of money on installing their own system in the USA would not budge an inch. They succeeded in persuading their neighbour Canada to support them. In the end neither side won a decisive victory, and both systems were installed by different countries in various parts of the world. In many areas both systems were installed. The result was, of course, that the long distance airlines had to equip their fleets with instruments to utilise both systems. Needless to say both systems today are largely obsolescent and being replaced by more sophisticated equipment.

In November 1953 the Queen and Prince Philip were due to fly to the Bahamas, there to join the royal yacht for a tour of the Pacific via the Panama Canal. The flight entailed passing through air space controlled by Britain, Canada and USA. Four weeks before the flight was due I was summoned to Ottawa for a meeting attended by representatives of MCA, the Air Ministry and their Canadian counterparts. The object of the meeting was to coordinate action for the safety and security of the royal flight. Our representative from London arrived with a lengthy document designed to safeguard every possibility. To this end the precautions embraced the stationing of British and Canadian destroyers to be used to keep constant communication with the aircraft and its supporting craft – both sea and airborne. The last stages of the flight entailed passage through air space controlled by the USA. It was my task to seek from the CAA similar safety measures.

The Americans could not have been more helpful. They provided coastguard cutters and rescue aircraft on a lavish scale. The Royal Party left Heathrow at 9pm GMT on 23rd November, and arrived at Montego Bay at 10am local time on 25th, after refuelling stops at Gander and Bermuda. Having been informed by BOAC that weather conditions at Newfoundland were far from perfect, we all heaved a sigh of relief. I often wonder what precautions are taken today when Her Majesty undertakes a long distance flight.

In November 1953 the Conservative Government introduced a white paper outlining their proposals to set up a system of commercial TV in competition with the BBC. The plan was to appoint a second corporation which would be empowered to lease its facilities to commercial firms, which would produce programmes and at the same time derive their revenue by showing advertisements.

I had as part of my duties been reporting regularly to the Post Office on TV practice and procedure in the USA. It bore, of course, no resemblance to our own BBC. All TV (and radio) stations were privately owned and relied on advertising. The only control by government was through the FCC (Federal Communications Commission) which licensed the stations. The result was a proliferation of TV stations, the majority of which were affiliated to the four national networks on condition that they transmitted certain programmes produced by the networks to which they were affiliated. In the large cities viewers had a choice of up to seven different programmes. They, of course, paid no TV licence fee.

In Canada broadcasting was a mixture of national and private enterprise. The nationalised Canadian Broadcasting Corporation (CBC) had recently opened its first three TV stations and was prepared to license privately owned stations provided they affiliated to the CBC network, and took some of the latter's programmes. All stations, whether CBC or private, derived their income from advertising. Viewers paid no TV (or radio) licence fee.

In January 1954 I flew home for a fortnight to confer with the Post Office and MCA. The former, as the controlling authority of broadcasting were deeply involved in the drafting of the Indepndent Television Bill concerning which there was much controversy in government circles, and consequently indecision. On my return to Washington therefore, I decided to spend some days in Ottawa and thoroughly investigate and study the workings of the CBC. I then sent the PO a full report including my recommendations.

Whilst at home it had been hinted that my term as Telecommunications Attache would terminate earlier than I had anticipated. Later this was confirmed. My friend Howard Read was within a year or so of the retiring age. Owing to a reorganisation within the Post Office his appointment was about to be abolished. It was decided therefore, to retire him prematurely and then appoint him to succeed me. At the time I was bitterly disappointed but as events turned out, the move was to my advantage.

I knew I was the only member of the PO staff who had lived with and studied commercial TV. The commercial TV door was about to open in Britain. I made up my mind to get my foot inside that door.

In June 1957 I left Washington with mixed feelings. During my 3 years in the States my wife and I had made many friends. Wherever we went we met with individual kindness and hospitality.

16

I join the staff of the Independent Television Authority—the birth of Independent Television

On our return I lost no time impressing on Ben Barnett and others in the Post Office my interest in commercial TV, and my hope to be associated with the new system which now seemed certain to be approved by Parliament. At Barnett's invitation I spent the afternoon and evening of the 30th in the House of Lords listening to a debate during the committee stage of the Television Bill. Although it was the brain child of the then Conservative Government its passage through Parliament was long and at times bitter. Apart from the Labour Party, there were not a few Conservatives in both houses who opposed it. Lord Hailsham made one of his typical gesticulatory, witty and hard-knocking speeches in condemnation of the bill, conjuring up the depth of cultural and moral degradation into which it would cast the nation, if ever it became law. Well known industrialists like Lord Iveagh, the Chairman of Guinness, and the Cadburys, were other opponents.

On 30th July the Television Bill received the Royal assent and on 3rd August the PMG announced the names of the nine members of the Authority. Sir Kenneth Clark was to be Chairman and Sir Charles Colston Vice-Chairman. In press interviews most of the members, with the exception of the Chairman, were reported to have confessed that they had hitherto neither possessed a TV set nor shown any interest in the medium. They had been chosen as men and women of the world, who had, in their respective spheres, attained a degree of success. As the Authority, or in plain terms the Board of Governors, I hasten to add that they succeeded.

Ben Barnett had very kindly asked Lord de la Warr, the PMG, to mention my name to Clark as a possible nominee for an appointment in

ITA. I was not, therefore, surprised a few days later to receive a summons to call on Sir Kenneth in his chambers in the Albany. On arrival I found Colston present. This was my first encounter with either of them. The contrast between them was striking.

Sir Kenneth Clark (later Lord Clark) was, according to his auto-biography, born into that strata of society known as 'the idle rich', his grandfather having made a fortune in the thread industry in Scotland. "Although in that golden age, many people were richer, there can have been fewer who were idler,"* is his frank assessment of his parents. Be that as it may, Sir Kenneth himself could by no means be classed as idle. By 1939, at the comparatively early age of 36, he had established himself as a leading authority amongst the international art set and one of the foremost art historians of our times. In appearance and manner of speech he struck me as out of place in the modern age of films and TV, and that he would have been more at home in the squirearchy of the eighteenth or early nineteenth century. I was later to learn that he had for a short period been Director of Films in the war-time Ministry of Information. Later still the public were to recognise him as an unusually competent performer on television, through his programme entitled *Civilisation*.

Sir Charles Colston was a highly successful business man. He had recently retired as Chairman and Managing Director of Hoover. He is reported to have turned the British company into a more profitable concern than its American parent. As an NCO in the First World War he had been awarded the coveted DCM. At 62 he was 11 years senior to Clark. He had climbed up the industrial ladder the hard way, and was a keen supporter of the Conservative Party. Clark on the other hand had no business experience. He professed to be a-political, but he was certainly no admirer of the Conservative Party. According to his own account he accepted membership of the Independent Television Authority partly to oblige his friend Lord de la Warr, the PMG.

The partnership of such opposite characters could only end in one of two ways. Either they would complement one another and form a strong team; or they would never see eye to eye and sooner or later part company. In the event the latter alternative proved to be the outcome. Clark's account* of the final rupture is described in terms which can only be described as mischievous and brimming with a good measure of

*Kenneth Clark – The Other Half (John Murray) p143

188

artistic licence. Colston invited Clark to lunch. He proceeded to soften up his guest with photographs of babies, prior to unfolding some machiavellian scheme to use commercial TV as a means of swelling the coffers of the Tory Party. Clark as head boy of ITA was horrified, rushed post haste to the headmaster, the PMG, and persuaded him to expel the sinful prefect. To save face Colston sent in his resignation and started a most succcessful washing machine business.

Two days after my interview in the Albany, Clark wrote inviting me to join the staff of ITA for a period of 3 months. I went straight up to London, found Clark in the PO Headquarters and accepted. Next day I started work which was to last 10 years. Incidentally the salary offered was appreciably more than I was earning when I retired after 35 years in the Army. Useful as that was, my main satisfaction lay in the fact that I had got at least a toehold in a constructive project of immense possibility. The opportunity to play some part, however minor, in that project appealed to me enormously.

Looking back over the years I still wonder why Clark accepted me. He had no managerial experience, and his appointment as Chairman was part-time. Therefore until a Director-General was appointed he had to find a skeleton staff to start the machinery rolling which would in time convert the Television Act 1954 from a piece of paper into a physical reality. The Authority was under pressure from the Government, who feared that, if the service had not been established before the election due in 1955, should Labour gain power, they would annul the Act.

The PMG had arranged to lend the Authority three of his administrative officers and the minimum clerical staff. Alan Wolstencroft was a most efficient and likeable administrator who later became Deputy Director-General of the Post Office. Tony Pragnall, his assistant, had joined the Post Office after distinguished war service resulting in the award of the DFC. He remained with ITA and ended up as Deputy Director-General. Tony Curbishley was from the finance side of the PO. He stayed with ITA and ended up as its Director of Finance. None of them, of course, had any knowledge of the technical side of broadcasting, and so, I suppose, it was the simplest course for Clark temporarily to make use of myself who had been the technical representative of the Post Office in America for the last three years. The fact that Alan Wolstencroft and I had got acquainted during that period, and that he had been a pupil of my brother* during his undergraduate days at Cambridge may have helped my selection.

*The late Professor E C S Wade QC LLD FBA

The first act of the Authority was to appoint a Director-General. On 6th August a brief notice appeared in *The Times* and other papers. No terms were quoted and no terminal dates for applications. By the time I joined a week later about 140 applications had been received. No doubt the list had increased further by 14th September when the Authority interviewed a final shortlist of five, two of whom were generals and one an air chief-marshal. Next morning the Chairman came into the office and announced that he had solved the problem of a DG by ringing up Sir Robert Fraser and persuading him to submit a last minute application. The Authority had appointed Fraser.

Bob Fraser was a good choice and I have very happy recollections of serving under him. He was an Australian-born journalist who was a leader writer on the staff of the *Daily Herald*. At the beginning of the war he joined the Ministry of Information and became a civil servant. At the time of his appointment to ITA he was head of the Central Office of Information.

I recently read Clark's own account* of the selection of the Director-General, as outlined in his autobiograhy. I must confess that it left me with feelings of disillusionment that a man, who in my short acquaintance I always found courteous and kindly, could descend to the level of claptrap journalism. It appears that he had from an early stage of the proceedings decided that he wanted Fraser as DG. He, therefore, kept his name up his sleeve as a trump card and produced it at the last minute of the game. Fair enough. But what is unfair and in doubtful taste is his description of the 140 plus applicants for the job. These he divides into two classes, "Troublesome claimants, in particular disgruntled members of the armed forces, whom the Treasury [why the Treasury is not explained] hopes to get rid of; and journalists, cranks, do-gooders and do-badders, mostly with influential sponsors."

Certainly there was a sizeable number of applications from high-ranking retired members of the armed forces.

This is only to be expected on such occasions, since retirement ages are much lower than those of other professions. To describe them as disgruntled is a gratuitous insult to men who had risen to the top of their profession by their own ability, and rendered distinguished service to the nation. By including journalists in the other class of applicants, he

*Ibid p139

makes subject to ridicule the chosen profession of his own nominee, Bob Fraser.

The Post Office had placed a couple of rooms in their St Martins-Le-Grand offices at the disposal of the Authority. These could not be retained indefinitely, and so, at the Chairman's request, I started to look for suitable office accommodation, bearing in mind the size of staff likely to be required to establish a nationwide service. Unfortunately there was no precedent on which to base these requirements. Unlike the BBC which provides a complete service, ITA was limited to providing the technical means of transmitting programmes to viewers, the programmes themselves being produced by private companies appointed under contract by the Authority. For our guidance the Post Office had made a tentative list of staff appointments, which they considered would be necessary in the initial stages of opening the service. These included, if I remember rightly, some seven or eight engineering staff. Fraser, quite rightly, no doubt remembering his war-time experience in the M of I, was most anxious that the staff should be kept to a minimum. It took me some time to convince him that in order to get the service started his engineering staff had to plan and execute the building of at least three high power transmitting stations. These involved high masts to carry the aerials and complex equipment to convert the weak signals received from the contractor's studios into powerful signals, carrying 40 or more miles to the roof-top TV aerials. They would also require buildings to house this equipment and the staff to run them; arrangements to monitor the technical standards of the programmes produced; and arrangements with the Post Office to ensure that the various programmes and advertisements from different studios were fed along circuits hired from the PO to the appropriate transmitter station at the exact second they were required to be seen by viewers. As a footnote let me add that up to the time the service came on the air in the London, Midlands and Northern areas (21 months later), the engineering staff at headquarters barely exceeded a dozen.

My instructions were to find a building capable of holding a total staff of 30-40 people, if possible to be on a short lease. (Later I got my terms of reference extended to cover freehold.) The Chairman impressed on me that the office must be in Mayfair in order to provide the right atmosphere in which to receive, and presumably impress, potential programme contractors and other important visitors.

Needless to say the number of buildings which met these requirements was limited. In the end the Office of Works came to the rescue and found us temporary accommodation in a war-time building in Woods Mews, off Park Lane. Of the houses which I considered worth showing to the Chairman or the Director-General two remain in my memory. The first was in Grosvenor Street. It had been occupied as a *haute couturerie*. When I showed it to Kenneth Clark he was much taken by it. It appealed to him because it was in the heart of Mayfair and very close to Grosvenor Square where he had lived as a boy. I remember when we reached the top floor he looked out with unfeigned delight over the familiar landscape of roofs and chimneys. The house itself was not really suitable for our purposes without considerable alterations. I was relieved when for some reason or other it fell through. The other was the American Ambassador's residence at Prince's Gate. This was due to become vacant, as the ambassador was shortly to move into Barbara Hutton's mansion in Regents Park. When I first visited the house, it appeared to be eminently suitable with very few internal structural alterations required. Moreover the price asked for the remainder of the ground lease was most reasonable. I was, therefore, disappointed when the DG told me that the Authority had turned it down as being too far west. I was not, however, surprised when ten months later the Authority changed its mind. In the meantime the price had increased appreciably. The Authority moved into Prince's Gate in August 1955. It remained there for five years, during which time the Queen and Prince Philip made an official visit to meet the staff and representatives of the programme contractors. By the time it moved into the present offices in Brompton Road the staff had mounted to well over 100.

With the move to Woods Mews in October 1954 – a small two storey building which, judging by the all-pervading smell of disinfectant, had been used for some medical purpose- my responsibility for searching for suitable office accommodation ceased. I became responsible for laying the foundations of ITV on the engineering side. This initially involved finding suitable sites for the transmitting stations, starting in the London area. In this task I received considerable help from the Post Office engineering staff, who had, in anticipation of the TV Act, done some preliminary search.

However, the selection of the site and the granting of planning permission for the London station at Beulah Hill, West Norwood within a matter of a few weeks was mainly due to the enthusiastic insistence of the Borough of Croydon Corporation. It appeared that Baird, whom they regarded as the inventor of TV, had lived in Croydon; therefore the new ITV station must be within the corporation boundaries. The fact that the BBC London TV transmitter literally towered over Crystal Palace grounds – just outside their boundary – was no doubt an additional incentive.

My responsibility for the engineering did not in fact last long. Having apppointed the Director-General, the Authority next advertised for a Chief Engineer. The response was not large, since apart from the BBC and two or three electrical firms, there was a dearth of engineers with practical experience in the TV field. The appointment went to a BBC engineer, as indeed did most of the subsequent engineering posts.

Pat Bevan was the senior trouble-shooter on the BBC engineering staff, and it was his task to sort out the problems when things went wrong on the technical side. Having been intimately connected with the build up of the BBC TV service after the war he was, therefore, well qualified for the appointment. He was a thoroughly likeable character and we took to one another the first time we met. I had been warned by the Chief Engineer of the BBC, whom I had entertained in Washington, that Pat was a nonconformist in the broadest sense of the word. He did not believe in routine office hours and his appearances were quite unpredictable. Punctuality was outside his ken. Being then unmarried, he was apt to get down to serious work half way through the afternoon, and forget that others had families to return to. He suffered considerably from ill-health. When I got to know him I realised that he was one of those people who slept badly, and therefore, found difficulty in keeping regular hours. Although his appointment was announced in October there was a delay of six or seven weeks before he joined us officially; due to difficulties over the transfer of his pension rights from the BBC. In the meantime we met frequently, and I have to thank him for the guidance he gave me in a branch of telecommunications of which I had no previous practical experience.

The task of building the London transmitting station without a proper staff to plan and supervise its construction was so urgent that even before Pat took up his appointment the Authority allowed us to place a contract with the Marconi Company to build it as a 'turn-key' project. For a fixed sum of about £110,000 they contracted to build the complete station and hand it over in working condition. Only in that way was it possible to open the service in the London area in the incredibly short period of 13 months after the passing of the TV Act. Today it takes at least that time to open a new local radio service. Bearing in mind the limited finance available to the Authority the cost of the London station was a sizeable sum. Under the Act ITA could borrow up to £2 million over a period of five years from the date of the passing of the Act. Of this sum not more than £1 million was to be available during the first year. In the event ITA never had to borrow the full amount and repaid to the Treasury its borrowings plus interest within the five year period. Thus commercial TV cost the British taxpayer not one penny.

To return to the very early days of ITV. The Act laid down that it was the duty of the Authority to appoint a number of 'programme contractors independent of each other both as to finance and to control' to provide the programmes. They were also to ensure that there was 'adequate competition' between contractors. In their turn the programme contractors were permitted to sell space for advertisements to be transmitted under strict conditions laid down by the Authority. One such condition was that sponsorship of programmes was forbidden. This method of advertising is, of course, a common feature of commercial TV in other countries in particular in the USA, where programmes frequently start with the words, 'This programme comes to you by courtesy of the XYZ Corporation, etc.' For political reasons which I have already stated, the Government was pressing the Authority to open the service as soon as possible in the three most populous areas of the United Kingdom, namely London, the Midlands and the North. These should prove the most rewarding as regards revenue from advertising. The simple solution would have been to appoint three contractors, one for each area. But in the interest of competition the Authority decided to appoint four, by dividing the contracts into weekdays and weekends, ie, a 5.2 day basis. The four companies appointed were Associated Rediffusion (A-R), Associated TV (ATV), ABC Television (ABC) and Granada TV. The contracts allotted were:

	Weekdays	Weekends
London	A-R	ATV
Midlands	ATV	ABC
North	Granada	ABC

Thus ABC became a weekends only company. This was really no disadvantage since the weekend audiences are larger than weekday ones and, therefore, justify the charging of higher rates for advertising during the most popular viewing periods.

No sooner had the names of the contractors been announced than ITA came under bitter attack from the *Daily Mirror*, which in more than one front page article accused them of bowing to Conservative newspaper interests, notably the Kemsley Press and the *Daily Mail*. This in turn led to heated scenes in the Commons on 3rd November where the unfortunate PMG (the late D Gammons) had to defend the Authority and indirectly the DG, on whose head any adverse criticism of the ITV – and there was plenty – invariably fell. This pattern of responsibility followed closely in the steps of the BBC as established by Lord Reith. In his early days as DG Sir John Reith (as he was then) *was* the BBC. There was without doubt a Chairman and Board of Governors somewhere in the background, but there they remained, whilst the spotlight of the press and publicity shone on the dictatorial figure of the puritanical DG. Following this tradition Bob Fraser soon became *the* ITA, and the members of the Authority faded into the obscurity of the Arts Council's plush offices in St James's Square; Kenneth Clark also being Chairman of that august body. There they remained well away from the austere conditions in Woods Mews.

One could not help feeling sorry for Fraser, speculating whether, after the sheltered life of a civil servant, he had realised what brick-bats he was to encounter as boss of a nationalised institution. Having been a staunch supporter of the Labour Party (he had once stood unsuccessfully for Parliament in their cause) he now found himself in the unenviable position of head of a controversial organisation laboriously set up by a Conservative government in the face of fierce opposition. Moreover it was an organisation which depended for its success, not to mention survival, on the provision of vast sums of capital needed to set up the programme companies. Such capital, initially at any rate, could only be attracted from the so-called press barons and the tycoons of the entertainment industry. This in the eyes of the Labour Party and even some Conservatives was anathema.

Even before he joined, the announcement of his appointment prompted *Punch* to print a somewhat scathing criticsm of Fraser, entitled "Sir Robert Fraser's Song", in the form of a parody of the First Lord's song in HMS *Pinafore*. After tracing Fraser's rise via the *Daily Herald* and the Ministry of Information, it concluded with this advice to civil servants,

Keep well out of entertainment's way,
and you may all be Rulers of the ITA.

It was only recently that I realised that the editorial chair of *Punch* was at that time occupied by that volatile 'vendor of words' (to use his own expression) Malcolm Muggeridge. I sometimes wonder if he himself had applied for the appointment of Director-General, ITA.

In the previous week's edition *Punch* had produced one of its typically witty full-page cartoons. In this Kenneth Clark, unexpectedly encountering Ian Jacob, DG of the BBC, in a forest of TV aerials, raises his hat and exclaims, "Sir Ian Jacob, I presume." Both safari-clad figures are accompanied by strings of native porters carrying loads on their heads. On the top of the load immediately behind Jacob crouches the monkey-like figure of the late Gilbert Harding.

With the two London programme contractors appointed and Marconi commissioned to build the London transmitting station, we were able to turn our attention to the next most urgent task of planning the opening of the service in the Midlands and the North. With the weekdays/ weekends pattern of appointing programme contractors, it was desirable to ensure that the proportion of the population which each could reach was, as far as possible, comparable.

On the engineering side we were hampered in two directions: the insistence of the PO that we should co-site our transmitting stations with those of the BBC and the shortage of steel. In the course of long debates in the Commons during the passage of the TV Bill through Parliament the assistant PMG, in reply to one question, had stated that there would be no proliferation of ugly great masts or towers; commercial TV would use those already erected by the BBC. It was only a question of adding another aerial on to the existing structure. Whoever briefed him to give this answer cannot have consulted the BBC. Technically it would have been impossible, at that time, from both the point of view of structural strength and electrical efficiency, for the ITA to produce a service comparable in coverage to that of the BBC under a policy of mast-sharing at existing BBC stations. (Ten years later with the introduction of colour TV and the use of very much higher frequencies it became possible and was adopted.) After a long struggle with the PO they finally agreed that mast-sharing was not a practical proposition. So we must do the next best thing, they pronounced, and put our stations as close as possible to the BBC – a policy which became known as co-siting.

By now finding sites for the transmitters had become my responsibility. In the case of London this had been comparatively easy: our station was within a mile of the BBC's at Crystal Palace. In the Midlands too I was fortunate in being able to negotiate a site near Lichfield within 4-5 miles of the BBC station at Sutton Coldfield. But when it came to the North we ran into real difficulties. The BBC had erected their station at Holme Moss, an excellent site on the backbone of the Pennines, just south of Huddersfield. Here they had mounted their aerial on a 750 feet high mast. From this they were able to give a good service, extending from coast to coast – from Liverpool to Hull.

Given equipment specially developed and a mast height of at least 1,000 feet it would have been possible from an adjacent site for ITV, bearing in mind the very high frequencies allotted to us by the PO, to have given a service comparable to that of the BBC. But this was out of the question. Owing to the shortage of steel – a legacy from the war years – the best we could produce was a self-supporting lattice steel tower – like a super pylon – with a height of 450 feet. With this we calculated we could only cover about half of the area required. In the end after a long struggle, the PO waived their co-siting policy and we were allowed to erect two stations: one at Winter Hill north-west of Bolton to cover the industrial north-west, and another at Emley Moor south-east of Huddersfield to cover Yorkshire. These both had 450 feet towers, as also did the Midlands station near Lichfield. Some years later, when ITV had been established nationwide, these towers were replaced by much higher masts; whilst London which had started with a 200 feet tower – the only structure immediately available at the time – had it replaced by one 300 feet higher.

On 3rd November 1956 the last of these four stations, Emley Moor went into service. Within 2¼ years of the passing of the TV Act, Independent Television had become available to 33 million people, ie, more than two thirds of the population of the United Kingdom. No mean feat. In the meantime the 1955 election had seen the Conservatives returned to power. ITV had come to stay.

17

ITV Service opens—appointed regional officer East Anglia—Anglia Television—educational TV

On 22nd September 1955 the ITV Service opened in the London area. To celebrate the occasion the Authority staged a dinner in the Guildhall, at which the Postmaster-General, Charles Hill (later Lord Hill), and the Lord Mayor were present. The Chairman of the BBC was duly invited – and refused. However, he appears to have had second thoughts, because eventually he did attend together with the DG. The dinner was an exclusive affair. Only the Director-General, Alan Wolstencroft and Pat Bevan were invited. The rest of us on the staff had to be content with what was called, 'a gala night at the Mayfair Hotel.' There the programmes could be watched on large TV sets accompanied by the usual cabaret and compere. The whole event lasted from 7.15 to 11pm. The individual programmes were brief and unremarkable. The only remarkable feature of the evening was the showing of advertisements for the first time on the screen. They were on the whole entertaining, tasteful and restrained.

The reluctance of the BBC top brass to attend the dinner was not unexpected. Their attitude towards ITV was that of an ageing *prima donna* whose nose had been put out of joint by the threat of a youthful rival who might usurp the leading role in a forthcoming production. Word had evidently gone out from the top that non-cooperation was to be the watchword in Broadcasting House. Members of staff who had transferred to the new upstart ITV were little better than deserters and should be cold-shouldered. Eventually, of course, BBC and ITV settled down to amicable rivalry, as was only to be expected, when so many men and women had worked in both organisations and formed lasting friendships. But this process of reconciliation took many months, if not years.

An example of the BBC's attitude which I well recall occurred the first time I went over to Northern Ireland to start the search for a transmitting site. Colonel Chichester, the member of ITA representing Northern Ireland (there were similar members for Scotland and Wales) kindly met me and introduced me to the appropriate officials in Belfast. After lunch we drove up to the Black Mountain just west of the city on which the BBC transmitting station, Divis, was situated. My instructions were, if possible, to co-site with the BBC. As a matter of courtesy and rather on the spur of the moment we decided to call on the engineer-in-charge of Divis. Our arrival was obviously a source of embarrassment to the staff, and the situation was only saved when suddenly the second engineer appeared and recognised me. Some weeks previously he had appeared at ITA before a selection board, of which I happened to be Chairman, as candidate for a vacancy on our staff. Subsequently the Colonel told me that at lunch next day in his club, the head of BBC in Northern Ireland had come up to him, and in no mean terms upbraided him for our trespass on his property!

One of the first acts of the Authority was to decide that the daily news bulletins should not rest in the hands of individual programme contractors, but should be provided by a separate company. They therefore arranged with the first four contractors – the 'big four' of ITV – to set up and finance Independent Television News (ITN). (At a later stage all 14 companies were required to participate.) ITN quickly proved to be popular, mainly because it set a new standard in newscasting. Hitherto viewers had become accustomed to stylised and impersonal presentation of the news by male figures, soberly dressed by day and dinner-jacketed by night, who read the news rather in the style of a cleric reading the lessons in church. Any sign of personal feeling or emotion was strictly taboo. Their appearance evoked the expression 'stuffed shirts'. The very idea of an Angela Rippon or Anna Ford as newscaster was beyond the pale.

ITN from the start set an entirely new fashion. Its earliest newscasters, such as Robin Day and Christopher Chattaway, were encouraged to dress as they pleased, and by their facial and vocal behaviour impress their personalities on viewers without in any way detracting from the imparting of news. Before long the BBC fell into line. Today the presentation of news on both channels, whether national or regional, is without doubt of the highest standard.

u45 By August 1957 we were in a position to extend the service to central Scotland. I had found an ideal site for the transmitter just north of the Edinburgh-Glasgow main road. It belonged to a small farmer by the name of Jock Muldoon. He and I became good friends and many were the drams we put down together in his house. I am happy to say that in return I was able to arrange with the Electricity Board that, in bringing power to the station, they would without charge extend a supply to Jock's farmhouse. Later he showed me with pride his electrified milking parlour.

Unfortunately a last-minute hitch caused me the worst headache I suffered during my 10 years with ITA. After planning permission had been granted for the station and the lawyers for either side had agreed on the contract for sale of the necessary land, Muldoon's advocate suddenly discovered that under some obscure covenant, peculiar to Scottish law, their client, although the lawful owner of the land, was not empowered to sell it without permission of the courts. After frantic to-ing and fro-ing between London and Edinburgh by our solicitor and myself, we were able to get the matter straightened out in the Scottish High Court, just in time before they went into their long vacation. Had the construction of the station been further delayed it would have placed the ITA in a very awkward position – and possibly liable to heavy damages – because, on hearing from our solicitor that the exchange of contracts had been agreed, I had informed the DG that all was clear to go ahead with the construction of the station. On the strength of this the ITA had appointed a programme contractor so as to give him ample time to set up his studio, staff etc. It so happened that at this period the existing 'big four' contractors, far from showing a profit on the £2-3 million each had invested in setting up their companies, were losing money heavily. The advertisers were just not spending the amount of money on TV advertising which everyone had anticipated. Whether this was due to the Suez crisis or other political or economic factors is not clear. Consequently when it came to advertising for the Scottish TV franchise there was only one worthwhile competitor. This was Scottish TV formed and owned by Roy Thomson,* the Canadian newspaper-owner. Being a hard-headed businessman with practical experience of the broadcasting media in his own country, he seized the opportunity of a buyer's market and only after some hard bargaining was the ITA able to confirm the contract with him. The sequence is ironical. Scottish TV came on the air in August 1957. By the time it did so TV advertising accounts were on the up and up. Not many months later Thomson was reported from Canada to have stated publicly that, 'being in commercial TV in Britain was like having a licence to print your own money.' This remark, needless to say, did not go down well in ITV circles. However, the germ of truth it contained seems to have withstood the test of time!

*The late Lord Thomson of Fleet.

By the time I left the engineering staff of ITA, my assistant and I had acquired twenty main transmitter sites from which to give coverage to over 95 per cent of the population of the United Kingdom and the Channel Isles. This had been accomplished in six years, and many thousands of miles of travelling by air, road, rail and on foot.

Since it might take anything up to two years before a suitable site could be tested, approved and acquired plus a further year in which to erect the building and mast, one was usually working in at least three areas at the same time. One got used to spending one day a week in the office and the remaining four travelling. Looking back on the six years I spent on the engineering staff of ITA I am reminded of the cooperation one received from local authorities including planning officers, electricity and water officials, and, with some exceptions, landowners and their agents. At times we were involved in somewhat unusual negotiations. For example, for our station at Burnhope, County Durham, I had to negotiate with the National Coal Board to purchase *in situ* a narrow seam of coal, which if worked, might have caused subsidence on our site with serious results to the building and mast.

As ITV spread across the country with more programme contractors being granted franchises, it became difficult for the ITA to keep close contact with up to 12 companies operating outside the London area. They, therefore, introduced a system whereby members of the staff were located alongside the principal companies. Known as regional officers, their tasks were twofold. Firstly, to act as the Authority's local representative so that minor matters raised by the companies did not have to be referred to London. Secondly, to act as public relations officers for ITV. Generally speaking the system was welcomed by the companies.

In October 1959 Anglia came on the air. I had applied for the appointment of Regional Officer, East Anglia. In doing so I was influenced by my wife's deteriorating health, which was not eased by my being away from home most of the week. Bob Fraser had been quite agreeable, but Pat Bevan intervened with the result that it was decided I should stay at Headquarters for another year in order to continue the finding of sites which would bring ITV coverage up to some 98 per cent of the population. In the meantime another officer would be posted to Anglia TV on a temporary basis.

In October 1960 I moved to Norwich. One could not have found a better company to work with. When the franchise for East Anglia was advertised there were only two serious applicants. One was a company the board of which represented county landowners, businessmen and the local press, but which was lacking on the entertainment side. The other headed by Lord Townshend of Raynham, a large landowner and a director of the Norwich Union, included a wide range of interests. The press was represented by Lawrence Scott of the *Guardian*; the theatre by Donald Aubrey; films by John Woolf; whilst Glyn Daniel, a Cambridge don, had become something of a TV personality through the BBC programme *Animal, Vegetable or Mineral?* Wildlife was represented by Aubrey Buxton (now Lord Buxton) whose *Survival* programmes have since become internationally famous.

At the Authority's request the local press changed sides and their Chairman joined the Board. This move was in accord with ITA policy. Since TV revenue from advertising would partially, at any rate, be derived at the expense of the Press (and other media) they encouraged newspaper interest to participate in programme companies. Anglia TV differed from most other programme companies, in that no officers of the company were members of the Board. The Board itself met in Norwich once a month, but the day to day running of the company was handled by an Executive Committee comprising the Chairman, Buxton, Scott and Woolf who met weekly in London.

As a regional company Anglia was expected to provide about 15 per cent of its programmes, the remainder being taken from the 'big four' and ITN. From its earliest days it started to build up a reputation based on three types of programmes – drama, natural history and agriculture. The company was fortunate in obtaining the services of George Moore O'Ferrall as head of their drama department. George had started his career in film production; then when the BBC opened their TV service in 1936 he joined them. He was the first person in the world to produce a TV play. This he did at the old studios at Alexandra Palace. Unlike the 'big four' Anglia made no attempt to produce serials, but concentrated on single plays with a running time of 60 or 90 minutes. They invariably included some well-known names in their casts. These productions were so successful that they were accepted by the other companies and shown over the entire ITV network. Anglia's *Survival* programmes are today so well-known that further comment is superfluous. However, it is worth recording that from the date of its formation in 1959 Anglia established a Natural History Film Unit to concentrate exclusively on the production of this type of programme. They were in fact the pioneers of the nature programmes, which today feature so frequently on our screens.

East Anglia being largely agricultural, a weekly programme for farmers was a *sine qua non*. *Farming Diary* appeared on the first Sunday that Anglia came on the air, and, to the best of my knowledge, has appeared every Sunday since. Incidentally it was the making of one of the best-known Anglia TV personalities. Before the opening day trial, *Farming Diary,* programmes were run with an established TV narrator. These were seen by the Chairman who was far from satisfied with his performance. In desperation Lord Townshend rang up Dick Joice, one of his tenant farmers and said, "Dick, for God's sake, come and help us out. You're a farmer, see if you can put it over. We can't send out *Farming Diary* like this." Dick responded so successfully that before long he was introducing *About Anglia*, and other programmes. Following a serious illness his appearances are today less frequent and confined to *Bygones* featuring early agricultural and domestic appliances, local characters and other reminders of days gone by.

Three characters, which Dick introduced on the screen, remain firmly fixed in my memory – a highly literate tramp, a poacher turned gamekeeper and the last surviving eel catcher in the region. Dick's latest achievement should not pass unnoticed. For years he has been building up what is probably the most comprehensive collection of early agricultural appliances in the country. These are now admirably housed in the stables of Holkham Hall on the north coast of Norfolk.

One of the regional officer's tasks is to watch the programmes produced by his local company to ensure that they in no way infringe the standards of what the public in general regard as good taste. Such standards have altered, some would say deteriorated, to a remarkable extent during the last 30 years. Two examples will suffice to illustrate this. In July 1964 I was rung up by Anglia one afternoon and asked to come over to the studios urgently to preview an item for that evening's edition of *About Anglia*. It concerned ladies-wear on display in a shop in the centre of Ipswich. The see-through garment had arrived and a freelance newsman had sent in shots of a model displaying this latest freak of feminine fashion. Did I think that these could be shown on the screen? The shots were taken in profile and in my view showed no more of the female bust than is frequently displayed by girls wearing bikinis on the beaches. I allowed the shots to appear, but at least one member of the programme staff expressed surprise at my decision. There were, I learnt later, adverse comments in the *Daily Express* and local press. Regional officers used to attend monthly conferences at ITA headquarters in London. On one of these occasions we were all asked to preview a recording of Harold Pinter's play *The Lovers*. In one scene the lady of the house, in her husband's absence, is entertaining her lover. She stands behind a piece of furniture in the living room. He crouches on the floor beneath it and strokes her legs. The programme staff were worried that this scene was too erotic to be shown on the little screen in people's sitting rooms. Unanimously we decided it was not.

It seems strange to recall these two incidents today, when practically no drama shown on TV is complete without depicting human abnormalities or amorous activities in the bedroom. The pendulum has certainly swung far. Not long ago the BBC showed a programme devoted to strip-tease artistes at a well-known Paris music hall, where female nudity was the norm, both on the stage and in the dressing room. One critic described it as, "cheerful, rude and strangely innocent". In that particular case he was probably right.

By this time broadcasting of schools programmes on radio by the BBC was established. In 1961 ITV started schools programmes on TV. The companies were asked to appoint education officers to act in liaison with the schools to obtain their reactions to the programmes. Whether or not the schools used the programmes depended primarily on the county education authorities who had to provide the TV sets and allocate them to their schools. In January 1962, therefore, I decided to invite county education officers and others interested parties to a conference. The object was to interest them in TV as a tool in the educational field and to hear their views on the subject. The Director-General agreed to come up and explain what ITV was trying to do. Only about two dozen attended and not much enthusiasm was aroused. Many thought TV was just a form of entertainment. Nothing discouraged two years later I held another similar conference. By this time the University of East Anglia had opened in Norwich and the Vice-Chancellor, Dr R Thistlethwaite, agreed to take the chair. To my astonishment nearly all those invited accepted and to my embarrassment many whom I had not invited, asked if they could attend. The hall which I had hired was limited in capacity, and I had to refuse some of the late applicants.

By now a few universities, polytechnics and colleges of education had started to explore the possibilities of closed circuit TV as an educational aid, thus opening a much wider field than the broadcasting of schools TV programmes. I was fortunate in getting two exceptionally able speakers to deal with both aspects of what is now commonly known as educational TV – Dr Lincoln Ralphs*, Director of Education for

*The late Sir Lincoln Ralphs.

205

Norfolk and a doyen of the scholastic world, and Mr Peter Laslett, a Cambridge don whose enthusiasm and drive for higher educational TV I was to witness and share in the coming years.

Soon after I moved to Norwich the Chairmanship of ITA fell vacant. Sir Ivone Kirkpatrick, a retired career diplomat, who had succeeded Kenneth Clark in 1957, had completed his term of office. He had been the conventional BBC-type Chairman, keeping well in the background and leaving everything, as far as possible, in the capable hands of Bob Fraser. The new Chairman was a very different character to his predecessors.

Lord Hill had first become known to the public as the radio doctor, Charles Hill, who in war time had advised and entertained the nation on matters affecting their health in general and, from all accounts, their bowels in particular. He had then become a politician and succeeded Lord de la Warr as PMG in 1955. Finally his political career came to an abrupt halt when he fell victim to Macmillan's 'night of the long knives'. However, his downfall was not without its rewards – a life peerage, the chair of one of the largest chemical concerns in the country, and now Chairmanship of the ITA.

Hill's arrival at 70 Brompton Road resembled the proverbial cat amongst the pigeons. He left no doubt in anyone's mind that he was, in military parlance, commanding officer of the ITA and that the DG was his adjutant. One of his first acts was to summon a press conference, over which he presided with a mute Bob Fraser sitting by his side. To our astonishment he invited the assembled press men to come and see him personally, whenever they wished to raise matters concerning ITV. Some of us conjectured as to how Bob Fraser would react to this apparent change in his status. To our surprise he adapted himself to the ways of his new master and soldiered on long after Harold Wilson had abruptly transferred Hill to the chair of the BBC with the scarcely concealed object of sacking the Director-General – Carleton Green – an object which Hill successfully achieved within a few months of taking up the appointment.

Like all ambitious politicians (and most are ambitious) Charles Hill was his own public relations officer. He loved to address the staff on all possible occasions, freely peppering his addresses with references to his past achievements in Parliament and making frequent repetitions from his repertoire of medical jokes. To his credit he took an interest in the staff and made a point of visiting many of the transmitting stations, the staff of which led lives remote from the glamours of Brompton Road.

In November 1964 I left ITA. I was 66 – a year above the normal retiring age. At the request of Anglia TV the Authority had allowed me to stay on an extra year.

In October 1963 an experiment in inter-university co-operation had taken place in what became known as the Cambridge TV week. In that period an exchange of lectures by closed circuit TV (CCTV) was arranged between the Universities of Cambridge and East Anglia (Norwich) and between Cambridge and Imperial College, London. Although terminal facilities were provided without charge by TV companies, the circuits between those terminals, ie, lecture rooms, had to be rented from the Post Office.

The driving force behind these exchanges was Peter Laslett of Trinity College, Cambridge. The results were successful in that they showed to a limited number of university dons the potential value of TV as a teaching aid, and as a means of making available, to more than one university, rare teaching skills. At the same time they emphasised what many of us already knew, that so long as such exchanges depended on hiring circuits from the Post Office the cost would be prohibitive, with the possible exception of those cases where two universites were located in the same city, eg, Glasgow and Manchester. The alternative was to record lectures on videotape and send them to other universities to be played back on their own TV equipment. This method suffered two drawbacks. At that time recording equipment of sufficient reliability and high standards was very costly.* Moreover, the recording system provided no feed-back, ie, the remote audience could not ask questions of the lecturer.

On the subject of expense it will be recalled that during the mid-sixties the programme of university expansion was at its height. New universities were being opened and technical colleges being upgraded to university status at the rate of two or three a year. Altogether between 1962/3 and 1967/8 the number of universities in Great Britain rose from 17 to 38 and the number of students from 217,000 to 376,000. Finance for these vast projects was derived from central government funds administered through the University Grants

---

*Today the situation is quite different. Videotape recording and playing equipment is a commonplace in thousands of homes.

Committee (UGC). It was unlikely that TV equipment would be regarded as of high priority by this body.†

In 1965 the Brynmor Jones Report on higher education had noted, "Universities and other centres of higher education tend to work in isolation. Although contact between departments in different universities may be maintained where there is common interest, there is little exchange of information with regard to teaching."

Obviously liaison in the field of higher education was remarkable more for its absence than its presence. There were some who thought that modern methods of communication, of which TV was the latest, might help to remedy the situation, and at the same time improve efficiency and effect economies by sharing facilities between different universities teaching the same subject. To examine the possibilities a working party of representatives from five universities* (Cambridge, East Anglia, Essex, Hull and London) was formed in July 1964, under the Chairmanship of Peter Laslett. With a grant from the Gulbenkian Foundation the working party established a small unit to carry out such research as they required. It was known as the Inter-University Research Unit and was based at Cambridge. Peter Laslett invited me to join it as technical consultant. We were a team of four including a secretary.

The work of the unit lasted just over three years during which time we visited nearly all the universities and many polytechnics and colleges of education. A number of experiments in inter-communications were carried out not only using TV, but also less sophisticated equipment which enabled a lecturer at, for example, Cambridge to address an audience in Edinburgh and accompany his lecture with simple diagrams using the normal telephone system.

In many forms of teaching the use of CCTV is self-evident; particularly those which depend on the teacher handling small, delicate or potentially dangerous objects or substances in an environment which does not allow mass observation. Many aspects of engineering and physics fall into this category. But to my mind the most impressive field lies in surgery. It is just not practicable to fill an operating theatre with

†Today however, the university without a CCTV system embracing a central studio and a network of distribution points is a rarity.

*Later four more universities (Glasgow, Leeds, Strathclyde and Sussex) were invited to join. These were chosen since at the time they had the most developed TV services.

students to watch a delicate operation on the human intestines. There is normally not room for them, nor is it possible for more than one or two to get a close-up view of the actual operation. With a TV camera suitably slung above the operating table any number of students can watch the operation on TV screens in an adjoining classroom. Moreover with the addition of a microphone the surgeon or his assistant can convey a running commentary.

It was at Moorfield Eye Hospital, London that the significance of this technique was amply demonstrated to me and one of my colleagues. The authorities had recently installed two operating theatres designed for teaching by CCTV. Round the sides of the theatre and at a height of about six feet above its floor the walls were replaced by large glass panels. Behind these panels and isolated from the theatre was a gallery fitted with rows of seats. Here TV screens were hung at suitable intervals. The students were thus able to look down into the theatre and view the general layout and procedure. Then as the delicate eye surgery started they could turn to the nearest screen and follow in detail the operation.

My interest in and connection with CCTV was not confined to the Research Unit. In the winter of 1967 the Vice-Chancellor of the City University took the opportunity of a CCTV conference to initiate a simple organisation aimed at coordinating the work being carried out in the numerous institutions of higher education in the London and Home Counties areas. I was asked to be Chairman of this body, which in due course operated under the title of the South East Forum (SEF). The first meeting was held at the City University on 13th March 1968 and over 100 delegates attended from universities, technical colleges, colleges of education, medical schools, local authorities and even the police and fire services. Thereafter the Forum held meetings three times a year, to which any organisation or individual was welcomed on payment of a small fee.

By now the higher education authorities were gradually acquiring CCTV equipment of their own with in some cases central studios manned by professional broadcasters and technicians. The object of SEF was to help coordinate these developments and to create a climate in which universities, particularly those located in a specific area, would cooperate with one another to ensure that material recorded in one establishment would be available, where appropriate, to other establishments.

I handed over the Chairmanship of SEF in 1973. By that date I was fully involved in work of an entirely different nature. Moreover the growing body of those involved in running the various educational CCTV services had formed themselves into a body with the imposing initials NECCTA, standing for the National Educational Closed Circuit Television Association, thus facilitating the exchange of ideas and information in the ever-widening CCTV field of Education.

Today when CCTV has become necessary – and in many cases indispensable – in the field of shipping, nuclear power, traffic control, the underground, not to mention prisons and supermarkets, it is interesting to recall that this aid to safety and security was still in its infancy some 15 years ago.

To return now to the Inter-University Research Unit. In 1969 we issued our final report. During the three years of its existence it had, in the opinion of many closely associated with its work, fully justified the comparatively small amount of money which the Gulbenkiam Foundation had generously allotted it. It had drawn attention to the need for cooperation between the universities and other educational institutions in the use of CCTV. It had drawn attention to less sophisticated methods of exchanging lectures and seminars using the existing PO telephone system. Finally it had encouraged British manufacturers of electronic communication equipment to study the needs of the educational world.

18

I join the HQ staff of WRVS—death of Lady Reading—views on psychiatric hospitals—I join the 'rag trade' and get involved in ladies garments

In April 1968 my wife died after a long and painful illness. For years she had struggled against ill-health. Her death was in some ways a merciful release.

I was fit despite my years and determined to keep my mind and body active. At the age of 71 one could hardly expect to find a job, as it were, on the open market. Eventually in response to an advertisement in the *Daily Telegraph* for, "Someone who was interested in the housing of old people", I found myself invited to spend a day at the Headquarters of the WRVS in London's Old Park Lane. It was the beginning of a connection with that organisation which was to last five years.

After a months' holiday in South Africa I started working for the WRVS. My work was concerned with the maintenance and construction of buildings. Hitherto my idea of the WRVS had been of ladies in green and maroon uniform delivering meals-on-wheels and dishing out cups of tea and buns in canteens. Apart, of course, from their overseas welfare work with the Forces, of which I had ample evidence in India and Malaya.

I now learnt that their welfare activities at home covered a very wide field. This entailed the ownership of a vast amount of property embracing old people's homes, nursing homes, clubs, canteen/shops, not to mention a home for 'old lags' and others for ex-Borstal boys. These institutions were run by local committees and my task was to act as guide, philosopher and friend to them so far as bricks and mortar were concerned. In addition the WRVS controlled three housing associations with blocks of flats scattered throughout the country. These were not my responsibility, though I was occasionally called to lend a hand.

Originally I had agreed to work on a part-time basis, but it soon became full-time. In my first week a part-time volunteer in the office warned me, "You don't know what you're letting yourself in for. The heads here are slave drivers. They'll work you to death, if you don't watch it." Granted her hyperbole, there was an element of truth in the remark. I must admit that I was a willing victim. Before long I found myself travelling hundreds of miles each week, clambering all over buildings inside and out, drawing up specifications and plans for new buildings, and arguing with contractors and fire precautions officers. It was work after my own heart. I thoroughly enjoyed it.

The leader and inspirer of all the multitudinous activities of the WRVS was the late Lady Reading. The first time I met her she said, "You'll be shocked at how we run things here. You'll probably think we're all crazy. But it works." And it did. It is hard to describe the immense drive and personality of this remarkable woman. I once said to a member of the HQ staff who had served her for a very long time, "You know I think Lady Reading must model herself on Winston Churchill."

"Don't you believe it," was her instant reply, "she models herself on Lady Reading and no one else."

When war seemed inevitable the then Home Secretary, Sir Samuel Hoare, had consulted Lady Reading as to how the womenhood of Great Britain could best be employed and organised in the event of hostilities. She replied, "Give me a few days to think it over." Or words to that effect. She was due to leave on a visit to Constantinople (Istanbul), where her father had been Consul-General when she was born. In the Orient Express she drew up her plans, and presented them to the Home Secretary on her return. Thereafter the Women's Voluntary Service for Civil Defence, to give it it's full title, was born. Today it remains a Service under the Home Office, from which it receives an annual grant towards the cost of administration. In other respects it is self-financing. The 'Civil Defence' has been dropped from its title, since it now embraces so many other fields and civil defence is but a skeleton.

Lady Reading died suddenly on 22nd May 1971. Only four days previously I had been to a small working lunch party with her in the

House of Lords. She seemed as energetic as ever. On 15th June a service of thanksgiving for her life was held in Westminster Abbey. Vast throngs of women in WRVS uniform from all over the country converged on and filled the Abbey. I was one of the few men present, apart from relatives and Home Secretaries. I shall always remember the scene, and in particular the rendering of the hymn, *Mine eyes have seen the glory of the coming of the Lord* to the thundering organ tones of the tune which I had always associated with the American Revolutionary song about the deceased John Brown.

I was not, of course, the only man working in the WRVS. In my time at HQ there were at any one period up to six of us, of whom three were generally in the accounts department. This incidentally was the only department presided over by a man. In the Regions, into which the Service was organised, and the various lower echelons under them, it was quite common to find men – usually husbands – assisting their wives, in the manning of canteens, the distribution of meals-on-wheels and similar activities.

The heads of departments and the heads of Regions were usually women with experience in business or in the Services. As an ex-serviceman I naturally found the latter particularly easy to work with, since we shared a common training. Key appointments were known by their titles, eg, Regional Administrator, but there were no ranks. Consequently no distinctive badges were worn.

In practically every large hospital (and many of the smaller ones) throughout the country the WRVS provides services to patients in the form of shops, canteens and trolley services for books, sweets, cigarettes etc. In most hospitals the authorities provide the accommodation to house and accommodate these amenities. But in many of the large psychiatric hospitals in particular the WRVS had to erect buildings to house their canteen/shops. The construction and maintenance of these was one of my responsibilities. In this way I saw a good deal of how the state cares for those suffering from mental diseases. To an outsider it seemed that in some hospitals there was crying need for improvement. In many cases hospitals were accommodated in former workhouse buildings. The dismal origins of these could hardly be disguised with coats of paint, however appealing the colours.

For the nursing staff in psychiatric hospitals one can have nothing but praise. Their task is an uncongenial one. Their only recompense can be the speed with which patients respond to the treatment and recover.

The really sad cases are those minority, in some case children, who are beyond known treatment, and must remain under care for the rest of their lives.

One aspect which came as a surprise to me, was to learn of the large number of people who voluntarily entered these hospitals suffering from nothing worse than fits of depression or a nervous breakdown. They stayed for a few weeks and then returned home. On reflection I am sure that it is sensible to regard mental sickness in the same way as any other illness and attach no stigma to it, as undoubtedly was the case when I was young.

On the subject of voluntary patients two incidents struck me as having an ironical side to them. One night at a large hospital outside Lincoln, entry was forced into the WRVS newly constructed shop/canteen. I hastened up to investigate the damage. At a meeting in the hospital secretary's office the local crime prevention police officer expressed the view that the break-in was an inside job by a patient. He added, "You know in this hospital you've got quite a few of our customers. So often we arrest someone for a petty crime, and when he or she comes up before the magistrates we are told that a doctor has given them a certificate to say that they are in need of psychiatric treatment, and they end up in here."

In another case I was visiting one of our canteen/shops in a large hospital at Epsom. I noticed the piano was frequently being played by a man, who was obviously a performer of no mean ability. On asking one of the sisters what was wrong with him, she replied, "Oh! there's nothing wrong with him really. He's one of our regulars."
"What does that mean?" I enquired.
"Well each winter he gets himself admitted. Then when the weather gets better he goes off and earns his living playing the piano. Sometimes he goes down to the South of France. Then he comes back here for the winter."

In 1975 I left the WRVS. I was 77. It was obviously time I sought some less strenuous occupation. Having recently re-married I wanted to spend more time with my wife than travelling all over the country permitted me. Furthermore, I was not anxious to serve under a new chairman. Since Lady Reading's death, her deputy Mrs Clode had taken over, on the understanding that as soon as there was a general election she would stand down in favour of Miss Mervyn Pyke MP. The latter had decided not to stand for Parliament again after a longish spell in the

House. In due course Lady Pyke, having been given a life peerage became Chairman of the WRVS.

It was obvious before I left that she was going to set about reorganisation and apply the proverbial new broom with vigour. Subsequently I learnt that in true political fashion she had used the axe, with a vengeance. Many who had served faithfully under Lady Reading for many years, were to receive their *conge*. What effect these sweeping changes had on the service I am in no position to judge. But of one thing I feel certain. The WRVS will continue to serve the country with that spirit of selfless dedication which has distinguished it over the last five decades.

On re-marriage I went to live in Leicester where my wife had a house. Her father owned a small factory manufacturing ladies outer-wear in that city. He had recently re-married and gone to live in Cornwall leaving my wife to manage the business. Nominally he remained the Chairman which left my wife in a very difficult position. The production side had for some years been in the hands of a manager, whilst Cynthia and another director looked after design and sales. As soon as my father-in-law died, a year after our marriage, the manager started to show his true colours. He did everything to thwart his two co-directors and offended some of the firms clients. In desperation my wife asked him to resign and offered him substantial financial compensation. This he accepted, and then immediately took his case to one of the recently introduced industrial tribunals. The result was disastrous.

A tribunal is not a court of law, but a board of three members whose task is to consider the facts, decide whether or not the plaintiff was unfairly dismissed and, if so, to award compensation according to a statutory scale. I consulted a friend who is an eminent QC. His advice was, "On no account let your wife's firm be legally represented. All the tribunal wants to know are the facts." Unfortunately solicitors representing the firm, without consulting my wife, briefed a young barrister to represent their case. The result was that, although the tribunal found the manager 20 per cent to blame, they awarded him the maximum compensation permissible.

This tore a hole in the company's resources. To make matters worse a few months later one of it's largest customers went into voluntary liquidation without warning. Among its major creditors were several firms in Leicester, of which my wife's was worst hit. Despite these two setbacks the company managed to survive.

To relieve my wife of the purely administrative side of the business, it was arranged that I should become secretary of the company without remuneration. By this time the rate of inflation was starting to rise and so were wages. To ease the shortage of cash we started to sell direct to the public by opening a factory shop and starting a mail order business through advertisements in the *Lady*. But like so many small businesses in the second half of the 70's the odds were too heavily stacked against us.

In the 'rag trade' there is a time lag of about six months between the receipt of orders and the delivery of goods. If we underestimated the rise in inflation, profit margins were eroded. If we overestimated, orders declined. Another difficulty lay in the supply of the raw materials of the trade, ie, fabrics. Here one was largely in the hands of the giant combines, in particular Courtaulds. In the early spring their representatives would come round with samples of their new fabrics for the autumn season. We would order a small number of rolls, sufficient to make up sample dresses to show our customers, the wholesalers. They might order six sample dresses in each of three or four styles for their representatives to show their customers, the retail shops. In due course, if one was lucky, a bulk order would come in from the wholesaler. We would accordingly order the requisite number of rolls from the manufacturer. It was then that he might turn round and say, 'There is not sufficient demand, so we are discontinuing the fabric you want.' And so you lost a bulk order and were left with a dissatisfied customer.

By 1977 it became obvious that continuation of the business could only lead to further losses. Therefore, the best and most honourable course was to close down whilst we were in a position to pay redundancy to our 40 or so employees and pay all our creditors. This we did. My wife sold her house in Leicester and we settled down on the outskirts of Norwich.

Now we have ample time to write, garden and take advantage of the many package holidays available. At the age of 89 I am active, healthy and very happily married; moreover I have numerous friends of all age groups. No man can ask for more.

Looking back over the last 80 years or so it is easy to be pessimistic and hark back to the good old days. But were they really so good? I think not. I recall scenes from my childhood. Scenes of children in ragged clothing and with bare feet, elderly couples forced to seek refuge in the workhouse, women with heavy bundles of firewood trudging along the roads. These were by no means exceptional sights.

Today, generally speaking, children are well-dressed and even if some boys and girls affect brightly coloured and spikey hairstyles, they are probably only trying to overcome a feeling of inferiority. Gone are the workhouses. Instead the old age couples draw their weekly pensions from the Post Office. The load of firewood has been replaced by the plastic shopping bag.

In this age of rapid communications the world has metaphorically shrunk. Outbreaks of disease, drought, famine and violence, which a century ago were scarcely brought to our notice, are now vividly depicted in our homes.

Despite the blight of unemployment, which in my view is the biggest problem facing us and indeed the Western World, we are still a great nation. It is surely up to us to set an example to other nations by caring for those less fortunate than ourselves.